D1327647

# MEGALITHIC REMAINS IN BRITAIN AND BRITTANY

BY

A. THOM

AND

A. S. THOM

CLARENDON PRESS · OXFORD

1978

*Oxford University Press, Walton Street, Oxford* OX2 6DP

OXFORD  LONDON  GLASGOW
NEW YORK  TORONTO  MELBOURNE  WELLINGTON
IBADAN  NAIROBI  DAR ES SALAAM  LUSAKA  CAPE TOWN
KUALA LUMPUR  SINGAPORE  JAKARTA  HONG KONG  TOKYO
DELHI  BOMBAY  CALCUTTA  MADRAS  KARACHI

**British Library Cataloguing in Publication Data**

Thom, Alexander
  Megalithic remains in Britain and Brittany.
  1. Astronomy, Prehistoric   2. Megalithic monuments
  – Europe   4. Astronomy, Prehistoric   4. Megalithic
  monuments – France – Brittany
  I. Title   II. Thom, A S
  936            GN799.A8              77-30637

  ISBN 0-19-858156-4

Set by Eta Services (Typesetters) Ltd., Beccles, Suffolk
Printed in Great Britain
by J. W. Arrowsmith Ltd., Bristol

# PREFACE

IN two previous books, *Megalithic sites in Britain* (Thom 1967) and *Megalithic lunar observatories* (Thom 1971), there will be found a study of various types of prehistoric free-standing stones in Britain with special reference to the metrology and geometry of their arrangement and to their astronomical significance. Since the publication of these books, we have extended the investigation to France in addition to surveying a number of important sites in Britain. As a result we now have highly accurate plans of the thousands of stones in the Carnac alignments with most of the near-by menhirs and we have precise plans of Stonehenge, Brogar in Orkney, and Avebury. These surveys necessitated six visits to Orkney, one to Shetland, and five to Carnac, where, in some years, we had as many as ten or twelve helpers. The analysis of the resulting mass of material required years of desk work. For example, the plan of the Kermario alignments was over 8 ft long and took several months to plot. Our Avebury survey demanded more than a plotted plan and, accordingly, we have given the coordinates of the centre of every stone.

The work in Carnac has shown that the erectors of standing stones in Brittany made use of the same units of measurement and the same geometry and were investigating the same astronomical phenomena as the erectors in Britain.

Our recent work in Britain has shown up the fundamental importance of the lunar observatory in Brogar in Orkney. Here, as in no other place, there are enough remains to prove conclusively that the movements of the moon were being fully observed.

The present volume can be read by itself but a knowledge of the material in the two previous books will make the reading easier. It may be found difficult to understand the complex movements of the moon in the sky, but we hope in this connection that Chapter 2 will be useful. To understand and to appreciate fully what we have found in Brogar (Chapter 10) it is necessary to have a reasonable knowledge of what happens at a standstill.

Acknowledgements and thanks are due to the thirty or forty people who have helped with the surveys but we cannot mention them individually here. We wish to say how grateful we are to all the members of our family, and especially to Beryl Austin (*née* Thom) and her family and to Dr. T. R. Foord and M. Jean-Luc Quinio.

We must also mention in connection with the astronomical theory Professor A. E. Roy of Glasgow University Astronomy Department, and Dr. A. T.

Sinclair of the Royal Greenwich Observatory. Much useful advice was also obtained from Professor P. R. Giot of the University of Rennes.

For over 25 years we ourselves financed the expeditions to sites all over Britain, but by 1970 it was necessary to obtain help. We now gratefully acknowledge assistance received from the Carnegie Trust, the Hulme Fund, Brasenose College, the B.B.C., and the Royal Society. We must specially mention Mr. R. L. Merritt, who obtained for us a number of grants from the Lloyd Foundation, Cleveland, Ohio. His personal encouragement and help have been invaluable.

*Dunlop, Ayrshire*                                                                                                A.T.
*August* 1977                                                                                                     A.S.T.

# CONTENTS

# LIST OF MAIN SYMBOLS
# AND ABBREVIATIONS

$\epsilon$    Obliquity of the ecliptic *or* residual (in statistical analysis)
$i$    Mean inclination of moon's orbit to ecliptic
$\Delta$    Perturbation of moon's orbit caused by the sun
$s$    Mean semidiameter
$p$    Parallax
$Az$    Azimuth
MY    Megalithic yards
MR    Megalithic rods
MI    Megalithic inches

# 1

## INTRODUCTION

**1.1.** MEGALITHIC remains are widely spread around Britain and France and indeed much further afield. We find isolated tall stones or menhirs on both sides of the English Channel, but rings of stones are much more common in Britain than in France. The Breton word 'cromlech' (*crom*, circle, *lech*, area) means practically the same thing as 'stone circle' but the five cromlechs we surveyed in the Carnac area are larger than the average British stone circle and none was circular. In both countries we find stones or menhirs arranged in straight lines, but multiple parallel rows are almost absent in Britain, whereas in France there are numerous examples. In fact the huge alignments near Carnac have made this area internationally famous.

**1.2.** The man who has perhaps done more than anyone else for the antiquities of Carnac is Zacharie Le Rouzic (1864–1939). As a youth he was taught by a Scotsman, James Milne, whose brother Robert ultimately founded the Carnac Museum in James's memory. Le Rouzic, by this time director of the museum, with the help of peasants re-erected the majority of the fallen stones in the alignments, and those he set up he marked by a square plug of red cement. He tried to put the stones in their original positions, but in this he was only partially successful. Things are the more uncertain in that some stones were apparently re-erected before Le Rouzic's time, and he may have been misled by these. Throughout whole areas of the alignments and cromlechs almost every stone carries the red mark; in fact in some sections it is difficult to find stones not so marked. In a paper published in 1939 Le Rouzic stated that he intended to write a note to explain the exact meaning of the red mark. His son-in-law, M. Jacq, before his own death told us that Le Rouzic died before this was done.

Surprisingly good large-scale plans of some parts of the alignments and cromlechs in the Carnac area were made in the last century by Lukis and Dryden. Small-scale maps of several of the main alignments were also made during the Second World War by German surveyors. We and parties surveying with us completed large-scale (1/500) surveys of all the Carnac alignments and in fact a great part of the present book will be devoted to a study of these.

**1.3.** Our normal equipment when surveying large important sites consists of a good theodolite, a chain, steel band, steel tape and cloth tape for off-setting.

We also carry a levelling tacheometer staff and numerous rods of wood, steel, and aluminium. One of the latter is provided with a spirit bubble which allows it to be placed accurately vertical. We also carry adjustable supports which can be used for holding the steel tape in a level position. Where less accuracy is required we make much use of tacheometry. When we started surveying sites in the 1930s we did not realize the necessity for extreme accuracy and most of our early surveys were made with a cloth tape.

The orientation of each of our surveys is normally determined by sun/azimuth observation made by a theodolite and a good watch keeping time to within one second. It is of course possible to determine true north without the use of a chronometer of any kind, but it is much quicker to make use of the broadcast time signals. In our work up to the present we have made twelve to fifteen hundred determinations of azimuth, most being correct to about one arc minute. The details of the method used will be found in Appendix B of *Megalithic lunar observatories* (Thom 1971).

As we shall see, one of the greatest difficulties in studying the sites is the determination of the altitude of the horizon. It is true that with *proper* use of a theodolite the apparent altitudes can be determined to a few seconds when the horizon is visible. For long distances it is very often not visible and it may be necessary to return to a site to measure a distant horizon. When the altitude has been measured there remains the still greater difficulty of knowing the value of astronomical atmospheric refraction to be applied. Tables of this exist of course, but these differ for low altitudes and the effect of temperature is by no means accurately known. We now use the tables and chart provided by the *Nautical Almanac*. It has emerged that a still further correction may be necessary to allow for the amount by which the ray coming from an astronomical body may be bent when it grazes over a hilltop. So far we have only managed to make half a dozen measurements of this grazing correction. It probably varies from place to place, hour to hour and from day to day and it almost certainly depends on the shape of the ridge over which the ray is passing. Where the ridge is sharp and narrow the effect is probably small, but where the ray runs for a considerable distance close to the ground, the correction may possibly amount to several minutes.

### 1.4. Causes of distortion of megalithic shapes

*Soil creep*. Most superficial deposits, including boulder clay, flow but the flow depends on the slope and must be affected by the rock surface below; if this is irregular then the movement of the soil is irregular in pattern. The surface flows at a different rate to the bottom and this shearing effect may upset stones. But if a stone is set deeply enough to reach down into ground which is stationary it will be 'left behind', as it were. Perhaps this explains what we find at Long Meg and her Daughters because this is a circle on a slope; the stones at the lower side are mostly fallen and of the upright stones shown further up there are one or two which seem out of place. At Loch of Yarrows the rows are irregular, almost certainly showing the effect of soil creep. A surface slope of 1° is reported to cause flow in boulder clay.

*Trees*. Another source of distortion is produced by trees. After the great gale in 1953 we noticed that an uprooted tree in the Dyce circle had lifted a large upright stone bodily in its roots. In cases like this the tree can subsequently rot away leaving no trace and the stone is left peculiarly out of place. In other places, for example, Winterbourne Abbas S4/1 and Shianbank P2/8 (see Thom 1967 for classifications), tree-trunks are pressing against upright stones, possibly pushing them over. What happens eventually to the stone depends on whether the tree falls over or rots away standing; if the latter, then the stone is perhaps left out of place but being upright is later assumed to be undisturbed.

*People*. The worst and most deceptive disturbances, however, are those produced by people who re-erect stones without leaving any record; the re-erectors have no knowledge of the original geometry and they have no survey. They simply replace the stone where they think it looks best; examples can be found at Seascale L1/10, Callanish H1/1, and Killin P1/3. Where Le Rouzic re-erected stones in Carnac he marked them with a plug of red cement but other people have not been so thoughtful and today it may be possible only by statistical analysis to estimate the original positions of the stones.

Many sites, for example Beagh More in Ireland, have been uncovered when peat has been cut. In this connection it is interesting to look at a drawing made of Callanish I in the nineteenth century. The artist shows clearly that at that time the stones still carried the marks of the peat on the first 6 ft or so. This has now weathered away. The drawing is important because it shows which stones were then fallen and which upright. All the fallen stones were subsequently re-erected and so without the drawing we could not determine the exact geometry of the great north avenue. The crofter at Callanish II told us that his father cut the peat from the stones there and it had been 6 ft deep. He also told us that when working in the fields the crofters watched the movements of the setting sun, day after day, along the horizon.

*Frost*. Another cause of movement is frost but its effects are unpredictable. We have seen the small stones in a gravel path arrange themselves into rings as a result of repeated freezing and thawing, and it appears that this can happen on a larger scale where boulders are lying touching one another. Is this what happened to the field of boulders near Merrivale?

Some stones and some circles have been disturbed by water. For example, the remains of the circle near Forse Latheron are now in a swamp. One of the circles on Er Lannic in the Sea of Morbihan is completely submerged by the rising level of the sea, and a portion of the circle called the Girdle Stones has been washed away by the River Esk.

In view of what has been said above it is only in exceptional circumstances that we can expect Megalithic stones to be accurately in their original places and this must be kept in mind when statistical examination of circles, alignments, etc. is undertaken. Even where the stones have been set in hard ground and re-erected the re-erectors may have raised the wrong end.

**1.5.** In the above connection we must consider how accurately the original erectors succeeded in placing the stones exactly where they intended them to be. They would mark out the position for a stone on the ground, but before the necessary hole could be dug they had to have four pegs round about so that the marked out position could be re-established or maintained as the hole was sunk. The stone was then let into the hole using, if necessary, antifriction guides on the sides. It would be most unlikely that the position it took up corresponded exactly with the four pegs round about. To move it in the hole would be difficult and the erectors might eventually be satisfied provided it more or less lined up with the neighbouring stones. At Stonehenge, the trilithons and sarsen stones in the main ring have been adjusted to within about an inch, but in the less important rings the same accuracy was perhaps not considered necessary. At Avebury it must have taken a great deal of work and skill to adjust the huge stones in the chalk sockets.

In the case of a stone used as a backsight it is unlikely that any subsequent displacement will affect the declination seriously. If we do find that the declination differs by an arc minute or so from what we expect, we ought not to be surprised by the error but surprised that the stone had been placed so near to the correct position. We have always to bear in mind how limited were the erectors' facilities and remember that they had no *Nautical Almanac* or theodolite.

Megalithic activity went on for a long time, perhaps for several thousand years. We must not expect to find that during this period the ideas governing the erection of the stones were static. During periods of political stability, knowledge would probably have increased either by natural development or by diffusion from elsewhere. We should expect this to be reflected in the stones. The cruder circles were probably earlier, and we must be prepared to find indications of growth in some of the sites where perhaps one scheme was being replaced by another. This development we can expect to find reflected in the geometry and in the knowledge of astronomy. The most ambitious geometrical design in Britain is that of the Avebury Ring and the most advanced lunar observatory is perhaps seen in the final stages of Brogar.

In Britain the theme of the ring persisted and the Carnac alignments, as we shall see, were associated with large, carefully set out cromlechs. We do not know what these alignments were for, but we suggest that they came late in the culture and probably replaced much that went before.

Archaeologists are increasing their knowledge of the rings and henges and of the activities which were associated with them. A study of the recent books by Dr. Aubrey Burl (1976) and Dr. Euan W. Mackie (1977*a, b*) show how far this has gone in Britain.

**1.6.** The radiocarbon method of dating and more especially its recent recalibration gives an entirely different range of dates. Everything is earlier than was previously thought. In view of this it is necessary to re-examine the histogram of declinations given in *Megalithic sites in Britain*, Fig. 8.1 (Thom 1967). The star declinations shown there are for the period 2000 to 1800 B.C. We must now look earlier; according to Burl very much earlier. Only two stars stand out in the histogram, Capella and Deneb, and today we would exclude a number of the lines which were in 1967 attributed to Capella. For example, the two long lines at Temple Wood are now considered to be lunar to the south whereas they were assumed to be for Capella to the north. Similarly the Callanish avenue which was assumed to be for Capella is possibly a lunar line showing the moon passing to the south, but here it should be pointed out that we have not yet obtained an accurately measured profile of the hills to the south; furthermore these hills are not visible from the north end of the avenue. Nevertheless it appears that the case for Capella is considerably weakened. The star Deneb is, however, indicated by one or two impressive lines, but the declination of Deneb changes so slowly that it cannot be used for dating. For the same reason, however, it should give the best value for the extinction angle or the lowest altitude at which a star is ever visible. The line from Callanish to the east showed perhaps Altair rising in 1760 B.C., a date only slightly earlier than that which we shall show in Chapter 10 is indicated by the Brogar lunar observatory.

**1.7. Le Grand Menhir Brisé**

We shall now discuss the most massive artificially cut stone in Europe, namely Le Grand Menhir Brisé at Carnac. It was about 70 ft (21 m) long, and weighed over 300 tons, and was put in position nearly 4000 years ago. It now lies broken in four pieces. Even today a load of 300 tons would be regarded as exceptional—and yet Le Grand Menhir Brisé must have been brought from some distance. It is most unlikely that the erectors found a suitable piece of rock loose and ready to be shaped, and it presumably had to be cut from solid rock by hand. One shrinks from trying to make an estimate of how many man-hours were necessary. We might guess that 20 men could work on each side cutting huge grooves, or rather valleys, into the rock leaving the stone to be eventually parted by the usual technique of cutting a row of slots, driving in dry wooden wedges and then pouring water on the wood. Atkinson has described how the Stonehenge menhirs were shaped by hammering the surface and removing the dust repeatedly. We can picture the men working until they had sunk a trench in the rock wide enough to work in and 10 or 12 ft deep. Then the stone had to be lifted and transported, inches at a time, using tree-trunks as levers—perhaps 40 levers lifting 8 tons each or perhaps lifting one end at a time. The fulcrums must have been of wood, but what bearing area of ground was needed for each? The organization and control of the labour force must have presented many problems, for example feeding and housing the men year after year. What was the urge behind it all and how were the labourers persuaded or forced to work?

Here we may note the heights of the stones at some of the known or suspected lunar sites in Scotland: Ballymeanach 13 ft, Beacharr 15 ft, Camus an Stacca 12 ft, Borgue 13 ft, Lund 13 ft, Ballinaby 17 ft, Lundin Links 14 ft, and Knockstaple 12 ft.

Since these are all higher than the average height of menhirs in the districts, we can say that the lunar backsights were often marked by exceptionally tall stones. Le Grand Menhir Brisé is an improbable backsight but we suggest that it was intended as a universal lunar foresight: we shall give our reasons for this belief in Chapter 9.

When did Le Grand Menhir Brisé fall? Closely connected with this question is another: how did it fall into the position in which we find the four pieces? The top three pieces presumably broke apart when they hit the ground; but the bottom piece lies turned over and faces away from the next section. Experiments with three or four child's building bricks on a tray show that there is only one way to induce them to fall like that, and that is to shake the tray. One can picture an earthquake bringing about this kind of fall if the menhir was initially separated into two parts. Lightning can break a stone provided that water has got into a crack, but if there was no crack at this junction then the earthquake must have been very violent.

A possibility worth considering is that the main break occurred before the stone was erected so that it was put in position in two parts. Provided that the lower part was properly founded then no wind could have upset the upper. An examination of the photographs in Fig. 9.2 shows that originally the stone was in one piece so that the job was not done by preparing two flat surfaces which would fit together. If this is the explanation we are still left with the question as to what caused the break.

From information passed to us by R. L. Merritt who has been in touch with Professor P. R. Giot of Rennes University, we understand that records exist of a series of earthquakes in the district in A.D. 1286.

The subject will have to be studied by an expert in the strength of materials with a knowledge of seismology. He would need to know the frequency and amplitude of the tremor and the natural frequency of the stone and the method of its support and consequent attachment to the ground or the underlying rock. The matter is in an unsatisfactory condition at present, but it ought to be possible to make an estimate of the likelihood of the fall being produced by an earthquake.

To make the car park at Le Grand Menhir Brisé necessitated the virtual destruction of the tumulus which ran up to the stone. Let us hope that the agitation to move the stone to Paris and re-erect it there has been finally silenced forever.

# 2

## ASTRONOMY—GENERAL BACKGROUND

**2.1.** IT is not possible to follow much of the later material in this book without a knowledge of the moon's movements. These are sufficiently described in Thom 1971 and so here we shall merely mention the main facts and give some extra details. Every month the moon's declination attains a maximum northerly value and two weeks later a minimum, that is a maximum negative, value. In fact in a month it goes through a similar cycle to that made by the sun in a year. There are, however, two important differences. Whereas the sun in a year goes from declination $+\epsilon$ at the summer solstice to declination $-\epsilon$ at the winter solstice and back to $+\epsilon$, where $\epsilon$ is the obliquity of the ecliptic, the limits of the moon's movements are not constant but vary from $\pm(\epsilon+i)$ at the major standstill or turning point, to $\pm(\epsilon-i)$ at the minor standstill (some 9 years later). Here $i$ is equal to $5° 08' 43''$, the mean inclination of the moon's orbit to the ecliptic. The period of this cycle is 18·61 years. In addition a small perturbation or continuous wobble of amount $\Delta$ in the inclination of the moon's orbit is caused by the sun. $\Delta$ has a value of about 8'. This wobble has a period of 173·3 days or half an eclipse year and, in fact, eclipses of the sun or moon occur only when $\Delta$ is at or nearly at a maximum. Tycho Brahé was the first European to discover this perturbation of the orbit. He pointed out that the maximum values occurred when the node was in conjunction with or in opposition to the sun and was at its minimum when the node was in quadrature.

One of the objects of our previous book (Thom 1971) was to show that the wobble, in spite of its small amplitude, was known to Megalithic man. This perturbation would have been visible to these people only at the standstills, when the variation in the declination produced by the main movement had approached zero. The small value of $\Delta$ made it necessary to use an observing method sensitive enough to detect a change of declination of one or two arc minutes. A technique which made this possible is described fully in Chapter 1 of Thom 1971. Briefly, on each night near the standstill the observer placed himself in a position from which the edge of the moon appeared to graze a well defined distant object, natural or artificial. The observer's position was marked by a stake each night and the resulting set of stakes could be studied afterwards. As the observations could be made only once a day, the moon would, in general, attain its maximum declination between two observing times, and a method of extrapolation had to be used.

We believe that the stone rows found in Caithness and some of those in Carnac are the remains of an arrangement for making this extrapolation (see Appendix B). Unless a method for extrapolation had been used the whole observatory would have been useless and, in fact, the observing sites which we have surveyed and describe later could not have been built.

To find out just how much Megalithic man knew and how he used his lunar observatories, it is necessary to measure up what we find and to have a complete understanding of a standstill. Figure 2.1 shows what happens at a typical major standstill, that of 1969. Here we see the top of the main declination cycle shown by the dotted line. The monthly declination maxima are shown and it will be seen how these are sometimes greater than the mean dotted line and sometimes less. This is the perturbation cycle already referred to, with a period of half an eclipse year and an amplitude which varies from about 7′ to about 9′. We shall now look at the factors which affect its value.

## 2.2. The amplitude of the perturbation

The inclination of the moon's orbit is given by Danby (1962) as

$$i_d = i + 8'\cdot7 \cos 2U + 0'\cdot65\{\cos 2u + \cos 2(u - U)\}, \qquad (2.1)$$

where $i$ — mean inclination of the moon's orbit to the ecliptic $= 5° \ 08'\cdot7$; this remains constant over thousands of years. $U = $ longitude of sun — longitude of node, and $u = $ longitude of moon — longitude of node. Longitude (celestial) is measured along the ecliptic anti-clockwise from the First Point of Aries.

At the standstill, as explained in Thom 1971, p. 18, with the moon at its extreme declination, longitude of node $= 0°$ or $180°$, and longitude of moon $= 90°$ or $270°$, hence

$$i_d = i + 8'\cdot7 \cos 2U + 0'\cdot65(-1 - \cos 2U), \qquad (2.2)$$

and the extremes are

$$i_d = i + 7'\cdot4 \qquad (2.3)$$

when $U = 0°$, and

$$i_d = i - 8'\cdot7 \qquad (2.4)$$

when $U = 90°$.

It follows that we can put $\Delta = 7'\cdot4$ when $i$ and $\Delta$ are of the same sign and $\Delta = 8'\cdot7$ when they are of opposite sign.

The fact that the top of the perturbation wobble shown at T, Fig. 2.2, does not in general happen at the top, $Q$, of the long-period oscillation of $\pm(\epsilon \pm i)$, produces another small effect: the height of T is reduced by an amount $b$. Since the period of the wobble is 173·3 days, T can be before (or after) $Q$ by one half of this, namely 86·6 days. When the crest is more than 86·6 days away from $Q$ then the next oscillation, V, will have a higher peak. In Thom 1971, p. 24, it is shown that $b$ is approximately $0\cdot00013 \ t^2$, where $b$

is in arc minutes and $t$ is the time difference between T and $Q$ in days. Thus $b$ might be as large as $1'\cdot0$. If we do not know $t$ then T may possibly have fallen anywhere up to 86·6 days from $Q$ and all we can do, when attempting to compare declinations ($\delta_O$, see later) obtained from sight lines with the moon's declination at standstills, is to take a time mean over this interval. From the expression given above for $b$, this angle is found to be $b_{\text{mean}} = 0\cdot3$ arc minutes.

Let us write the declination at T as $\epsilon + i + \Delta_E$ where $\Delta_E$ might be called the effective perturbation or the value which we should use for comparison with observed declinations. Then at the major standstill, for example at T,

$$\delta_T = \epsilon + i - b + \Delta, \tag{2.5}$$

$$\Delta_E = \Delta - b = 7'\cdot4 - 0'\cdot3 = 7'\cdot1. \tag{2.6}$$

Eight different cases exist. Examining them we find that when $i$ and $\Delta$ are of the same sign $\Delta_E = 7'\cdot4 - 0'\cdot3 = 7'\cdot1$, and when they are of opposite sign $\Delta_E = 8'\cdot7 + 0'\cdot3 = 9'\cdot0$.

The total effect of such adjustments while comparing declinations is always small, but it seems desirable to put the matter on record, more especially as the actual value of $b$ might, in a given case, be as large as $1'\cdot0$. It would then appear to be better to use $b_{\text{mean}} = 0'\cdot3$ rather than neglect the correction.

### 2.3. Parallax

Parallax is produced by the fact that instead of viewing the sky from the centre of the Earth, we observe it from a point distance $r$ from the centre, where $r$ is the radius of the Earth, some 4000 miles. When a body is seen on the horizon the line of sight is normal to the line to the Earth's centre. Parallax is then at a maximum, the so called 'horizontal parallax', and is approximately $r/R$, where $R$ is the distance to the body from the Earth's centre. Because the lunar orbit is an ellipse, $R$ is not constant and so parallax varies from a minimum of $53'\cdot9$ to a maximum of $61'\cdot5$, the mean being $57'\ 02''\cdot7$.

We can, however, go into the subject in greater detail by making use of the full expression for parallax, $p$, namely:

$$p = 3422''\cdot7 + 186''\cdot5 \cos l + 28''\cdot2 \cos MS + 34''\cdot3 \cos(l - MS)$$
$$+ 10''\cdot2 \cos 2l + 3''\cdot1 \cos(l + MS), \tag{2.7}$$

where $l$ = mean anomaly, and $MS$ = longitude of moon − longitude of sun, which is $u - U$ in (2.1). For our present purposes the mean anomaly can be thought of as the mean position of the moon measured anticlockwise from its position at perigee.

We are interested only in values of the longitude of the sun and moon near to $0°$, $90°$, $180°$, and $270°$, and this makes things much simpler. When $l$ is $0°$

or 180°, the second term in (2.7) is numerically 186″·5 and so is larger than any of the later terms in the expression. Hence we shall not be far wrong in assuming that maximum parallax occurs when $l = 0°$ and minimum when $l = 180°$. Further examination shows the values given in Table 2.1.

**Table 2.1.** *Values for parallax*

| Moon's maximum declination | p max | p min | Mean p | Mean semidiameter, s (0·2725 p) |
|---|---|---|---|---|
| $\pm(\epsilon+i+\Delta)$ | 60′·3 | 54′·2 | 57′·2 | 15′·6 |
| $\pm(\epsilon+i-\Delta)$ | 61′·4 | 54′·0 | 57′·7 | 15′·7 |
| $\pm(\epsilon-i+\Delta)$ | 61′·4 | 54′·0 | 57′·7 | 15′·7 |
| $\pm(\epsilon-i-\Delta)$ | 60′·3 | 54′·2 | 57′·2 | 15′·6 |

We do not know at which particular standstill any particular foresight was erected; hence we do not know the value of the mean anomaly and so have no knowledge of the exact parallax and can take only the appropriate mean value from Table 2.1.

### 2.4. Time of year of maximum declination

At a major standstill the ascending node of the moon's orbit is near the First Point of Aries but conditions are complicated by the perturbation induced by the sun on the inclination of the orbit. This perturbation causes the plane of the orbit to wobble so that only when the node is in conjunction with or in opposition to the sun can the moon's monthly maximum declination attain its greatest values and these are separated by 173·3 days, that is, half an eclipse year.

Any monthly declination maximum happens when the longitude of the moon is near to 90° (or 270°). The highest declination will be that occurring, as has just been said, when the node is near conjunction with, or opposition to, the sun; but as we have just seen, the node is near the First Point of Aries and therefore the sun's longitude is near to 0° or 180°. Thus for a maximum declination we must have

(1) moon's longitude near 90° or 270° and
(2) sun's longitude near to 0° or 180°.

As a result of (1) and (2) the moon is at its first or third quarter when the maximum occurs and as a result of (2), the maximum declination occurs near either the vernal or the autumnal equinox. This is clearly shown in the values for 1969 plotted in Fig. 2.1 where the three consecutive maxima occurred either at the end of September or the end of March, whereas the minima happened at the end of December or the end of June, that is at the solstices.

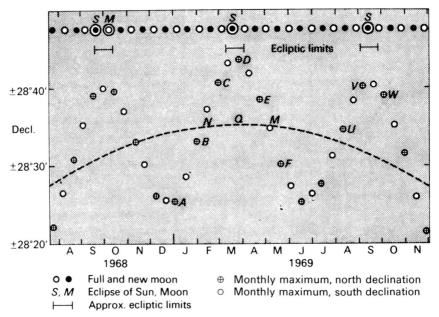

FIG. 2.1. Declination maxima (north and south) at the 1969 standstill.

## 2.5. Time of day when the moon is on the horizon

We must now consider the hour of the day when the moon is found on a foresight. We calculate the hour angle of the foresight measured from the south, add the moon's longitude and subtract the sun's longitude. The result, converted into time units, is approximately the required hour in old astronomical time, and this places zero hour at midday.

Consider a foresight for the moon *setting* with maximum positive declination. The hour angle measured from the south is between 90° and 180°, and if we take the case when the sun's longitude is 0° and apply the above rule, we find that the time is between 12 hours and 18 hours (zero hour at midday). Since we are dealing with a date near the equinox, the sun will be below the horizon between the hours 6 and 18, that is the moon will set during the hours of darkness. If we consider a foresight for the *rising* moon we find that we must adopt the case when the sun's longitude was not 0° but 180°, that is the autumnal equinox, otherwise we find that the moon rose in daylight.

It follows that we must have information (declination, parallax, etc.) for the two greatest maxima of the perturbation oscillation. One of these is for the sun's longitude near to 0° and the other for 180°. We choose the one which suits in that it shows that the moon was on the foresight in darkness.

The same arguments apply to the greatest south declination but here the longitude of the moon is 270°.

The above deals with the cases $\pm(\epsilon \pm i \pm s \pm \Delta)$ in which $s$ is the moon's semidiameter, and $\Delta$ and $i$ are of the same sign. If we wish to consider a foresight that we think has been used when $\Delta$ and $i$ are of opposite sign, that is when the perturbation is at its lowest, then we have to put the node in quadrature with the sun, and we find that the sun's longitude is near to $\pm 90°$, and this is at the solstices. In other words, the maxima of the wobble occur at the equinoxes and the minima at the solstices (Fig. 2.1).

## 2.6. The Greenwich calculations

It is obviously desirable to have definite information regarding the moon's declination, parallax, etc. throughout the period in which we are interested. Thanks to the good offices of staff of the *Nautical Almanac* Office at the Royal Greenwich Observatory, we now have the information we need in full detail. To calculate all the necessary values seemed a very long task, but Dr. A. T. Sinclair (personal communication) found a somewhat simplified method which, on examination, gave values agreeing closely with those from the full theory. Nowhere, in fact, did the difference in declination attain a value of 1 arc minute. Figure 2.2 shows how the declination maxima behave near a standstill. With no perturbation the maxima would have lain on a smooth curve coming to its greatest value when the node of the orbit was at the First Point of Aries. Greenwich provided us with particulars from 2100 to 1300 B.C., of the moon's longitude, declination and parallax for times T, U, V, and W,

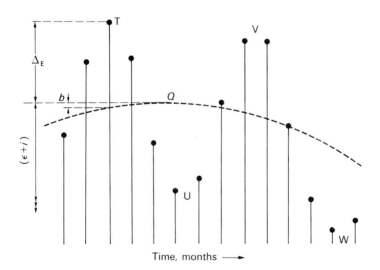

FIG. 2.2. The moon's monthly declination maxima at a major standstill, showing the effect of the perturbation $\Delta$, period = 173·3 days. The declination, had there been no perturbation, is shown by the dotted line which has its maximum $(\epsilon + i)$ at $Q$ when the node is at the First Point of Aries.

along with the longitude of the sun. There is, as has been already explained, an important difference between T and V in Fig. 2.2; one of these happens near the vernal equinox and the other near the autumnal equinox. Similarly for U and W; one happens near midsummer and the other near midwinter.

We present here, in a manner which we shall now describe, such of the Greenwich results as we require for a detailed study of Brogar, the most complete lunar observatory so far discovered. Most of the field measurements given in our previous publications including Thom 1971 have been used to obtain the 'observed' declination $\delta_O$ of the foresights by using the figure of 57'·0 for mean parallax. Let the parallax, $p$, be 57'·0+$q$. Had we used $p$ instead of 57'·0 to deduce the declination, the result would have been $\delta = \delta_O + q \, d\delta/dp$. But $d\delta/dp$ is equal to $d\delta/dh$, where $h$ is the altitude, and this can be evaluated by using the appropriate formula (see equation (2.6) Thom 1971, p. 27); for any particular case of $\pm(\epsilon\pm i)$ we have found it sufficiently accurate for our present purpose to use for $d\delta/dh$ a mean value from one end of Britain to the other, namely 0·95 at major standstills and 0·86 at minor standstills. Note that when we know $p$ we also know $s$, the semidiameter; in fact $s = 0\cdot2725p$.

Let $D_G$ be the appropriate value of the declination given by Greenwich. We want to compare $\delta$ (that is $\delta_O \pm q \, d\delta/dh$) with $D_G \pm s$ or, what is the same thing, to compare $\delta_O$ with $D_G - q \, d\delta/dh \pm s$ which we shall call $D_O$. Accordingly, we evaluate $D_O$ for all the required cases and present the results in such a form that we can see at a glance if the value of $\delta_O$ found at any foresight is sufficiently close to $D_O$ at some or other standstill or range of standstills to make it possible that the backsight and foresight were arranged at that date.

To have all the values of $D_G$ ready to be used on any possible foresight we have prepared 16 sets of derived values of $D_O$ but here we shall give only the values needed for Brogar, Fig. 2.3. It will be seen that there is a long-period sinusoidal oscillation in all the curves produced by the peculiar manner in which lunar parallax affects the results. By extending for several thousand

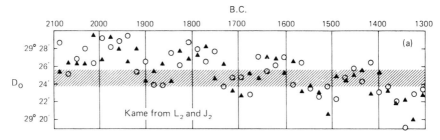

(a) Kame from $L_2$ and $J_2$ compared with
    ○  ($\epsilon+i+s+\Delta$) autumn 8 p.m. Longitude of moon (LM) approx. 90°, Longitude of sun (LS) approx. 180°, and
    ▲  ($\epsilon+i+s+\Delta$) spring 8 a.m. LM approx. 90°, LS approx. 0°.

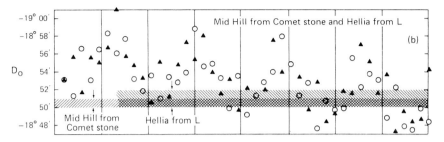

(b) Mid Hill from Comet Stone compared with
   ○   $-(\epsilon-i+s-\Delta)$ autumn 3 p.m. LM approx. $-90°$, LS approx. $180°$, and
   ▲   $-(\epsilon-i+s-\Delta)$ spring 3 a.m. LM approx. $-90°$, LS approx. $0°$,
   and Hellia from $L$ compared with $-(\epsilon-i+s-\Delta)$ autumn 9 p.m. and spring 9 a.m.

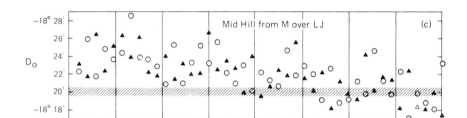

(c) Mid Hill from $M$ ground level over $L$ and $J$ compared with
   ○   $-(\epsilon-i-s-\Delta)$ spring 3 a.m. LM approx. $-90°$, LS approx. $0°$, and
   ▲   $-(\epsilon-i-s-\Delta)$ autumn 3 p.m. LM approx. $-90°$, LS approx. $180°$.

*Note.* A narrower band has been used for Mid Hill because Mid Hill lines are
probably less liable to be affected by the graze.

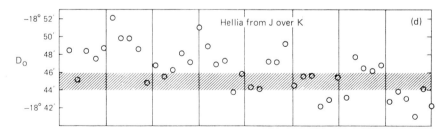

(d) Hellia from $J$ over $K$ compared with
   ○   mean of $\left\{ \begin{array}{l} -(\epsilon-i-\Delta) \text{ autumn 9 p.m. LM approx. } -90°, \text{ LS approx. } 180° \\ -(\epsilon-i+\Delta) \text{ summer 3 a.m. LM approx. } -90°, \text{ LS approx. } 90° \text{ (Full} \\ \text{moon).} \end{array} \right.$

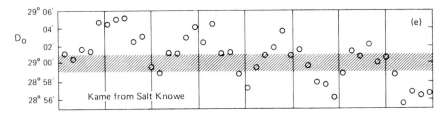

(e) Kame, lower, from Salt Knowe ground level, compared with

　　○　mean of $\begin{cases} (\epsilon+i-\Delta), \text{ winter 2 p.m. LM approx. } 90°, \text{ LS approx. } 270° \text{ (Full moon)} \\ (\epsilon+i+\Delta), \text{ spring 8 a.m. LM approx. } 90°, \text{ LS approx. } 0°. \end{cases}$

FIG. 2.3. Values of moon's declination, $D_O$, for Brogar deduced from the values of $D_G$ provided by Greenwich. As an illustration these are compared with values measured at Brogar (Chapter 10).

years the argument given in Thom 1971, p. 81, we found that the oscillation has a period of about 65 456 days or 179 years and this agrees in broad outline with the values provided by Greenwich. The mean amplitude, however, appears to be smaller than that shown in Thom 1971. Note that the values of $D_O$ in Fig. 2.3 are all falling gradually with a slope of about 39″ per century, i.e. the rate of decrease of obliquity. It is this very slow rate of fall of $\epsilon$ which makes it so difficult to date the sites astronomically.

　　Use will be made of Fig. 2.3 in Chapter 10 on Brogar.

# 3

## CIRCLES AND RINGS

**3.1.** ALTOGETHER there are probably well over a thousand remains of stone rings still visible in Britain, the smaller ones being only a few yards in diameter while at the other end of the scale the Avebury ring is over 1000 ft across. As the Megalithic culture lasted for perhaps 2000 years, ample time existed for the knowledge of geometry to develop; and develop it certainly did so that, long before the Greeks, people in north-west Europe were setting out ellipses and other much more complicated geometrical shapes.

The majority of the rings were true circles but in Fig. 3.1 we give for reference the commoner variations. Of the 900 Megalithic rings known to Burl he thinks that about 600 are circles, 150 are flattened circles, 100 are ellipses, and 50 are egg-shaped (Burl 1976). There were also the compound rings (Thom 1967) leading finally to the most advanced of all, that at Avebury.

An important difference exists between the flattened circles and the other types. All type A rings, whatever their size, are geometrically similar; and the same applies to type B. Neither type incorporated a triangle with integral sides. Nearly all the others (egg-shaped, ellipses, and mixed) are based on right-angled triangles, and in every triangle the sides are integral or nearly integral in Megalithic yards (MY). Provided that the sides of the triangles are integral then all the other dimensions required for setting out the figure can also be integral. It seems that in all types a primary aim was to have an integral number of Megalithic rods (MR) in the perimeter.

We shall show in Chapter 5 that the designs of the petroglyphs or cup and ring marks cut in the rock were largely controlled, at least in north England and in Scotland, by the same rules: as far as possible all lengths had to be integral multiples of a unit that we shall call the Megalithic inch. Thus Megalithic man's geometry became based on integral lengths. He had no graduated rules and tried to do without them.

The incommensurate value of $\pi$ evidently worried him. Perhaps taken at first to be 3, it was later found to be nearly $3\frac{1}{8}$; witness that we find more circles with a diameter of 8 MY than any other number. The product $3\frac{1}{8} \times 8$ is 25 and so the circumference was assumed to be 10 MR of $2\frac{1}{2}$ MY each. Still later it was obviously realized that $3\frac{1}{8}$ was not perfect; witness that at Brogar a value of 3·140 was accepted.

It is shown in Thom 1967, p. 47, that when the diameter was irreconcilable with the circumference in integers it was often slightly adjusted in order to make both approximately integral.

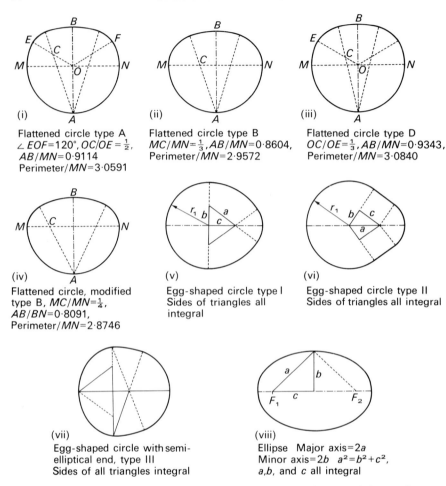

Flattened circle type A
$\angle EOF=120°$, $OC/OE=\frac{1}{2}$,
$AB/MN=0.9114$
Perimeter/$MN=3.0591$

Flattened circle type B
$MC/MN=\frac{1}{3}$, $AB/MN=0.8604$,
Perimeter/$MN=2.9572$

Flattened circle type D
$OC/OE=\frac{1}{3}$, $AB/MN=0.9343$,
Perimeter/$MN=3.0840$

Flattened circle, modified
type B, $MC/MN=\frac{1}{4}$,
$AB/BN=0.8091$,
Perimeter/$MN=2.8746$

Egg-shaped circle type I
Sides of triangles all
integral

Egg-shaped circle type II
Sides of triangles all integral

(vii)
Egg-shaped circle with semi-
elliptical end, type III
Sides of all triangles integral

(viii)
Ellipse   Major axis$=2a$
Minor axis$=2b$   $a^2=b^2+c^2$,
$a,b$, and $c$ all integral

FIG. 3.1. Types of rings found in standing-stone circles and in cup and ring marks.

## 3.2. Ellipses and eggs

Before we can call a shape a 'Megalithic egg' or a 'Megalithic ellipse' it must
have all linear dimensions nearly integral in Megalithic yards or half-yards
and the perimeter must be integral, or nearly integral, in Megalithic rods.
We say 'nearly integral' because we must bear in mind that the difficulty of
measuring the length of a curve was added to the difficulty (theoretically the
impossibility) of finding a design with integral linear dimensions that would
have an integral perimeter.

*Some French cromlechs.* There are not so many rings or circles in Brittany as
in Britain. In the Carnac area we know of six cromlechs as they are called

and these are all partly destroyed. Nevertheless the Megalithic yard shows up in five—the two Le Ménec cromlechs, the two at Kerlescan, and the Crucuno rectangle. The west cromlech at Le Ménec is seen in Fig. 6.1. All but five of the stones in this ring carry the plug of red cement put there by Le Rouzic to show that the stone has been re-erected and, of these five, all lie on or close to the egg-shaped ring we have superimposed. This type I egg shape is based on a 3, 4, 5 triangle having sides 15, 20, and 25 MR. There can be little doubt that this was how the ring was set out. The manner in which the cromlech was connected to the alignments here and at the east cromlech will be shown in Chapter 6 on Le Ménec.

Figure 6.1 shows how, by dropping a perpendicular from the centre to the hypotenuse, we get another 3, 4, 5 triangle, namely 12, 16, 20 MR and this triangle forms the basis of the type II egg-shaped circle that we find at the east cromlech (Fig. 6.2). The modern road runs through the south end of the east cromlech and much of the remainder is probably built into the road or the near-by houses.

The perimeter of the west cromlech calculated from the dimensions shown is 304·41 MY or only 0·2 per cent short of the ideal 305 and that of the east cromlech is 369·94 MY or less than 0·02 per cent below 370.

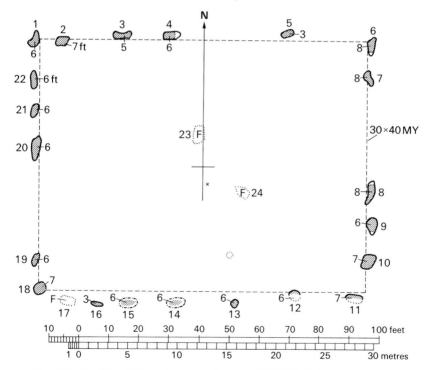

FIG. 3.2. The Megalithic rectangle at Crucuno, 19003059 (47° 37'·5, 3° 07'·3).

Another example of the use of Megalithic rods in France is the rectangle at Crucuno (Fig. 3.2), where the tall stones are built round a rectangle 30 × 40 MY with diagonal 50 MY.

### 3.3. The cromlech at St. Pierre

The greater part of this cromlech was removed certainly before 1868 when the remains were surveyed by Dryden and Lukis. Their survey does not show much more than ours made in 1970 and in fact we have an extra stone at the

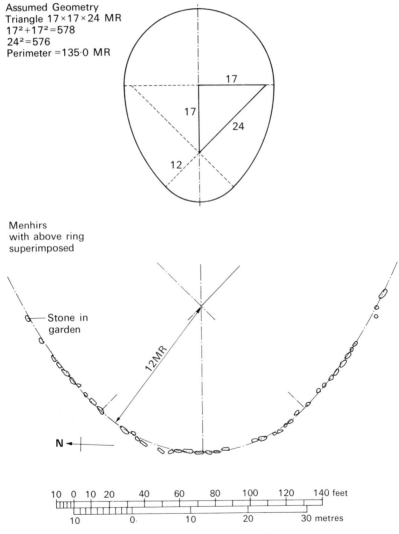

Assumed Geometry
Triangle 17×17×24 MR
$17^2 + 17^2 = 578$
$24^2 = 576$
Perimeter = 135·0 MR

Menhirs
with above ring
superimposed

Stone in garden

12MR

N

10  0  10  20     40      60      80     100    120    140 feet

10          0·          10        20        30 metres

FIG. 3.3. The cromlech at St. Pierre, Quiberon.

north end of the arc; we found it enclosed in a garden. The surveys agree
closely and both show the two changes of curvature in the remaining part of
the ring. Using this slender evidence we give in Fig. 3.3 a possible reconstruction of the geometry of the ring. This egg-shape shown is based on a triangle
of 17, 17, and 24 MR. Note that $17^2 + 17^2 = 578$ and $24^2 = 576$. The perimeter of the ring is 135·02 MR. There can of course be no certainty until the
site is excavated but the triangle is excellent and the perimeter is almost
perfect according to the rule.

### 3.4. Egg shapes with elliptic ends

There are two examples of a type III ring to be found among the cup and
ring plans (in Figs 5.6 and 5.7). Both of the rings at Newgrange probably

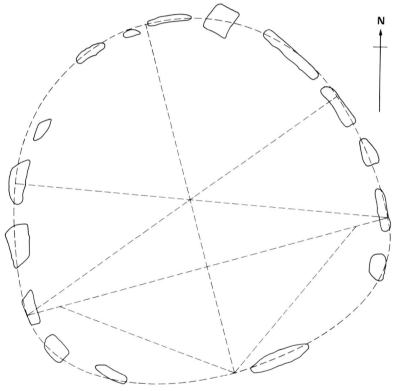

N

Ellipse (MY): $2a=7$, $2b=4$, $2c=5\frac{3}{4}$            Triangle for arcs (MY): $-a=3\frac{3}{4}$, $b=3\frac{1}{2}$, $c=1\frac{1}{4}$
$5\frac{3}{4}^2+4^2=49·06$, $7^2=49$                              $3\frac{1}{2}^2+1\frac{1}{4}^2=13·81$, $3\frac{3}{4}^2=14·06$

Perimeter $=21·58$ MY

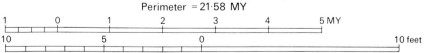

FIG. 3.4. Hirnant Cairn Circle, SN 753839.

belong to this type as does perhaps the ring at Whitcastles (G7/6), but the stones at Whitcastles are so big that it is equally possible to fit a modified type B ring with its diameter divided into 4 instead of 3.

In Fig. 3.4 we show a survey made by John R. Hoyle of another Type III ring. This is the ring called Hirnant Cairn Circle. The theoretical perimeter is 21·58 MY but there were two triangles to be satisfied in integers and it would thus have been remarkable if the erectors had achieved a perfect result.

### 3.5. Spacing of the stones round the circles

In some rings the stones are placed so as to touch one another, for example at Moel ty Ucha in Wales and the west cromlech at Le Ménec in France, but in most cases the stones are spaced widely apart. In only one or two examples were the spacing and orientation controlled by the desire to indicate the rising or setting positions of the sun and moon at important times. The outstanding example is Castle Rigg near Keswick, for which reference should be made to Thom 1965 or to Thom 1967. But at the great majority of circles the spacing of the stones has nothing to do with astronomy.

We shall now look at the spacing in a number of circles chosen because they are in a reasonable state of preservation and because they are not too small. It does not appear that the stones were ever placed an integral number of Megalithic yards or rods apart, but in many of the better circles the spacing seems to have been uniform. In other words the circumference was divided into an integral number of parts $(n)$.

Particulars of the circles which we propose to examine are given in Table 3.1. We wish to show that in these circles the stones were intended to be equally spaced and we wish to find out if the erectors started at the north point. The azimuth $(Az)$ of each stone was measured as seen from the centre of the circle. This was then compared with $(360/n) \times m$, where $n$ is the number of stones and $m$ is the order number of the stones with zero in the north.

Put $\epsilon_1 = Az - (360 \, m/n)$ and find $\epsilon_m$, its mean value. This we shall call the node, and we shall define the quantum as $360/n$.

We illustrate by an example, namely the circle at Loch Buie in Mull (Table 3.2). There are nine stones in the ring and so the mean space, $2\delta$, is $360°/9 = 40°$. With this as the quantum (Thom 1967, Ch. 2), the node, $\epsilon_m$, is $-0·2$. Hence the intended position of a stone in degrees is $40m - 0·2$ and the amount by which the stone is away from this position is $\epsilon = Az - (40m - 0·2)$. The variance is $s^2 = (1/n)\Sigma\epsilon^2$; $s^2/\delta^2 = 0·071$, and for such data Broadbent's tables (Thom 1967, Fig. 2.1) show a value of 1 per cent for the 'probability level'. This is the probability that the stones if randomly placed would be as nearly uniformly spaced as we found them. Actually nine stones is too small a sample for the probability level to be accurate but this hardly matters.

As is shown in textbooks on statistics, it is quicker to obtain $s^2$ from

**Table 3.1.** *The positions of stones in some circles chosen for their reasonable state of preservation*

|  | Site | Diameter (ft) | $n$ | Node | $s^2/\delta^2$ | Probability level (%) |
|---|---|---|---|---|---|---|
| M2/14 | Loch Buie | 44·1 | 9 | −0·2 | 0·07 | 1·0 |
| B1/26 | Loanhead | 67·2 | 11 | −2·2 | 0·022 | 1·0 |
| G4/9 | Loch Mannoch | 20·9 | 10 | 15·0 | 0·01 | 0·3 |
| B1/6 | Aquorthies Manor | 64·2 | 11 | −13·2 | 0·07 | 1·0 |
| B2/2 | Sunhoney | 83·2 | 11 | −12·8 | 0·03 | 1·0 |
| L1/16 | Blakeley Moss | 54·4 | 11 | 15·9 | 0·08 | 1·0 |
| S1/16 | Botallack | 71·6 | 21 | 8·6 | 0·02 | 0·01 |
| S1/14 | Merry Maidens | 77·8 | 19 | 12·9 | 0·18 | 1·0 |
| S1/6 | Leaze | 81·5 | 12 | 2·2 | 0·11 | 1·0 |
| S2/3 | Brisworthy | 81·4 | 24 | −0·8 | 0·19 | 1·0 |
| — | Trezibbet | 106·2 | 32 | 3·1 | 0·10 | 0·01 |

Merry Maidens, Trezibbet, and perhaps others have been re-erected. Blakeley Moss is reported to be a fake but it is interesting that its diameter is exactly 20 MY!
$n$, number of stones in ring.

**Table 3.2.** *The spacing of stones at Loch Buie Mull, diameter 44·1 ft*

| $m$ | $Az$ | $40°m$ | $Az-40°m$ |
|---|---|---|---|
| 0 | 1·2 | 0 | 1·2 |
| 1 | 31·5 | 40 | −8·5 |
| 2 | 75·2 | 80 | −4·8 |
| 3 | 113·4 | 120 | −6·6 |
| 4 | 159·5 | 160 | −0·5 |
| 5 | 202·7 | 200 | 2·7 |
| 6 | 249·3 | 240 | 9·3 |
| 7 | 280·8 | 280 | 0·8 |
| 8 | 324·5 | 320 | 9·5 |

$m$, order number of stone
$Az$, azimuth in degrees

$s^2 = (1/n)\Sigma(\epsilon_1{}^2)-([1/n]\Sigma\epsilon_1)^2$ and this has been used for the other circles in Table 3.1. The low values of probability level show that for these circles the stones are intended to be uniformly spaced. There are other examples where the same result holds.

Some circles (Table 3.1), notably Loch Buie, Loanhead, Loch Mannoch, and Brisworthy, have small numerical values for the node position indicating that the first stone was placed very nearly at the north point. The circle at Trezibbet is interesting. Burl tells us that it has been re-erected. We shall assume that the stones were replaced in or near their original positions. The

survey we used was made by Major A. F. Prain and it shows the stones
accurately as they are today. The statistical diameter measured from the
survey is 106·9 ft, which is close to 39 MY (106·2 ft). The probable reason for
the choice of 39 MY for the diameter lies in the fact that the perimeter,
$39 \pi$ MY, is equivalent to 49·01 MR. It may be noted that the perimeter
divided by the diameter is $49 \times 2\frac{1}{2} \div 39$ or 3·1410. This is a better approximation to $\pi$ (3·14159) than that given by the Ring of Brogar or by the inner rings
at Avebury.

### 3.6. The Ring of Brogar

Our first survey made in 1971 showed how important was this ring and so later
we made a new and particularly accurate survey using steel tapes. We
measured from the centre to each corner of each stone with allowance for
ground slope where necessary. Full details will be found in Thom and Thom
1973a, where it is shown that the large slabs, which are up to 15 ft high and
average only some 9–15 inches thick, are placed in a circle with a diameter,
measured to the stone centres, of 340·7 ± 0·44 ft. Taking this diameter to be
50 MR we find 1 MR = 6·813 ft. Adopting the method used earlier in this
chapter we found that the 60 stones were equally spaced 6° apart (probability
level = 0·05 per cent) starting from an azimuth of 9′. It is quite likely that for
this important circle the north–south line was determined as accurately as
possible and that the angle of 9′ is the error in the determination. This error is
comparable with the error at Callanish of about 6′, or that at Stonehenge.

To determine true north in the latitude of Brogar was no mean task. There
was no 'pole star' and the method was almost certainly to use a long plumb
line and from behind it to sight the east and west elongation of a star near the
pole. Bisecting the two positions on the ground would give a point due south
from the plumb line. At Brogar the chief difficulty was that the altitude of the
pole, being equal to the latitude, was 59° and so a long plumb line was
necessary.

It will be seen that the circle is surrounded by a deep ditch. Professor Colin
Renfrew has recently established that this ditch is cut through the surface soil
into the underlying rock. It is true that the rock is not particularly hard, but,
even so, cutting a ditch over 1200 ft long must have been a formidable task.
Evidently the site was considered important. It will be discussed again in
Chapter 10.

Dr. Graham Ritchie (1975–6) has shown that the nearby Ring of Stenness
was also surrounded by a ditch cut into the rock. This ring is much smaller,
with a diameter close to 103 ft.

A team from the Department of the Environment has explored both of
these Orkney rings by magnetometer. There are some interesting apparent
lines visible but the marks shown are too diffuse to give azimuths with any
certainty.

## 3.7. The perimeter of ellipses and eggs

In Table 3.3 we give particulars collated from Thom 1967 of 28 ellipses with Stonehenge added. A slight change has been made in the presentation; it makes but little difference. Previously we took exactly integral values of $2a$ and $2c$ and calculated $2b$. Here we have chosen to make $2a$ and $2b$ integral and to calculate $2c$. Then for $2a$ and $2b$ we found the perimeter $P$ (from Table 4.1, Thom 1967). The last column gives the discrepancy, $\epsilon = P - N$, from the nearest number ($N$) of multiples of $2\frac{1}{2}$ MY.

Tables 3.4 and 3.5 give similar particulars for the egg-shaped rings taken again from Thom 1967 with the Shetland rings, the Hirnant Cairn Circle, and the Ménec cromlechs added.

It will be seen that in both the ellipses and the eggs, $P - N$ is usually small and this indicates that these rings were set out with a standard unit of length

**Table 3.3.** *Dimensions of elliptical sites*

| Site | $2a$ | $2b$ | $2c$ | $P$ | $\epsilon = P - N$ |
|------|------|------|------|-----|--------------------|
| A9/2 | 18 | $13\frac{1}{2}$ | 11·91 | 49·73 | −0·27 |
| B1/24 | $10\frac{1}{4}$ | 9 | 4·91 | 30·27 | +0·27 |
| B1/26 | 14 | 13 | 5·20 | 42·47 | −0·03 |
| B1/27 | $16\frac{1}{2}$ | $15\frac{1}{2}$ | 5·66 | 50·29 | +0·29 |
| B7/4 | $17\frac{1}{2}$ | 16 | 7·09 | 52·65 | +0·15 |
| B7/5 | $18\frac{1}{2}$ | $17\frac{1}{2}$ | 6·00 | 56·56 | −0·94 |
| P1/3 | 12 | 10 | 6·63 | 34·63 | −0·37 |
| P1/16 | $9\frac{1}{2}$ | 8 | 5·12 | 27·53 | +0·03 |
| P2/2 | $9\frac{1}{2}$ | $7\frac{3}{4}$ | 5·49 | 27·17 | −0·33 |
| S2/7 | 7 | $5\frac{3}{4}$ | 3·91 | 20·08 | +0·08 |
| S2/8 | $10\frac{1}{2}$ | 10 | 3·20 | 32·21 | −0·29 |
| S4/1 | 11 | $9\frac{1}{2}$ | 5·55 | 32·24 | −0·26 |
| W2/1 | 31 | $29\frac{1}{2}$ | 9·53 | 95·05 | +0·05 |
| W11/4 | 25 | 23 | 9·80 | 75·43 | +0·43 |
| P1/19 | 11 | 8 | 7·55 | 30·03 | +0·03 |
| Tormore | 18 | $15\frac{1}{2}$ | 9·15 | 52·70 | +0·20 |
| Auchengallon | 18 | 17 | 5·92 | 54·99 | −0·01 |
| Claughreid | 13 | 11 | 6·93 | 37·77 | +0·27 |
| Braemore | 34 | $29\frac{1}{2}$ | 16·90 | 99·87 | −0·13 |
| Learable Hill | 26 | $20\frac{1}{2}$ | 12·48 | 70·01 | +0·01 |
| H1/2 | 26 | 22 | 13·86 | 75·53 | +0·53 |
| H1/4 | $15\frac{1}{2}$ | $11\frac{1}{2}$ | 10·39 | 42·54 | +0·04 |
| H1/10 | 21 | $16\frac{1}{2}$ | 12·99 | 59·12 | −0·88 |
| L2/12 | $8\frac{1}{2}$ | $7\frac{1}{2}$ | 4·00 | 25·16 | +0·16 |
| P2/9 | 12 | $8\frac{1}{2}$ | 8·47 | 32·41 | −0·09 |
| P2/11 | 9 | $7\frac{1}{2}$ | 4·97 | 25·97 | +0·97 |
| S3/1 | 39 | 36 | 15·00 | 117·86 | +0·36 |
| S3/1 | 52 | 48 | 20·00 | 157·14 | −0·36 |
| Stonehenge | 27 | 17 | 20·98 | 70·08 | +0·08 |

$2a$ = major axis, $2b$ = minor axis, $2c$ = distance between foci; $P$ = perimeter, all in Megalithic yards, $N$ = nominal perimeter = nearest multiple of $2\frac{1}{2}$ MY to $P$; $\epsilon$ = discrepancy; $\Sigma\epsilon^2 = 4\cdot15$.

**Table 3.4.** *Dimensions of egg-shaped rings, type I and type III*

| Site | $a$ | $b$ | $c$ | $r_1$ | $P$ | $\epsilon = P-N$ |
|------|-----|-----|-----|-------|-----|------------------|
| B2/4 | 5 | 3 | 4 | 14 | 90·95 | 0·95 |
| B7/1 | 10 | 6 | 8 | 19 | 125·36 | 0·36 |
| B7/18 | 5 | 4 | 3 | 7 | 47·28 | −0·22 |
| G9/15 | $8\frac{1}{2}$ | $5\frac{1}{2}$ | 6·48 | 8 | 55·58 | 0·58 |
| Le Ménec (W) | $62\frac{1}{2}$ | $37\frac{1}{2}$ | 50 | $42\frac{1}{2}$ | 304·41 | −0·59 |
| East Burra | $19\frac{1}{2}$ | 18 | $7\frac{1}{2}$ | $10\frac{1}{2}$ | 79·14 | −0·86 |
| Stanydale | $\left\{\begin{array}{l}13\\25\end{array}\right.$ | 11<br>24 | 7<br>7 | $4\frac{1}{2}$<br>$5\frac{1}{2}$ | 39·32<br>43·01 | −0·68<br>0·51 |
| Hirnant | $3\frac{3}{4}$ | $3\frac{1}{2}$ | $1\frac{1}{4}$ | — | 21·58 | −0·92 |

See Fig. 3.1 for definitions.
All dimensions in Megalithic yards.

**Table 3.5.** *Dimensions of egg-shaped rings type II*

| Site | $a$ | $b$ | $c$ | $r_1$ | $P$ | $\epsilon = P-N$ |
|------|-----|-----|-----|-------|-----|------------------|
| G9/10 | $15\frac{1}{2}$ | $9\frac{1}{2}$ | 12·25 | 25 | 164·27 | −0·73 |
| W11/3 | 3 | 2 | 2·24 | 11 | 70·24 | 0·24 |
| Le Ménec (E) | 50 | 50 | 40 | 55 | 369·94 | −0·06 |

See Fig. 3.1 for definitions.
All dimensions in Megalithic yards.

and that the perimeters were in general intended to be multiples of $2\frac{1}{2}$ times this unit.

Taking all 41 together we find $\Sigma\epsilon^2 = 8\cdot52$ and this, from Thom 1967 Fig. 2.1, shows a probability level of less than 0·01 per cent. Since we did not in any way adjust the values of $a$, $b$ or $c$ to make $P-N$ small, we are fully entitled to assume that such a low value indicates that our hypothesis is probably true.

We know that this process does not satisfy the modern statisticians who want to be shown a least square solution for every ring. An examination of typical rings (Thom 1967, Figs 6.14–6.23) shows that this would usually be completely unrewarding. For example how could one deal with the egg at Allan Water, or at Borrowston Rig? Which stones would one include and which exclude? These would be subjective decisions and it seems to us to be much better to make the decisions on the drawing board where one can see what one is doing and not hand the decision over to a computer. One cannot in fact take a site in isolation but must allow the knowledge acquired from them all to play its part in deciding that a particular site is an ellipse or an egg of a certain size.

The method we used above is independent of the exact value of the

Megalithic yard and so nothing would be gained by a least squares solution, unless we wanted to compare two suggested designs.

We give in Fig. 3.5 a graphical presentation of the values of $P-N$ by plotting $100(P-N)/P$ on $P$. In other words we express $P-N$ as a percentage of $P$ and show how this varies with size of ring. The extreme values that $P-N$ can have are $\pm(\frac{1}{2}$ of $2\frac{1}{2})$, that is $\pm 1\frac{1}{4}$, and these limits are shown. It will be seen how the points for both ellipses and egg-shapes nowhere reach these limits and of course this is what produces the low probability level. The figure shows how satisfactory the two cromlechs at Le Ménec really are.

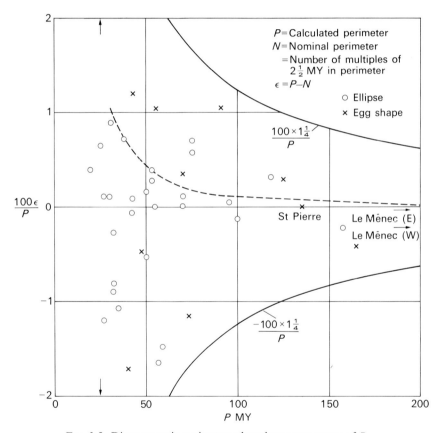

FIG. 3.5. Discrepancy in perimeters plotted as a percentage of $P$.

## 3.8. How was the perimeter measured?

It is interesting to speculate as to what size of measuring stick was used for measuring perimeters. Presumably shorter measuring sticks were used for the smaller rings, but let us try sticks 1 MR long and see what happens. In Thom 1967 we give that for an arc of radius $R$,

$$\text{arc minus chord} = c^3/24R^2,$$

where $c$ is the chord or the length of the measuring sticks. Taking $R = P/2\pi$ and bearing in mind that there are $P/c$ chords in the perimeter we find that the difference between true perimeters and measured perimeters is $\pi c^3/6P^2$. This value is shown in Fig. 3.5 by a dotted line.

The value taken above for $R$ is possibly too large and so the line is on the low side for a stick 1 MR long. For the smaller rings a stick 1 MY long may have been used and the line for this would have ordinates about 1/6 of those of the dotted line, and this might be said to be representative of the values at the lower range of perimeters.

**Table 3.6.** *Dimensions of pairs of circles*

|  | Site | Map reference | A diameter | B diameter | Distance between centres |
|---|---|---|---|---|---|
| P1/10 | Fowlis Wester | NN 924250 | See Fig. 13.5 |  | 86 |
| N2/3 | Shin River, Lairg | NC 582049 | 13·6 | 20·5 | 119·8 |
| P2/8 | Shianbank | NO 156272 | 27·5 | 27·5 | 70·5 |
| B3/3 | Raedykes (S) | NO 832907 | 57 | Ruinous | 315·4 |
| P1/14 | Tullybeagles | NO 010361 | 23 | 31·4 | 54·0 |
| B4/1 | Carnousie Ho. | NJ 678505 | 27 | 84 | 163·1 |
| S2/1 | Grey Wethers | SX 639831 | 104·5 | 108·7 | 128·3 |
| W11/4 | Usk River | SN 820258 | Ellipse | 68·2 | 364·9 |
| W11/2 | Trecastle | SN 833310 | 76·3 | 43·7 | 140·1 |

These are mostly ruinous, except Grey Wethers but c. 1879 Lukis shows most of the stones in this pair prostrate.
All dimensions in feet.

**Table 3.7.** *Pairs of circles, astronomical functions*

| Site |  | Azimuth | Altitude | Declination | Function |
|---|---|---|---|---|---|
| N2/3 | A to B | 147°·5 | 4° | −23° | Solstice? |
|  | B to A | 327°·5 | 1°·9 | 28° | — |
| P2/8 | A to B | 317°·5 | 0°·6 | 24°·5 | Solstice |
|  | B to A | 137°·5 | 2°·6 | −21°·9 | Calendar? |
| B3/3 | A to B | 314°·2 | 2°·1 | 23°·9 | Solstice |
| P1/14 | A to B | 84° | 0°·1 | 2°·9 | Equinox? |
|  | B to A | 264° | 3°·8 | −0·3 | Equinox? |
| B4/1 | A to B | 181° | — | — | Meridian |
| S2/1 | A to B | 181°·4 | — | — | Meridian |
| W11/4 | E to W | 295°·3 | 1°·2 | 16°·0 | Calendar? |
| W11/2 | B to A | 53°·3 | 0°·1 | 21°·3 | Calendar? |
| P1/10 | W to E | 88° | 0°·1 | 0°·5 | Equinox |
| P1/11 | E to W | 26°·8 | 1°·8 | 0°·1 | Equinox |

### 3.9. Pairs of circles

At nine places we found pairs of circles as opposed to sets of three or more. Most of the circles in pairs are decrepit but we measured them up as well as we could. The particulars are given in Table 3.6 while Table 3.7 has the astronomical details. It will be seen that they all give calendar declinations or lie in the meridian. Those at Lairg are very small and unimpressive. In no case was any prominent horizon mark noticed so it is presumed that these were all early types before the accurate solar observatories like that at Ballochroy were being built.

# 4

## AVEBURY AND THE MEGALITHIC YARD

**4.1.** In the book *Megalithic sites in Britain* (Thom 1967) will be found particulars regarding over 200 circles together with an analysis of the diameters using Broadbent's method. The conclusion was that the value of the Megalithic yard was 2·720 ft and that this was used from one end of Britain to the other. More powerful methods of analysing the diameters listed have been given by Kendall (1974) and by Freeman (1976). The conclusion arrived at in their papers was that the Megalithic yard had support from Scottish data but in England the evidence was not sufficiently clear. But there are many other strong indications that the yard really existed apart from a list of diameters. A number of these will be found in Thom 1967, among them a survey of the ring at Avebury.

We consider that because of its size and the fact that we know its geometry, Avebury provides the best site for determining, from a single site in England, the value of the Megalithic yard. Accordingly we decided to make an entirely new survey of the site using methods of greater accuracy and to make a mathematical analysis of the data obtained.

An authoritative description of the site at Avebury will be found in the volume *Windmill Hill and Avebury* (Keiller 1965) prepared by Dr. I. S. Smith to record the excavation and restorations carried out by Alexander Keiller and his associates. Miss Smith deals not only with the ring and the internal constructions but with the bank and ditch and also with the West Kennet Avenue. The main ring itself probably had a perimeter of about 3545 ft and is estimated to have had originally 98 stones. Some of these are very large, but in 1936 there were only 9 upright and another 10 lying fallen. The remainder had been destroyed or buried by the villagers. Stukeley has described methods used for the destruction and indicates that the villagers seemed to take a fiendish delight in breaking up the monument. The destruction would have made it quite impossible to discover the original design were it not for the fact that the stones had been socketed into the underlying chalk. Keiller and his associates, including Professor S. Piggott, were thus able by excavation to find approximately the original positions of some of the stones. His success in pinpointing each exact position depended on the size of the hole in the chalk, which in some cases had been enlarged by subsequent disturbances. For example, when the villagers felled a stone they dug out one side of the foundation and toppled the stone across a suitably excavated burning pit in which a fire was lit to destroy the stone. Keiller and his associates have excavated most of the western side of the ring and placed concrete plinths in what they considered to be the original stone positions. But it will be understood from what has been said above that these plinths and indeed also the re-erected stones cannot always have been accurately placed in the original positions and may in some cases have been misplaced by several feet.

With steel tapes and a theodolite capable of reading angles to within $\pm 5$ arc seconds, we ran a closed seven-sided traverse round the ring and checked the azimuth astronomically at three of the stations. The traverse closed to within an inch or two and so we could fix the position of every stone and plinth accurately. It will be understood that to do justice to this new survey it would be necessary to plot it to an unmanageably large scale. Accordingly we calculated from the measurements made in the field the coordinates of the centre of every stone in the ring and these are given in Table 4.1. The origin was chosen so as to give positive $x$ and $y$ values over the whole site. The problem then was to find a method whereby a 'least squares' solution would give the value which had most probably been used for the Megalithic yard in setting out the ring. Before we describe how this was done it is necessary to examine the geometry in detail.

**Table 4.1.** *Coordinates (in feet) of stones in the Avebury main ring*

| Stone | $x$ | $y$ | | $\Delta$ |
|---|---|---|---|---|
| 1 | 733·7 | 44·0 | | +1·4 |
| 3 | 659·7 | 28·0 | | −0·9 |
| 4 | 624·2 | 19·3 | centre $C$ | +1·9 |
| 5 | 588·4 | 13·9 | ($x' = 520·9$, | +2·4 |
| 6 | 551·6 | 12·3 | $y' = 720·8$) | +1·5 |
| 7 | 515·1 | 9·5 | | +3·6 |
| 8 | 478·0 | 16·6 | | −2·2 |
| 9 | 445·3 | 23·4 | | −0·8 |
| 10 | 413·8 | 46·2 | | −1·1 |
| 11 | 377·9 | 74·1 | | −2·1 |
| 12 | 357·1 | 94·1 | | −4·7 |
| 13 | 327·7 | 112·4 | | −1·2 |
| 14 | 300·6 | 136·2 | | −2·3 |
| 15 | 272·0 | 158·8 | | −0·9 |
| 16 | 243·5 | 183·0 | centre $W$ | −0·1 |
| 17 | 216·3 | 205·0 | ($x' = 1\,612·8$, | +2·2 |
| 18 | 188·9 | 229·8 | $y' = 1\,697·1$) | +3·1 |
| 19 | 163·5 | 255·5 | | +2·7 |
| 20 | 140·0 | 285·0 | | −1·1 |
| 21 | 120·6 | 305·7 | | −1·2 |
| 22 | 103·1 | 323·1 | | −0·2 |
| 23 | 85·9 | 344·0 | | −1·3 |
| 24 | 61·8 | 371·3 | | −1·1 |

**Table 4.1.**  *(continued)*

| Stone | $x$ | $y$ | | $\Delta$ |
|---|---|---|---|---|
| 30· | 19·3 | 624·4 | | +1·4 |
| 31 | 24·9 | 663·0 | | +1·6 |
| 32 | 33·3 | 698·3 | | +0·4 |
| 33 | 43·7 | 731·3 | | −1·4 |
| 34 | 55·5 | 764·4 | centre $A$ | −2·9 |
| 35 | 62·9 | 790·1 | ($x' = 723·2$, | −1·1 |
| 36 | 69·2 | 815·0 | $y' = 538·6$) | +2·3 |
| 37 | 85·0 | 849·8 | | +2·3 |
| 38 | 98·5 | 884·6 | | +6·4 |
| 39 | 123·6 | 910·5 | | −2·1 |
| 40 | 146·8 | 936·9 | | −3·5 |
| 41 | 175·2 | 962·4 | | −0·3 |
| 42 | 206·7 | 984·7 | centre $B$ | +0·6 |
| 43 | 237·6 | 1 002·9 | ($x' = 586·6$, | +0·3 |
| 44 | 270·3 | 1 022·5 | $y' = 386·9$) | +2·2 |
| 45 | 292·5 | 1 031·2 | | +0·5 |
| 46 | 315·8 | 1 042·0 | | +1·2 |
| 50 | 461·1 | 1 085·4 | centre $Z$ ($x' = 844·1$, $y' = -921·7$) | +1·8 |
| 68 | 1 033·4 | 946·2 | centre $P$ ($x' = 489·2$, $y' = 560·6$) | −1·3 |
| 98 | 769·9 | 64·9 | centre $D$ ($x' = 611·0$ $y' = 584·6$) | −1·0 |

The values given are the estimated centres of each stone referred to an arbitrary zero, $x$ towards east and $y$ towards true geographical north. The table also gives the coordinates $(x', y')$ of the centres of the arcs on which the stones were placed and the displacements $\Delta = \sqrt{((x-x')^2+(y-y')^2)} - R_a$, where $R_a$ is the intended radius, now using 1 MY = 2·722 ft.

## 4.2. The geometry of the ring

This ring is almost unique in that it consists of circular arcs meeting at an angle instead of running smoothly into one another. It thus has what might be called corners. An interesting fact is that the distance along the arcs between these corners is in every case close to an integral number of rods (Table 4.2). It will be understood that to invent a design dependent on a geometrical construction which has this peculiarity presented a very difficult problem. It will be shown how successful the designers were.

The basic geometry is shown in Fig. 4.1. To set out the ring construct a triangle $ABC$ with $AB = 75$, $AC = 100$, and $CB = 125$ MY. The angle $A$ is

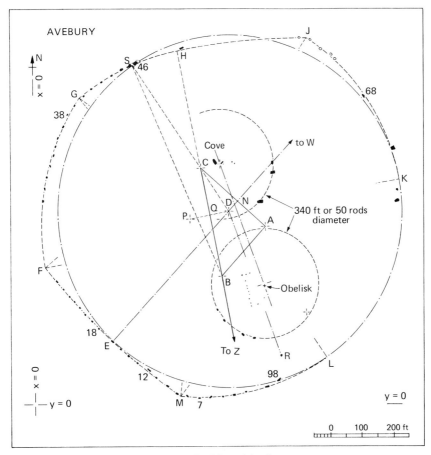

FIG. 4.1. The Ring of Avebury.

obviously a right-angle. Now find a point $S$, 260 MY from $B$ and 140 MY from $C$. Produce $SC$ to $D$ making $CD = 60$ MY; $DN$, the perpendicular distance to $CA$, should then be 15·061 MY, presumably assumed to be 15. But the triangle $BSC$ is so badly conditioned that it is almost impossible to construct it accurately. Perhaps $DN$ was made 15 MY and $DC$ produced to give $S$. $D$ is evidently considered as the main centre so with $D$ as centre and radius 200 MY, describe a circle. Now make $PQ$ equal to $QD$, the angle at $Q$ being a right-angle. It seems possible that in an early attempt the designers tried to make the figure symmetrical about $CB$ and this may explain the position of $P$. However there is no further indication of symmetry and so we proceed as follows: with centre $A$ and radius 260 MY describe an arc $FG$; similarly with centres $C$ and $B$ describe arcs $ML$ and $GH$. $EDN$ is parallel to $BA$ and must be produced until a point $W$ is found 750 MY from $E$. With this centre draw the arc *FEM*. Similarly produce *CB* until we find a centre *Z* 750 MY from *H* and with this describe the arc *HJ*. The remaining arc *JK* is drawn with centre at *P*. Even an experienced draughtsman will find this design difficult to set out on paper unless the perpendicular distance of *S* from *BC* produced be first calculated.

In view of the importance of the site we have calculated with the greatest care the lengths of the arcs between the corners on two different assumptions: (a) that the triangle *BCS* was set out first, and (b) that *DN* was made exactly 15 MY. The two assumptions are seen to give practically identical values and every one of the values lies close to an integral multiple of $2\frac{1}{2}$ MY which might be called the nominal value (Table 4.2). In a private communication Dr. Heggie tells us that he has checked these calculations. He has also estimated by several methods the probability that all the arcs should be accidentally so nearly integral as they are, and finds values between 0·1 and 1 per cent.

Note that the above calculations and the results depend entirely on the assumed geometry and so come only indirectly from the measurements made in the field.

**Table 4.2.** *Lengths of the Avebury arcs in Megalithic yards, computed from the geometry in Fig. 4.1*

|  | ME | EF | FG | Arc GH | HJ | JK | KM | Total |
|---|---|---|---|---|---|---|---|---|
| Length (i) | 97·16 | 117·31 | 199·99 | 129·68 | 149·94 | 195·59 | 412·63 | 1 302·30 |
| Length (ii) | 97·23 | 117·43 | 199·87 | 129·68 | 149·72 | 195·75 | 412·58 | 1 302·26 |
| 'Nominal' | 97·50 | 117·50 | 200·00 | 130·00 | 150·00 | 195·00 | 412·50 | 1 302·50 |

Assumptions used are:
  (i) $CS = 140$, $CB = 125$, and $SB = 260$ MY, so that $DN = 15·062$;
  (ii) $CS = 140$, $CD = 60$, and $DN = 15$, so that $SB = 259·97$ MY.

## 4.3. The results of field work

It is now necessary to see how nearly the geometrical construction agrees with the field survey. The construction was set out carefully on tracing paper assuming 1 MY = 2·720 ft and placed on the survey. It was moved about until the agreement seemed as good as possible. The coordinates of the central point *D* were then read off along with the azimuth of *DCS*. From these values were calculated the coordinates of all the other centres *A*, *B*, *C*, etc. The next step was to calculate from Table 4.1 the distance of the centre of each stone from the arc on which it stands. Comparing these distances with the theoretical radius we found the discrepancies (Δ) for each stone. It was proposed from these discrepancies to find the best position for the construction and for the value of the Megalithic yard. There were four unknowns, namely the corrections to the two coordinates of $D$, the correction to the azimuth of $DCS$ and the correction to the scale; we had taken 2·720 ft to be a Megalithic yard and this might need alteration.

In the *Journal of the Royal Statistical Society* (Thom 1955) the following method of dealing with this problem was suggested. Using Fig. 4.2, which shows a typical part of the ring, let the size be specified by $R$, here taken to be the radius of the main circular part, 200 MY; $\Delta = CS_1$ and is the perpendicular distance of a stone $S_1$ outside the ring; $\rho = OC$; and $\beta$ is the angle between $OC$ and the normal to the ring at $C$.

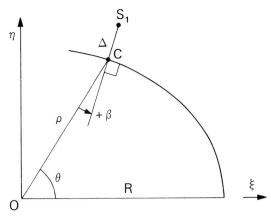

FIG. 4.2. Definitions of $R$, $\rho$, $\beta$, and $\Delta$.

Suppose that we scale up the whole size of the outline so that $R$ becomes $R+r$, $OC$ then increases by $\rho r/R$, and $\Delta$ decreases by $(\rho r \cos \beta)/R$. Suppose also that the assumed position of $O$ moves a small amount by $(\xi, \eta)$ and that the whole outline rotates through a small angle $\phi$, then $CS_1$ becomes

$$\Delta' = \Delta - r(\rho \cos \beta)/R - \xi \cos(\theta + \beta) - \eta \sin(\theta + \beta) - \eta \sin(\theta + \beta) - \phi \rho \sin \beta.$$

$$(4.1)$$

We want $S_1$ to be on the ring, that is, we want

$$\Delta' = 0. \qquad (4.2)$$

Every stone gives us an equation like (4.2). There are four unknowns to be found; namely the coordinates $(\xi, \eta)$ of the final position of the centre, the amount $(\phi)$ the outline has to be rotated and the amount $(r)$ by which its size has to be increased. Thus we have in all 42 equations to solve for four unknowns, that is, one equation for each stone and plinth.

We began by assuming (a) the centre $D$ to be at 611·0, 584·0 (ft), (b) the line $DCS$ to be at azimuth 146° 42′, (c) the radius of the main ring to be 544 ft, and (d) the Megalithic yard to be 2·720 ft (200 × 2·720 = 544). With these values we calculated the coordinates $(x', y')$ of the centres $A$, $B$, $C$, etc. of all the arcs. It was then easy to calculate the distance of each stone from the centre of the arc on which it lies. Subtracting the nominal radius then gave $\Delta$.

The coefficients in (4.1) were then found and the equations (4.2) were solved. However, as we wanted several solutions the help of the computer laboratory in Glasgow University was obtained.

The position of stone 38 (Figs. 4.1 and 4.3) is so far away from the ring that we ignored it, but the first solution (Table 4.3) retains all other stones and plinths. Stone 12 seems very far inside the ring and we tried the effect of omitting it. Similarly with stones 7 and 18. We may be completely wrong in assuming stone 98 to be on the circular arc (with radius 200 MY) produced and so we tried the effect of assigning it to the arc of 260 MY radius.

**Table 4.3.** *Solution of equations with various assumptions*

|  | $\xi$ (ft) | $\eta$ (ft) | $r$ (ft) | $\phi$ (radians) |
|---|---|---|---|---|
| Omit stone 38 | +0·59 | +1·15 | +0·73 | +0·0101 |
| Omit 12 and 38 | +0·29 | +0·28 | +0·43 | +0·0019 |
| Omit 7, 12, 18, and 38 | −0·23 | +0·75 | +0·09 | +0·0024 |
| Omit 38, and assume that 98 belongs to | | | | |
| outer arc | +0·02 | +1·25 | +0·35 | +0·0101 |
| For plotting Fig. 4.3, use arbitrarily | 0·00 | +0·60 | 0·40 | +0·0030 |

Note that the above uses the usual mathematical convention with positive rotation anti-clockwise; but azimuth is measured clockwise and so the assumed correction to azimuth is −0·0030 radians or −10 arc minutes.

It might be worthwhile to assign double weight to those stones which were upright in 1936, namely 1, 8, 32, 33, 44, 46, 50, 68, and 98, but this has not been tried.

On any of the selections tried in Table 4.3 it will be seen that $R$ needs to be slightly increased. It seems reasonable to take the increase as being about +0·4 ft. Hence $R$ becomes 544·0+0·4 ft and since this is 200 MY, the Megalithic yard becomes 2·722 ft.

Taking the values given in the last line of Table 4.3 we then calculated the revised positions of the centres $A$, $B$, $C$, etc. (Table 4.1) and so were able to obtain by calculation the exact position of the arcs. These are shown in Fig. 4.3 plotted in the correct positions. On the large scale of our drawing we could not use trammels to draw the circular arcs and so these were plotted from the equation:

$$y = x^2/2R + x^4/8R^3 + \ldots,$$

where the origin is at the mid-point of the arc.

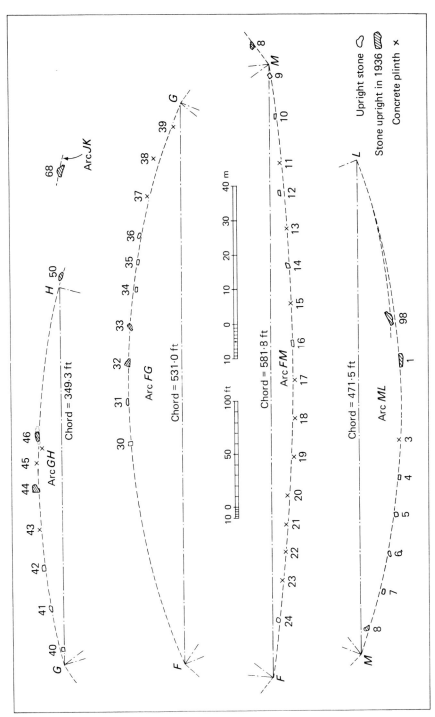

FIG. 4.3. Positions of stones relative to arcs. Enlarged from Fig. 4.1.

To appreciate fully what is happening here, it is necessary to be quite clear that these arcs are not independent, that is they have not been independently derived (Fig. 4.1). They are all part of the complete geometrical construction, so that, for example, if the arc *ML* is pushed to the north by a foot the arc *GH* will also be moved by a foot. The computer technique used is analogous to sliding a tracing of the geometry about over a plotted survey to find the best position and orientation. It is more powerful in that it minimizes the sum of the squares of the discrepancies and in that it will, as necessary, contract or expand the geometrical design.

The accuracy with which the ring has been set out is clearly remarkable; the stones fit every theoretical arc and the overall dimensions are satisfied within close limits. Both of us have considerable experience in setting out roads and railways using modern equipment and we know that even using such equipment it would be quite a task to complete this ring satisfactorily. Any engineer asked today to do this would begin by making a number of trigonometrical calculations. The erectors did it without theodolites, without steel tapes, and without trigonometric tables.

Let us now look at the dimensions which they actually used. Converting to Megalithic rods we find for the basic triangle 30, 40, 50; *BS* is 104, *CS* is 56, and *CD* is 24. The radii of the arcs are 80, 104, and 300. Thus all the dimensions with the exception of *PK* are integral in Megalithic rods and five are integral in multiples of 10 MR. Until it is excavated we cannot be certain of the geometry of the east side and so there may be some doubt of the exact length of *PK*.

We have assumed that stone 98 lay on the 200 MY radius (but see Table 4.3) from *D*, but this is somewhat doubtful because of the direction in which the axis of this large stone lies. It is possible that there was another 'corner' 105 MY along the arc from *M*. The next arc would then pass nearly through stone 98, but until this part of the ring has been excavated, this can only be guess-work. The assumed arc (Fig. 4.1) runs parallel with the edge of the ditch and until one or two stone holes here have been uncovered, it seems best to retain the geometry as shown.

Various claims have been made that the rings were set out by simple pacing but we cannot accept this hypothesis. The statistical analysis we have made above shows a value of 2·722 ft and in Table 4.4 this is shown to be close to values found elsewhere. In view of the great care which was obviously taken to get the Avebury ring set out to agree exactly with the postulated geometry, and in view of the care which we have taken in our survey and analysis we consider that the most accurately determined value of the Megalithic yard in England is that found above, namely 2·722 ft or 0·8297 m.

### 4.4. How was Avebury set out?

The centres for the flat arcs are outside the ditch and bank. It thus seems *likely* that the ring was laid out before the ditch and bank were constructed. It is difficult to believe that these arcs were set out by means of a long rope. Think of a rope 2044 ft long being used in this by no means level piece of country. We imagine the rope being supported by a row of men along its length but even so what about the stretch in the rope? A varying pull on a 2000-ft rope would give large differences in length. Such a technique may have been used in the early stages of the design until approximate positions were found, but for the final setting out we consider that the rope can be ruled out. Distances were almost certainly set out by two rods, lifted over one another alternately. Having found the centre of the arc, the two ends and the mid-point of the arc would be set out. This would give the versine or sagitta. One quarter of this sagitta would be the sagitta for the half arcs. Thus five points were found along the arc and as many more subdivisions could be made as were considered necessary. It is quite likely that the arcs with radius 200 and 260 MY were set out by the same method. All this presupposes that the design was specified and all the dimensions known. But how was the design discovered? It probably took years of trial and error. It would be an interesting exercise with an electronic computer to try to invent a similar design with all the linear dimensions integral and with the lengths along the arcs between the corners as near to integers as those found in Avebury. Once the difficulty of the problem is fully appreciated one begins to understand how difficult it must have been on the ground.

As a result of our analysis we now know the coordinates of *A*, *B*, *C*, and *S*. The important point *S* lies just under the overhang of the west end of stone 46, almost exactly where its position was previously estimated (Thom 1967) to be. The importance of stone 46 cannot be exaggerated and yet passing traffic is allowed to knock into it. This has happened at least twice and we hear on good authority that in one case a lorry knocked it well out of the vertical. It is a disturbing thought that in 1975 we were still allowing the destruction of the Avebury ring to continue.

## 4.5. Internal features

We could record only surface features and our own measurements are not sufficient to demonstrate the existence of the northern of the two large inner circles, but ample evidence for this circle is given by Dr. Smith. The southern circle is more definite and has a diameter close to 340 ft. This is 50 MR and in Chapter 10 we have shown this to be the *exact* diameter of the Brogar ring. It is our belief that the reason for using 50 MR or 125 MY is that this diameter makes the circumference 392·699 MY, very nearly an integral multiple of $2\frac{1}{2}$ MY. Taking the circumference to be 392·5 MY, that is 157 MR, corresponds to taking $\pi$ to be 3·140. A line joining the centres of the circles is 145 MY long and if we set off 90 MY along this line from the centre of the south circle and construct a perpendicular 10 MY long, the end falls on D, the main centre of the outer ring.

The 'ring stone' $R$ seems to have had some importance (Keiller 1965, p. 202). It will be noticed that the line joining the ring stone to the main centre $D$ is exactly parallel to the line joining the circle centres (with 10 MY separation) and the azimuth of this line is $340°·2$. Standing at the 'obelisk' on the line of the centres and looking through the stones at the 'Cove' one would be looking along the line to the place where Deneb 'set' in Megalithic times. The magnitude of Deneb is $1·3$ and we see from Fig. 13.1 in Thom 1967 that a star of this magnitude has an extinction angle of about $1°·4\pm0°·5$. By this we mean that with even the clearest atmospheric conditions it is impossible to see the star below an altitude of $1°·4$ and this is greater than the actual horizon altitude by over $1°$. The declination corresponding to azimuth $340°·2$, altitude $1°·4\pm0°·5$ in latitude $51°\ 43'$ is $36°·6\pm0.5$ which is that of Deneb about $2000\pm700$ B.C. The declination of Deneb was, however, changing due to precession so very slowly that it is not possible to use Deneb for dating. Deneb is one of the first magnitude stars for which the declination remains almost constant century after century, and this was probably one of the reasons for the interest obviously taken in this star (Fig. 8.1, Thom 1967). The other reason may have been the particularly long run of usefulness of Deneb as a timekeeper throughout the year (Thom 1967, p. 104). As confusion with other stars in Cygnus was possible, a method of identifying it was necessary.

### 4.6. Other indications of the value of the Megalithic yard

In Fig. 4.4 we reproduce from Thom 1967 a set of histograms of the deviation of actual measured radii and lengths from multiples of the Megalithic yard. We write for circles and rings $\epsilon = |R-2·72m|$, where $R$ is the measured radius and for the distances between circles we take $\epsilon = |l-2·72m|$, where $l$ is the measured distance between circles.

Both lots together are shown in Fig. 4.4(c). The high pile at the left is the evidence for the Megalithic yard. The smaller pile at the right is an indication that sometimes the half-yard was used while the slight lump in the middle may indicate that occasionally the quarter-yard was used.

We have in our files numerous surveys of lines of stones. Excluding the fan-shaped sites in Caithness, we scaled the distances between the stones in all the rows available and found we had 190 such measurements under 30 feet. Thom 1962 is the first review of the data, and a remeasurement of all the plans (Thom 1964) showed some differences in selection, but the overall picture remains the same.

Figure 4.4(b) shows a histogram of the deviation from the integral number of yards. Notice that here again there is definite evidence for the yard and the half-yard. We have in each figure sketched in three Gaussian distributions

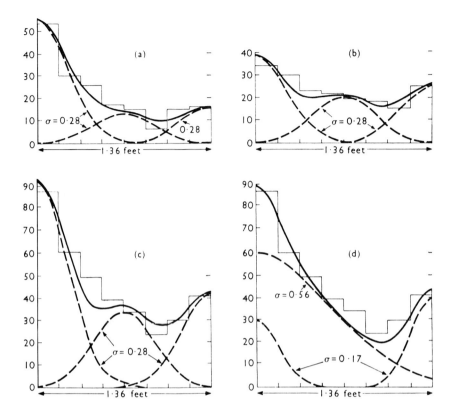

FIG. 4.4. Histograms of deviations, $\epsilon = |l - 2\cdot72\,m|$, compared with some suggested gaussians. In each case the full line shows the sum of the gaussians. (a) Radii and distance between circles. (b) Distance between stones. (c) and (d) Radii and distance between circles and distance between stones.

which, when summed, give the full line. It is clear that there is no evidence that the yard was divided into three.

### 4.7. The case for the Megalithic yard

There are therefore in Britain four strong indications, if not indeed proofs, of the reality of the yard:

   (i) Analysis of the diameters (Thom 1967, p. 41).
  (ii) Avebury.
 (iii) Histograms of distances between stones and the distances between circles.
 (iv) The perimeters of ellipses, egg-shaped rings, etc.

Consider also the histogram of observed diameters (Thom 1967, Fig. 5.1) and the reality of the egg-shaped rings and ellipses which depend on right-angled triangles built from integral numbers of yards and consider the evidence from the Brogar ring.

It seems to be impossible to combine mathematically the results given above so as to give an overall probability level but *philosophically* the conclusion is quite clear. There cannot be the slightest doubt about the reality of the Megalithic yard. Values found are given in Table 4.4.

**Table 4.4.** *Values for the Megalithic yard*

| Source | length (ft) |
|---|---|
| Diameters of circles (Thom 1967, p. 43) | 2·720 |
| Diameters of circles and rings (Thom 1967, p. 51) | 2·721 |
| Le Ménec (§6.8) | 2·721 |
| Kermario (§7.7) | 2·724 |
| Avebury (Chapter 4) | 2·722 |
| Brogar (Chapter 10) | 2·725 |
| mean | 2·722 |

How then was this length carried from one end of the country to the other and probably much further afield? The answer seems to be that wooden rods were used. Perhaps these were 1 MY long or perhaps 1 MR. Professor J. E. Gordon tells us that *along the grain* the expansion of wood when it becomes wet is very small, being in fact comparable with the expansion due to a rise of atmospheric temperature. We do not need to think about such materials as whale bones or walrus tusks. Hard wood could easily be obtained.

It has been stated in public that it would be impossible to use wooden rods to measure with the accuracy which we claim for the Megalithic yard. Accordingly we made an experiment on the ground under conditions identical to those under which Megalithic man must have worked. We made two wooden rods each exactly 6 ft long, and used them to set out a length of 198 ft (33 lengths of 6 ft) along the top of a rig in a grass field, each rod supported on two pieces of wood. We then measured with a steel tape the length we had set and found it to be 197 ft 11$\frac{3}{16}$ inches. Thus the error was $\frac{13}{16}$ inch, or 1 in 2924.

We then repeated the experiment and set out 96 ft, but this time we measured across the rigs which were about 33 ft pitch and 16–18 inches deep. This was more difficult, but we did not use any special equipment. The error was $\frac{3}{4}$ inch, or 1 in 1536. Thus there is no real difficulty in attaining an accuracy of 1 in 1500 in the field and this is equivalent to 0·0018 ft in the length of the

Megalithic yard. This is of the same order as the difference which we find in the yard from various sites.

It is interesting to compare the value of the Megalithic yard with that of the Spanish *vara* found in different places.

| | | |
|---|---|---|
| 2·766 ft | Burgos | Szymański 1956 |
| 2·7425 | Madrid | |
| 2·749 | Mexico | W. Latto and W. S. Olsen (personal |
| 2·788 | Texas and California | communication) |
| 2·75 | Peru | |

We take from Henri Michel's book (1967) that the Tyrolean perch has a length of 837 mm and the unit of length used in the mines is the klafter of 1·674 m. Since 837 mm is 2·746 ft, a unit of the same length as the vara was presumably in use in the Tyrol. It is possible that the vara was taken to America by the Spaniards and it spread as far north as California.

### 4.8. The West Kennet Avenue

Two avenues led to Avebury. That from the west is almost completely destroyed but there is still enough of the avenue from the south-east left to allow it to be followed from the concentric rings at the Sanctuary almost to the entrance of the main ring.

It is not yet clear how it made the ultimate approach but the last 2400 ft has been excavated and plinths put in the stone holes. A careful survey of this part was made by one of us (A.S.T.) assisted by Mr. K. McWhirter; a small-scale reproduction is given in Fig. 4.5. Details of the exact coordinates of the stones and plinths will be found elsewhere (Thom and Thom, Alexander S., 1976). Figure 4.5 shows that the lengths of the various straights measured on the centre line were all multiples of 5 MR. We suggest tentatively that the angles of the bends were intended to be arc sin $1/n$, where $n$ has the values 14, 16, 8, 3, and 14 for the bends $a$ to $e$. Unfortunately it is impossible to decide on the present evidence whether the builders used arc sin $1/n$ or arc tan $1/n$, but the former is slightly easier to set out on the ground. We believe that the sides of the avenue are made 18 MY apart, measuring to the stones centres, but this is so near to 50 ft that the excavators probably used 50 ft as a guide when placing the plinths. To the south-east of stones 37 no serious excavation seems to have been done. Perhaps if excavated and surveyed this part might throw some light on the reason for the peculiar geometry of the whole length.

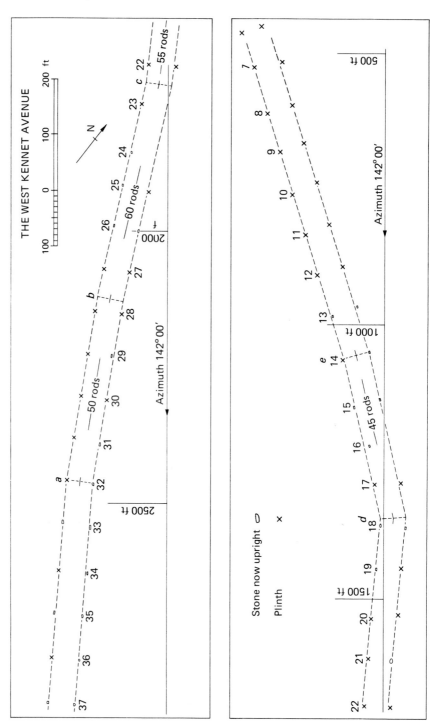

FIG. 4.5. The West Kennet Avenue from stones 37 to stones 6.

# 5

## CUP AND RING MARKS

**5.1.** A T many places in Britain and apparently throughout Europe there are the so-called 'cup and ring' marks cut into the rock or into a large stone. Sometimes there are only cups or holes scattered about on the surface, but often there are concentric rings round the cups. We also find spirals, egg-shaped rings and more complicated designs. It seems that at least for Scotland and north-east England, these designs were set out with a common unit of measurement; the Megalithic inch. Instead of using dividers or compasses as we would do today, the designer probably used beam compasses or trammels with the points set at *fixed* distances apart. He would have had a set of these with the points at perhaps 3, 4, 5, and 6 inches apart and also intermediate sizes at $3\frac{1}{2}$, $4\frac{1}{2}$, etc.

The interesting thing is that the terms of reference to which the designs were made were identical to those used in setting out the rings of standing stones. In both we find integral values of the unit used and in both the designs are usually based on right-angled triangles with all sides integral. In Argyllshire, Miss Marion Campbell has found some of the rubbers which she believes were used to polish the surfaces before the designs were drawn.

No satisfactory explanation has been given for the cup marks but doubtless they contain a message of some sort. For instance there is a set on the most important stone of the lunar observatory at Temple Wood, perhaps telling what the stone was for, but if this idea is correct the key has not been found. Sets of cup marks are also found in Brittany where there are also examples of complicated petroglyphs in some of the tumuli.

### 5.2. The unit of length

In 1967 Mr. R. W. B. Morris and Mr. D. C. Bailey brought us a number of rubbings and measurements of rings and suggested that we might examine these with a view to finding the unit of length, if any, which had been used. The measurements are given in Table 5.1 and are included in the histogram in Fig. 5.1, on which it appears that the diameters seem to cluster into a number of clumps. Further work shows that these clumps are spaced about 0·816 inches apart.

In the table, $y$ is the measured diameter of the ring in inches, $2\delta$ is the quantum or unit, $m$ is the whole number nearest to $y/2\delta$ and so is the number

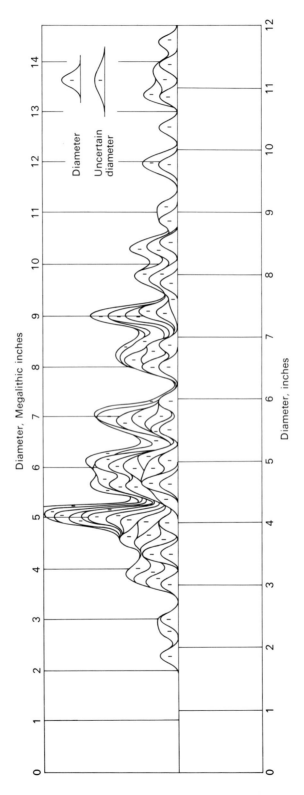

FIG. 5.1. Histogram of measured diameters, circular rings only.

of units in the diameter. The ideal diameter is $2m\delta$, and $\epsilon$ is the discrepancy or the difference between the diameter and $2m\delta$.

We analysed the diameters by Broadbent's method (Thom 1967, Ch. 2) and showed that the value of the quantum was 0·816 and that the additive constant was negligibly small. This means that the designers had in fact measured, as we tried to do, to the middle of the groove forming the ring and not to either edge of the groove. We can therefore use the expression given by Broadbent for cases when there is no additive constant and this is $2\delta = \Sigma my/\Sigma m^2$. From this we find $2\delta = 0·815$ inches. From the 57 values of $\epsilon$ in Table 5.1 we obtain a probability level of 4 per cent for the existence of the quantum.

**Table 5.1.** *Cup and ring marks, circular rings only; diameters* (y) *compared with the quantum* ($2\delta$)

| Site | Map ref. | $y$ (inch) | $m$ | $2m\delta$ (inch) | $\epsilon$ (inch) |
|---|---|---|---|---|---|
| Achnabreck, Argyll | NR 855908 | 11·37 | 14 | 11·42 | 0·05 |
| | | 8·50 | 10 | 8·16 | 0·34 |
| | | 6·50 | 8 | 6·53 | 0·03 |
| | | 4·62 | 6 | 4·90 | 0·28 |
| | | 4·25 | 5 | 4·08 | 0·17 |
| | | 6·62 | 8 | 6·53 | 0·09 |
| | | 8·37 | 10 | 8·16 | 0·21 |
| | | 10·37 | 13 | 10·61 | 0·24 |
| Ardgowan, Argyll | NS 098045 | 6·75 | 8 | 6·53 | 0·22 |
| | | 10·87 | 13 | 10·61 | 0·26 |
| Point Farm, Argyll | NR 992645 | 3·71 | 5 | 4·08 | 0·37 |
| | | 3·79 | 5 | 4·08 | 0·29 |
| Blackshaw, Ayrshire | NS 231484 | 5·45 ± | 7 | 5·71 | 0·26 |
| | | 9·75 | 12 | 9·79 | 0·04 |
| | | 4·62 | 6 | 4·90 | 0·28 |
| | | 5·50 | 7 | 5·71 | 0·21 |
| North Blochairn, Stirlingshire | NS 581762 | 4·52 | 6 | 4·90 | 0·38 |
| Craigston Wood, Renfrewshire | NS 435616 | 6·87 | 8 | 6·53 | 0·34 |
| Bombie, Kirkcudbrightshire | NX 723498 | 11·12 | 14 | 11·42 | 0·30 |
| | | 8·87 | 11 | 8·98 | 0·11 |
| | | 6·50 | 8 | 6·53 | 0·03 |
| | | 5·00 | 6 | 4·90 | 0·10 |
| | | 3·00 | 4 | 3·26 | 0·26 |
| | | 1·87 | 2 | 1·63 | 0·24 |
| Broughton Mains, Wigtonshire | NX 457457 | 4·88 | 6 | 4·90 | 0·02 |
| | | 7·87 | 10 | 8·16 | 0·29 |
| | | 4·00 | 5 | 4·08 | 0·08 |
| Cairnholy, Kirkcudbrightshire | NX 515546 | 3·27 | 4 | 3·26 | 0·01 |
| | | 5·60 | 7 | 5·71 | 0·11 |
| Castleton, Stirlingshire | NS 863880 | 4·37 | 5 | 4·08 | 0·29 |
| | | 8·00 | 10 | 8·16 | 0·16 |
| | | 11·75 | 14 | 11·42 | 0·33 |
| | | 15·25 | 19 | 15·50 | 0·25 |

**Table 5.1.** *(continued)*

| Site | Map ref. | $y$ (inch) | $m$ | $2m\delta$ (inch) | $\epsilon$ (inch) |
|------|----------|------------|-----|-------------------|-------------------|
| Claunch, Wigtonshire | NX 428485 | 6·8± | 8 | 6·53 | 0·27 |
| | | 3·20 | 4 | 3·26 | 0·06 |
| Glasserton Mains, Wigtonshire | NX 407375 | 7·37 | 9 | 7·34 | 0·03 |
| | | 4·92 | 6 | 4·90 | 0·02 |
| Glencorse Church, Midlothian | NT 247630 | 4·87 | 6 | 4·90 | 0·03 |
| Killean, Argyllshire | NR 706445 | 7·6± | 9 | 7·34 | 0·26 |
| | | 5·02 | 6 | 4·90 | 0·12 |
| Tongor Croft, Kirkcudbrightshire | NX 603483 | 10·90 | 13 | 10·61 | 0·29 |
| | | 9·09 | 11 | 8·98 | 0·11 |
| | | 7·41 | 9 | 7·34 | 0·07 |
| | | 5·71 | 7 | 5·71 | 0·00 |
| Senwick Croft, Kirkcudbrightshire | NX 647467 | 3·75 | 5 | 4·08 | 0·33 |
| Whitehill, Dunbartonshire (Various sites on farm) | NS 5073 | 3·49 | 4 | 3·26 | 0·23 |
| | | 5·98 | 7 | 5·71 | 0·27 |
| | | 3·99 | 5 | 4·08 | 0·09 |
| | | 4·55 | 6 | 4·89 | 0·34 |
| | | 8·00 | 10 | 8·16 | 0·16 |
| | | 5·76 | 7 | 5·71 | 0·05 |
| | | 4·09 | 5 | 4·08 | 0·01 |
| | | 2·45 | 3 | 2·45 | 0·00 |
| | | 3·50 | 4 | 3·26 | 0·24 |
| | | 4·03 | 5 | 4·08 | 0·05 |
| | | 4·10 | 5 | 4·08 | 0·02 |
| | | 3·10 | 4 | 3·26 | 0·16 |

From rubbings by Morris and Bailey.
$n = 57$, $\Sigma\epsilon^2 = 2\cdot482$, $s^2 = 0\cdot0435$, $s^2/\delta^2 = 0\cdot261$, probability level = 4 per cent.

It is important to note that all the values in Table 5.1 were measured by Morris, Bailey, or by us *before* the analysis was started and so can be considered as completely objective and unaffected by knowledge of the final value of $2\delta$.

These sites all lie in Scotland but some years later Mr. Evan Hadingham gave us some rubbings he had made in Yorkshire. The results of our measurements of Hadingham's rubbings are shown in Table 5.2.

An examination of any of the rubbings in Figs 5.2 to 5.11 shows that however neatly the rings may have been cut originally, today weathering and other damage has widened the grooves and made them difficult to measure. Indeed it is impossible to get accurate values. This makes it necessary to use as many as possible in an analysis of the kind we are making, but care must be taken to include circular rings only and to exclude any which show signs of being elliptical or egg-shaped. Taking the values from both tables together we find

$n = 74$, $\Sigma y = 465\cdot8$, $\Sigma my = 4278\cdot4$, $\Sigma m = 571$, $\Sigma m^2 = 5237$, $\Sigma\epsilon^2 = 3.185$,

**Table 5.2.** *Cup and ring marks, diameters* (y) *compared with the quantum* 2δ

| Site | Map ref. | $y$ (inch) | $m$ | $2m\delta$ (inch) | $\epsilon$ (inch) |
|------|----------|-----------|-----|--------|--------|
| Panorama Stone | SE 116473 | 4·0 | 5 | 4·08 | 0·08 |
| | | 4·5 | 6 | 4·90 | 0·40 |
| | | 7·3 | 9 | 7·34 | 0·04 |
| | | 5·1 | 6 | 4·90 | 0·20 |
| | | 8·4 | 10 | 8·16 | 0·24 |
| | | 12·3 | 15 | 12·24 | 0·06 |
| | | 4·3 | 5 | 4·08 | 0·22 |
| | | 6·9 | 8 | 6·53 | 0·37 |
| | | 9·8 | 12 | 9·79 | 0·01 |
| | | 4·2 | 5 | 4·08 | 0·12 |
| | | 7·3 | 9 | 7·34 | 0·04 |
| Baildon Moor | SE 138402 | 4·7 | 6 | 4·90 | 0·20 |
| | | 5·7 | 7 | 5·71 | 0·01 |
| Knock Edge | SE 076450 | 2·2 | 3 | 2·49 | 0·29 |
| | | 5·9 | 7 | 5·71 | 0·19 |
| | | 7·3 | 9 | 7·34 | 0·04 |
| | | 12·5 | 15 | 12·24 | 0·26 |

From rubbings by Hadingham.
Combined with values from Table 5.1, $n = 74$, $\Sigma\epsilon^2 = 3\cdot185$, $s^2 = 0\cdot0430$, $s^2/\delta^2 = 0\cdot259$, probability level = 2 per cent.

and these yield

$$2\delta = \Sigma my/\Sigma m^2 = 0\cdot817 \text{ inches}$$

with a probability level of 2 per cent.

The simplest expression for $2\delta$ is $\Sigma y/\Sigma m$ and this gives 0·816 inches. We shall call this the Megalithic inch.

Since the Megalithic yard is 2·722 ft and one-fortieth of this is 0·817 inches it appears that we can write:

1 Megalithic yard (MY) = 40 Megalithic inches (MI)
1 Megalithic rod (MR)  = $2\frac{1}{2}$ MY = 100 MI

**5.3.** A good illustration of the reality of the unit is seen in Fig. 5.2 which is a rubbing by Morris of five cups that are on the rock on the golf course at Gourock. Superimposed on the rubbing we show by rings the apices of triangles with sides 3, 4, 5 and 6, 8, 10 Megalithic inches. It seems to us that the manner in which our rings fit into the cups is in itself proof of the existence of the Megalithic inch. Further proof comes from the numerous designs found in Scotland and Yorkshire, some of which are given in Figs 5.3 to 5.11. Knowing the unit of measurement we can examine the designs more carefully.

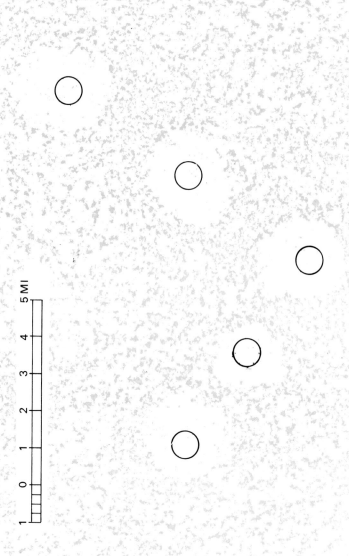

FIG. 5.2. Cups on rock at Gourock golf course.

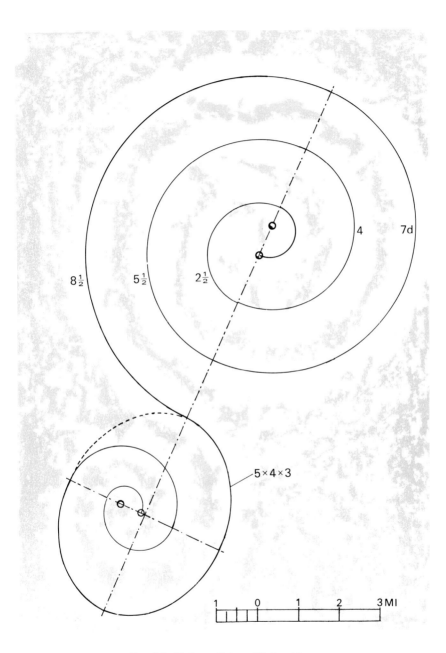

FIG. 5.3. Gallows Outon, Wigtonshire.
Ellipse: $5 \times 4 \times 3$ at small spiral
Semicircle diameters at small spiral: $2\frac{3}{4}$ and $1\frac{3}{4}$; at large spiral: $8\frac{1}{2}$, 7, $5\frac{1}{2}$, 4, $2\frac{1}{2}$

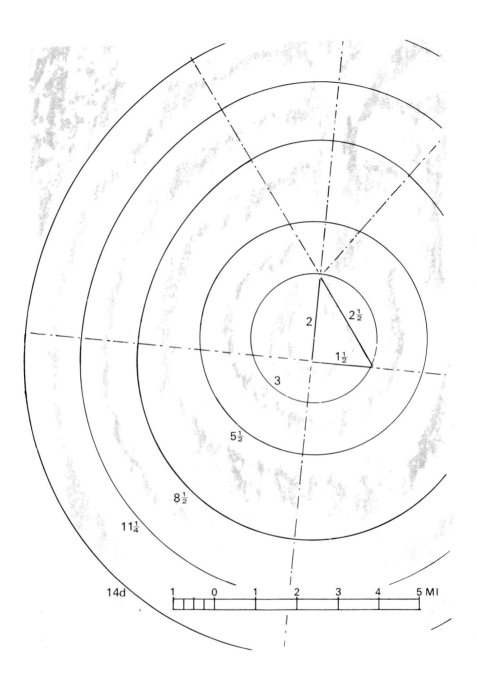

FIG. 5.4. Mossyard. Basic triangle $1\frac{1}{2}$, 2, $2\frac{1}{2}$ (3, 4, 5).

In Fig. 5.3 we have a spiral built up from semicircles. This seems to be connected to an ellipse that has basic dimensions of $5 \times 4 \times 3$ Megalithic inches. In Fig. 5.4 we show how the rings at Mossyard can be represented by two circles and by three egg shapes based on a 3, 4, 5 triangle. The perimeters of the egg shapes are 89·95, 72·18, and 54·8 MI, almost certainly intended to be 90, $72\frac{1}{2}$, and 55.

In Fig. 5.5 we show a set of concentric egg shapes based on a 3, 4, 5 triangle in the form $\frac{3}{4}$, 1, $1\frac{1}{4}$ MI. We have calculated the radii to make the perimeters 10, 15, $22\frac{1}{2}$, and 30, and find for the radii of the large ends of the egg 1·47, 2·27, 3·46 and 4·66 MI. These radii were used by us to draw the

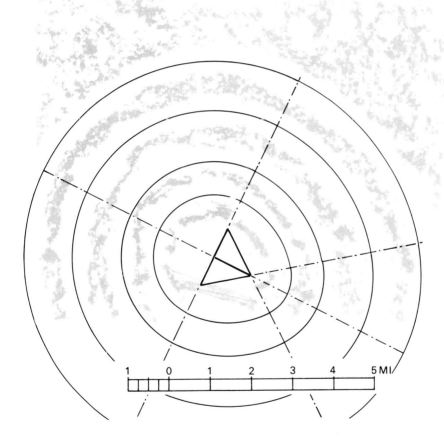

FIG. 5.5. Cardrones House
Basic triangle $\frac{3}{4}$, 1, $1\frac{1}{4}$ (perfect)
Basic radii about $4\frac{5}{8}$, $3\frac{1}{2}$, $2\frac{1}{4}$, $1\frac{1}{2}$
giving perimeters 30, $22\frac{1}{2}$, 15, 10

superimposed egg shapes, but we suggest that the designer used $1\frac{1}{2}$, $2\frac{1}{4}$, $3\frac{1}{2}$, and $4\frac{5}{8}$ MI. It is evident that it was considered important to have the perimeters as multiples of $2\frac{1}{2}$ units, and we suggest that this rule was given priority to the extent that it was allowed to control the radii, otherwise why did the designers use $4\frac{5}{8}$ MI for the largest radius?

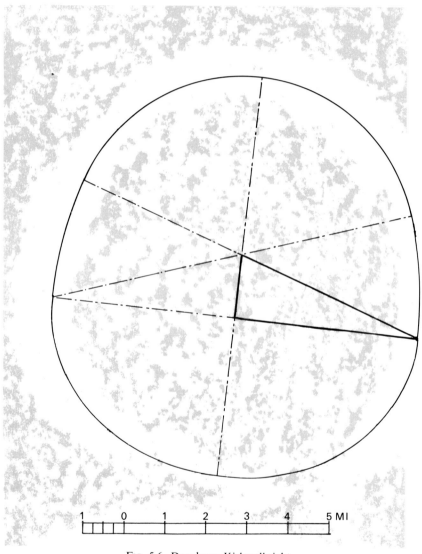

FIG. 5.6. Douchray, Kirkcudbright.
Half ellipse      $9 \times 7\frac{1}{2} \times 5$     324 v. 225+100
Triangle for egg   $4\frac{1}{2} \times 1\frac{1}{2} \times 4\frac{3}{4}$   361 v. 36+324

The ring at Douchray, Fig. 5.6 is interesting because the small end follows the usual construction, based on a $4\frac{1}{2} \times 1\frac{1}{2} \times 4\frac{3}{4}$ triangle, but notice that the outer apex of the triangle falls on the perimeter of the ring. The large end instead of being a semicircle is one half of an ellipse with major axis 9, minor axis $7\frac{1}{2}$, and distance between the foci 5 MI. The squares, in half units, are 324 versus $225 + 100$.

The design at Glasserton Mains, Fig. 5.7, has its outer ring identical with

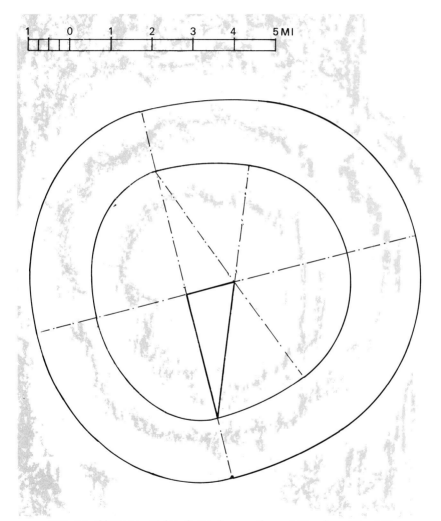

FIG. 5.7. Glasserton Mains. Outer ring exactly as at Douchray (Fig. 5.6).

| | | |
|---|---|---|
| Inner ring ellipse | $6 \times 4\frac{1}{2} \times 4$ | 144 v. $81 + 64$ |
| Egg | $3\frac{1}{4} \times 3 \times 1\frac{1}{4}$ | 169 v. $144 + 25$ |
| Perimeters | 29·39 and 19·49 | |

that at Douchray. It has also an inner ring with the same properties but based on two other triangles as shown in the caption to Fig. 5.7. It is remarkable that the designer succeeded in finding triangles which allowed him to construct two rings which nest inside one another but have the apices of the triangles on the perimeter. He also obtained reasonably good values for the perimeters, these being 29·38 and 19·49 for 30 and 20 MI. The designer doubtless considered he had succeeded in producing a perfect design without overstepping his terms of reference. The ring at Douchray was probably a copy of the outer ring.

We show in Fig. 5.8 the ring at Knappers Farm (NS 504713, but now in

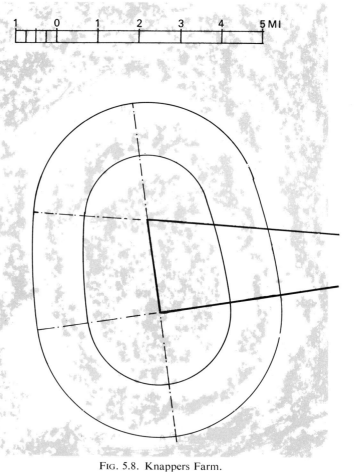

FIG. 5.8. Knappers Farm.
Basic triangle   $10\frac{1}{4}$, 10, $2\frac{1}{4}$   1681 v. 1600+81
Basic radii      3 and $1\frac{3}{4}$
Perimeters       22·60 and 14·75

FIG. 5.9. Panorama Stone, Ilkley SC 116475.

FIG. 5.10. The spiral from the Panorama Stone.

Kelvingrove Museum, Glasgow) because, in trying to find rings to suit the design, we ended up with the perfect triangle 9, 40, 41 in quarter Megalithic-inch units. This is the largest (numerically) exact triangle which we have found anywhere among the Megalithic remains and obviously lends some support to the idea that Megalithic man knew the theorem of Pythagoras. It would be very difficult to discover this triangle by actual construction in the field. It is unfortunate that the rock is badly weathered, for this makes it difficult to be sure that we have uncovered the intended design. However, strong support comes from the fact that the perimeters are 22·60 and 14·75 MI (for $22\frac{1}{2}$ and 15 MI).

A photograph of Mr. Hadingham's rubbings of some of the marks on the Panorama Stone at Ilkley (SC 116475) is given in Fig. 5.9. Our measurements of the circular rings on the rubbing are included in Table 5.1. Two of the little 'ladders' seen in the figure have a rung spacing of $1\frac{1}{2}$ MI and the other of 2 MI.

We have superimposed the design of a spiral in the middle of the figure and we show this again to a larger scale in Fig. 5.10. The spiral is built up from five half-ellipses, one being a semicircle. The particulars are given in Table 5.3.

**Table 5.3.**

| $a$ | $b$ | $c$ | $c$ taken as |
|---|---|---|---|
| 6 | 4 | 4·472 | $4\frac{1}{2}$ |
| 8 | 8 | 0 | 0 |
| 10 | 8 | 6 | 6 |
| 12 | 11 | 4·796 | $4\frac{3}{4}$ |
| 14 | 12 | 7·211 | $7\frac{1}{4}$ |

We give the value of $c$ to suit the major and minor axes. Taking $4\frac{3}{4}$ from 4·796 leaves only 0·046 MI or 0·038 inches in error, an amount which would hardly be apparent working on a stone surface.

Lastly we give the beautiful little design found at Knock and shown in Fig. 5.11. The spiral is built from seven half-ellipses and all the ellipses are based on triangles which satisfy the Pythagorean theorem. Values for $a$, $b$, and $c$ (where $a$ is the major axis, $b$ the minor, and $c$ the distance between foci), including the semicircle, are listed in the underline. We also give a comparison of the sum of the squares using a unit of a quarter of a Megalithic inch.

This remarkable set of triangles produces a spiral as shown, with the spacing between the whorls 1 unit along the major axis and $\frac{7}{8}$ unit on the minor.

This is surely one of the most perfect little designs left by Megalithic man. It is remarkable how well this design fits the rubbing, but it is more remarkable that *it exists*. A spiral can be drawn easily from a series of half-ellipses, but a spiral so perfectly proportioned and built from ellipses which satisfy the Pythagorean relation is indeed a surprising achievement.

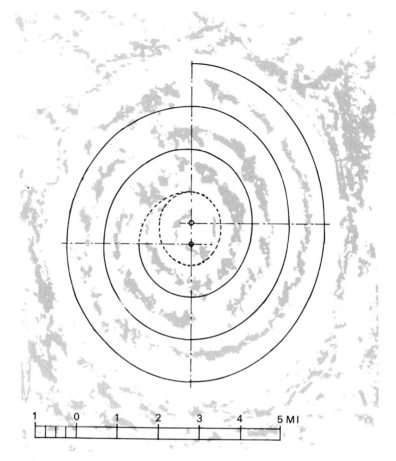

Fig. 5.11. The spiral at Knock. Spiral built from 7 half-ellipses, etc.

| | | |
|---|---|---|
| $7\frac{1}{2} \times 6\frac{1}{2} \times 3\frac{3}{4}$ | 900 v. 676 + 225 | or 901 |
| $6\frac{1}{2} \times 6 \times 2\frac{1}{2}$ | 169 v. 144 + 25 | or 169 |
| $5\frac{1}{2} \times 4\frac{3}{4} \times 2\frac{3}{4}$ | 484 v. 361 + 121 | or 482 |
| $4\frac{1}{2} \times 4\frac{1}{4} \times 1\frac{1}{2}$ | 324 v. 289 + 36 | or 325 |
| $3\frac{1}{2} \times 3 \times 1\frac{3}{4}$ | 196 v. 144 + 49 | or 193 |
| $2\frac{1}{2} \times 2\frac{1}{2} \times 0$ | 100 v. 100 + 0 | or 100 |
| $1\frac{3}{4} \times 1\frac{1}{2} \times \frac{7}{8}$ | 49 v. 36 + 12$\frac{1}{4}$ | or 48$\frac{1}{4}$ |

The last four columns show the comparison between the square of the hypotenuse and the
sum of the squares of the other two sides—all in units of $\frac{1}{4}$ MI.


## 5.4. The method of drawing used

A simple method of drawing an ellipse on a drawing board is to put a drawing
pin at each focus, put a loop of thread round them and scribe the ellipse with
a pencil point in the loop. This method could have been used for large ellipses
on the sand or on level ground but it would have been difficult on smooth or

polished rock. Suppose that an assistant held little rods at the foci, how was the thread adjusted? The rods being of bone or wood would probably be too thick.

The thread or rope method would have shown the draughtsman that the sum of the distances of any point on the ellipse from the foci was constant and equal to the major axis $2a$, and so he could use his set of trammels as follows (and illustrated in Fig. 5.12). He could set out an arc with radius $r$ from $F_1$

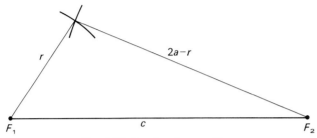

FIG. 5.12. Constructing an ellipse.

and then an arc with radius $(2a-r)$ from $F_2$. This gave one point and by interchanging $r$ and $2a-r$, altogether 4 points. He seems to have had trammels advancing by $\frac{1}{4}$ units so he could put in enough points. Then he could by eye scribe the whole curve and peck it out.

There are, in Britain, other types of designs that we believe were geometrically set out, but some are so badly weathered that it is difficult to be certain about the outlines (for example Thom 1969a, Fig. 3).

There does not seem to be any direct method of dating cup and ring marks but the material in this chapter shows how closely they are related to stone rings. First there is the unit, giving the relation:

$$100 \text{ MI} = 2\frac{1}{2} \text{ MY} = 1 \text{ MR}$$

and then there is the geometry. In the stone rings and cup and ring marks we find egg shapes and ellipses based on integral Pythagorean triangles and in both we find that the perimeters are integral in multiples of $2\frac{1}{2}$ times the basic unit.

# 6

# LE MÉNEC

**6.1.** IT will be seen in Fig. 9.6 that there are four main sets of alignments near Carnac, namely Le Ménec, Kermario, Kerlescan, and Petit Ménec. In association with the alignments, we find the remains of several cromlechs or stone rings. There was a cromlech at each end of Le Ménec, and presumably also at each end of Kermario.

About a mile northward from Carnac lies the hamlet of Le Ménec, part of which is built inside the west cromlech (Fig. 6.1). It will be seen that this cromlech consists of an egg-shaped ring of upright stones. The egg shape is based on a 3, 4, 5 triangle, the sides being 15, 20, and 25 MR. The fact that some of the stones do not lie on the geometrical construction is easily explained because all but five or six of the stones carry the re-erection mark (§1.2), and those which do not have the mark lie in the outline. This cromlech is important in that it shows unequivocally that the type I egg shape which we found in Britain was also used in France, and that the *same unit of measurement was used*. The perimeter of the ring is 304·4 MY. Figure 6.1 shows also that by dropping a perpendicular from the centre on to the hypotenuse we obtain another 3, 4, 5 triangle, the sides being 12, 16, and 20 MR. An examination of Fig. 6.2 shows that this triangle was applied at the east end of the Le Ménec alignments to form the type II egg which was used there. Note that the perimeter of this egg is 370·0 MY so that both eggs conform to the usual practice of having the perimeter close to an integral number of rods. One of the stones on the north-east side of the ring was difficult to find and difficult to survey as it was in the middle of deep whins, but the existence of these stones seems to prove our suggested construction. It may also be remarked that the straight distance from the centre, *e*, of the east cromlech to the centre, *w*, of the west cromlech (Figs. 6.3(a) and 6.3(b)) is 495·0 MR and row IX, produced as necessary, cuts the axis of each cromlech 1 MR from its main centre.

## 6.2. The alignments at Le Ménec

A modern road runs from Le Ménec to the east and passes along the south edge of the alignments at Le Ménec, Kermario, and Kerlescan. While this is a convenience for the tourist its construction has damaged the alignments badly. The road builders were almost certainly guilty in places of moving some of the stones without leaving any record of their original positions. This vandalism is particularly evident on Fig. 6.3 where the south row of Le

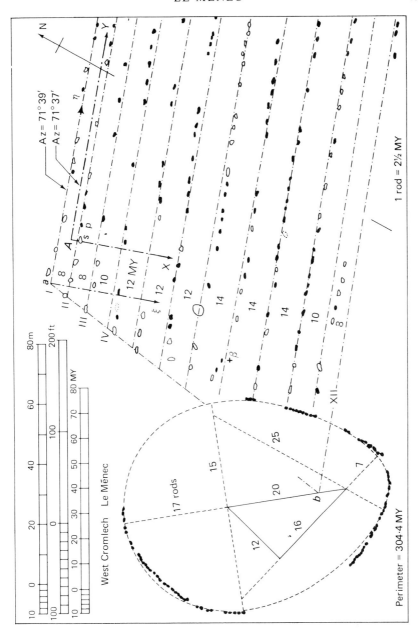

FIG. 6.1. Le Ménec, west end and cromlech. $A$ is 9·4 ft and 18·7 ft respectively from the nearest corners of stones $s$ and $p$. The line $AY$ passes 11·5 ft north of the corner of an isolated stone 1203 ft from $A$. Triangle shown in full is that used at east end. The coordinates of $a$ relative to $A$ are $x = -13·2$ ft, $y = -52·6$ ft. Position $\beta$, of zero of coordinates, in Table 9.3.

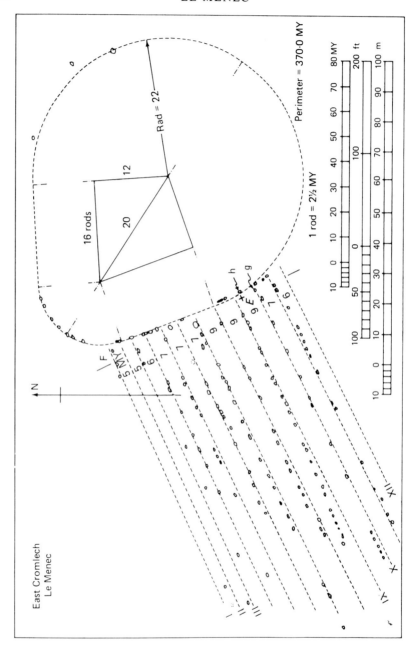

FIG. 6.2. Le Ménec, east end and cromlech. E is 17·1 ft and 7·2 ft respectively from the nearest points on stones g and h. The coordinates of E relative to A (Fig. 6.1) are x = −12·3 ft, y = 2948·2 ft.

Ménec near the knee has suffered. This leaves us with a feeling of uncertainty regarding the south row in Kermario (Fig. 7.3) as this is practically on the edge of the road.

A great many of the stones in the alignments carry the re-erection red plug; in some sections it is in fact difficult to find a stone not so marked. We believe that Le Rouzic died before he committed to paper exactly what he meant by these marks. We were told by a peasant that he marked stones which he had not re-erected and so it seems likely that Le Rouzic marked stones which he believed had been re-erected earlier as well as those he had re-erected himself.

At the west end of the alignments the menhirs are larger and stand on rocky ground, but towards the east end there is a length where the ground is better, so much so that the stones have been removed to make way for agriculture (Fig. 6.3(b)). Just before the east cromlech the lines, or some of them, start again, as shown in detail and on a larger scale in Fig. 6.2.

### 6.3. Le Ménec details

Our survey made in 1970 was plotted to a scale of 1/500 which made it much too big for reproduction but we show the cromlechs to a reasonable scale (Figs 6.1 and 6.2) and the remainder of necessity to a very small scale (Fig. 6.3). We recorded which stones carried the red plug but in the subsequent analysis we retained all the stones because, had we attempted to exclude the marked stones, in places there would have been little left. In many places we think that stones had been re-erected before Le Rouzic's time. Where the stones had all fallen one way is it possible that the wrong end was lifted so that the whole line was displaced? After the knee in the middle it looks very much as if the re-erectors had been guided by rows III and VII on the west side when they replaced some of the stones on the east side, but perhaps these are remnants of an earlier construction left by Megalithic man. The tall menhir shown on Fig. 6.3(a) is 12 ft high and possibly has nothing to do with the rows. It may have been bypassed by rows III and IV; but the re-erectors were perhaps guided by the menhir and deflected rows III, IV, and possibly V and VI in order to incorporate it in a row.

### 6.4. The spacing of the stones along the rows

Here we wish to find out if a quantum existed and to find its magnitude. It is explained in Thom 1967 that in analysis of this problem there are two cases, the first being when we have an *a priori* knowledge that a quantum of an approximately known value probably exists, and the second when we have no idea what to expect. Before coming to Le Ménec we had found values for both the Megalithic yard and the Megalithic rod in Britain and we found evidence for the rod being used in both Le Ménec cromlechs. Accordingly we are entitled to look for these units in the rows and so we use Broadbent's first

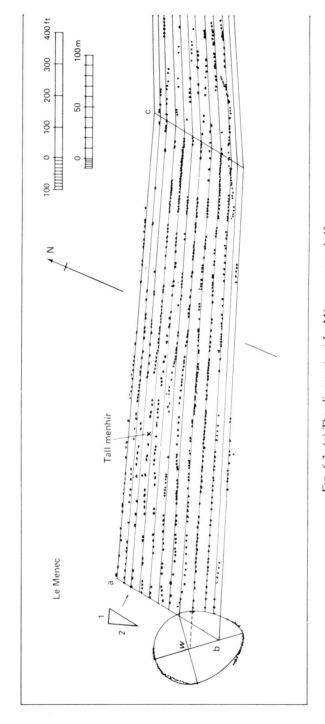

Le Menec

Tall menhir

N

100    0    100   200   300   400 ft

100m

0    50    100m

FIG. 6.3. (a) The alignments at Le Ménec, western half.

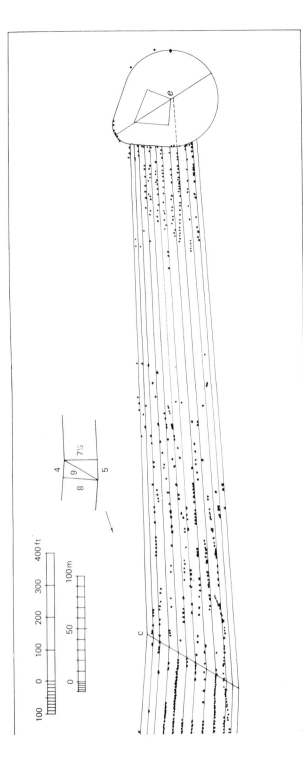

(b) The eastern half.

Without excavation it is not possible to be certain of the *exact* position of the axes of the cromlechs but the following dimensions represent closely those used in the original setting out. Distance from centre $w$ of the west cromlech to centre $e$ of the east cromlech is 495·0 MR. Row IX produced cuts the main axis of each cromlech 1 MR from the centres $w$ and $e$. The principal axis of the west cromlech makes an angle of 45° with the line $ab$ and meets it very close to, if not on, Row XII produced. The principal axis of the east cromlech makes an angle of 30° with the line $EF$ which is normal to the mean direction of the rows.

method with 1 MY or 1 MR. On a preliminary trial the former was so poor
that we concentrated on the value of the rod of 6·80 ft.

Suppose that we mark off on the edge of a strip of paper, ticks spaced
uniformly one rod apart to the scale of the survey, and try to fit the marked
strip to a row of stones. Perhaps in the less disturbed lines we shall find enough
coincidences to suggest that this unit was indeed used. We do not expect to
find stones at every 6·8 ft but perhaps spaced at twice, three, or even four
times this distance, with large gaps where stones have been removed. This
visual demonstration cannot however decide the matter; the disturbances
have been too great. Having chosen the best position for the strip of paper,
let us transfer the ticks to the row or line. We shall call these points 'nodes'.
What a statistical analysis does is to tell us the probability level at which we
can accept the quantum, and the most likely positions for the nodes. If the
quantum needs a small adjustment a revised value will emerge.

Let us write the positions of stones along the line as

$$y = b + 2m\delta + \epsilon,  \tag{6.1}$$

where $m$ is an integer, $2\delta$ is the quantum, and $b$ is the unknown distance to
the first node from the zero being used. The ideal or expected position of a
stone is $(b + 2m\delta)$ and $\epsilon$ is the divergence of the stone from this position (see
Fig. 7.6).

A full exposition of the statistical theory has been given by Broadbent. The
method of using the necessary formulae for the determination of $b$, $2\delta$, and
the probability level will be found in Thom 1967, Chapter 2, where a graphical
presentation of the probability level is also given.

We propose to give here only a short account of the analysis of the rows.
Details will be found in Thom and Thom 1972a.

The distance $y$ of a stone from the zero being used is taken from the survey.
With a trial value for $b$ we calculate the value of $\epsilon$ for each stone from
equation (6.1). The best value for $b$ is that which makes the sum of the squares
of $\epsilon$ a minimum. A difficulty is that as $b$ is altered some of the stones will have
to be assigned to a different node. Illustrations of the method of finding $b$
by examining the values of $\epsilon^2$ will be found in Chapter 7 on Kermario.

Another method is to get $b$ from $b = (1/n)\Sigma\epsilon_1$, where $\epsilon_1 = y - 6\cdot80m$.
Alternatively we can use Broadbent's full method using the case where we
have an a priori knowledge of the quantum. This method will give a revised
value of the quantum as well as a value for $b$ but shortly we shall show a
much better method of finding the quantum at Le Ménec. The engineers who
set out the rows would naturally have started their measurements from some
zero line crossing the alignments. We had expected that this line would be at
right-angles to the rows. However knowing the approximate value of $b$ for
each row we were able to plot the nodes to scale on the rows and found that
only lines at a gradient of 2 in 1 across the rows picked up all the nodes.

It can be shown that unless the rows are equally spaced there can, in general, be only one straight line crossing the rows which will pick up a node on every line. The rows are *not* equally spaced. Only one set of straight cross lines through nodes could in fact be found and the existence of this set shows that the spacing we assumed (Fig. 6.1) for the 12 lines was that used by the builders. Thus it appears that the starting point for each row was displaced relative to its neighbour by half the space between them. It will be seen that the cut-off for rows I–V at the west end (Fig. 6.1) follows closely the line drawn through *a* at a gradient of 2 in 1 to the row. Almost certainly this is the zero line from which the measurements started; they did not start at the east cromlech.

The analysis also gives us the position of the zero at *a* (Fig. 6.1) relative to the origin *A* of our original survey and so in future work we can use the line through *a* as the zero line. Measuring from this cross line we get the mean value of *b* for the row from $b = (1/n)\Sigma\epsilon_1$. The values of *b* are plotted in Fig. 6.4 with a vertical bar to show the calculated standard error. Note how small are the values both of *b* and its standard error relative to the quantum 6·80, indicating that the line *ab* is indeed a line of nodes.

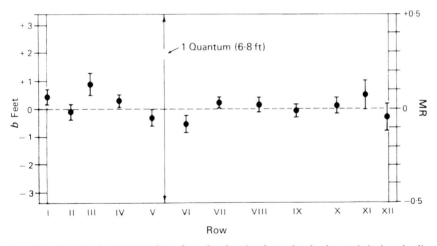

FIG. 6.4. Graphical representation of results showing how closely the statistical nodes lie on the line through *a* in Fig. 6.1.

In Thom and Thom 1972 we show that taking all the rows together and applying Broadbent's method we obtain a probability level of about 1 per cent. Some statisticians, however, prefer to ignore the above and want to work without any *a priori* value for the quantum but we believe that the disturbances in the rows have been too great to allow any method of this kind to give a conclusive result. It is here necessary to have the support of an *a priori* value. When this is invoked as above things fall into place.

## 6.5. East end

The stones in the western part of Le Ménec alignments are standing on the solid rock, but towards the eastern end the ground improves and has been cleared of menhirs to permit the practice of agriculture. But *at* the east end there is a group of about 127 stones in rows running up to the cromlech (Fig. 6.2).

Our survey point $E$ is shown on Fig. 6.2 with the reference distances given so that it can, if required, be picked up on the ground. Analysis has indicated that we can safely take the quantum to be 6·80 ft here also, and so we proceed to find the mean node $(1/n)\Sigma\epsilon_1$ for each row exactly as for the west end. In Table 6.1 these are given referred to the cross-line EF defined in Fig. 6.2. Here, as at the west end, we take the positive direction along the rows towards the east.

## 6.6. The geometry

The geometry of Le Ménec site is shown in Fig. 6.3 with the ends in larger detail in Figs 6.1 and 6.2. The knee of each row has been assumed to be exactly 220 MR (550 MY) from its nominal start. While it is not yet possible to be sure that this was the exact length used, we know that the uncertainty is only a rod or two, and later we shall see that this has no effect on the ultimate conclusions to be drawn from the analysis.

The first four rows are parallel up to the knee and spaced 8, 8, and 10 MY. The nodes in row III obviously lag (by $\frac{1}{2} \times 8$ MY) behind those in row II, which similarly lag behind those in row I. But after the knee we find that the nodes in all three rows are almost exactly in step. That this is so will be seen when we come later to examine Fig. 6.6 where the nodes in these lines at the east end are shown to be equidistant from the cross line. Another peculiarity is that at the knee the transverse spacing drops automatically from 8 to $7\frac{1}{2}$ MY. The explanation is that the angle of the bend is almost exactly that given by the juxtaposition of two triangles in the manner shown in the inset in Fig. 6.3(b). These triangles have sides 4, 8, 9 and 5, $7\frac{1}{2}$, 9. Since $4^2+8^2$ and $5^2+7\frac{1}{2}^2$ are both close to $9^2$, both triangles are nearly right-angled and thus permit at the same time of an integral change in step and an integral change in spacing.

Since this peculiar relation is only possible for the spacing used for the first three rows, we might argue that these rows were the first to be set out and so we number the rows from the north. The transverse spacing $S$ we have assumed is:

| | | | | | | | | | | | |
|---|---|---|---|---|---|---|---|---|---|---|---|
| at west end ($S_w$) | 8 | 8 | 10 | 12 | 12 | 12 | 14 | 14 | 14 | 10 | 8 | (MY) |
| before knee ($S_c$) | 8 | 8 | 10 | 11 | 11 | 11 | 12 | 12 | 12 | 8 | 7 | (MY) |
| at east end ($S_e$) | 5 | 5 | 6 | 7 | 7 | 7 | 9 | 9 | 9 | 7 | 6 | (MY) |

These spaces were found to fit the large-scale survey, but if the analysis given

**Table 6.1.** *Comparison of nodes: calculation versus survey*

| Row | ΣSw ξL | ΣSe ξM | ηM | ΣSe | e | ηN | ξN | l MY | l rods | c node (calc.) | b node (survey) | Diff. b−c |
|---|---|---|---|---|---|---|---|---|---|---|---|---|
| I | 0 | 0 | 550 | 0 | +57·57 | 1095·73 | −57·23 | 548·72 | 219·49 | 0·51 | 0·66 | +0·15 |
| II | 8 | 8 | 546 | 5 | +52·57 | 1096·38 | −52·27 | 553·67 | 221·47 | 0·53 | — | — |
| III | 16 | 16 | 542 | 10 | +47·57 | 1097·03 | −47·31 | 558·63 | 223·45 | 0·55 | 0·64 | +0·09 |
| IV | 26 | 26 | 537 | 16 | +41·57 | 1097·81 | −41·36 | 564·84 | 225·94 | 0·06 | 0·14 | +0·08 |
| V | 38 | 37 | 531 | 23 | +34·57 | 1098·73 | −34·42 | 572·21 | 228·88 | 0·12 | 0·24 | +0·12 |
| VI | 50 | 48 | 525 | 30 | +27·57 | 1099·64 | −27·48 | 579·58 | 231·83 | 0·17 | 0·28 | +0·11 |
| VII | 62 | 59 | 518·99 | 37 | +20·57 | 1100·55 | −20·54 | 586·97 | 234·79 | 0·21 | 0·32 | +0·11 |
| VIII | 76 | 71 | 511·98 | 46 | +11·57 | 1101·73 | −11·62 | 595·51 | 238·20 | 0·80 | 0·80 | 0·00 |
| IX | 90 | 83 | 504·95 | 55 | +2·57 | 1102·90 | −2·70 | 604·06 | 241·62 | 0·38 | 0·70 | +0·32 |
| X | 104 | 95 | 497·93 | 64 | −6·43 | 1104·08 | +6·22 | 612·62 | 245·05 | 0·95 | 0·80 | −0·15 |
| XI | 114 | 103 | 492·89 | 71 | −13·43 | 1104·99 | +13·16 | 618·66 | 247·46 | 0·54 | 0·82 | +0·28 |
| XII | 122 | 110₁ | 488·87 | 77 | −19·43 | 1105·78 | +19·11 | 623·57 | 249·42 | 0·58 | — | — |

Mean difference = +0·11

below is studied, it will be seen that at the west end no other integral spacing is possible. From what has been said above about the first three rows, it seems almost certain that all the spaces were intended to be integral in Megalithic yards.

### 6.7. Comparison of the nodes at the east and west ends

We now proceed to compare the nodes determined on the ground at the east end with the theoretical positions obtained by assuming that the setting out of the rows proceeded from west to east so that the nodes were carried right through. It is to be noted that Fig. 6.5 contains all the data needed to calculate the length of each line up to the cross-line $EF$ apart from the spacings of the rows I–XII which have just been given.

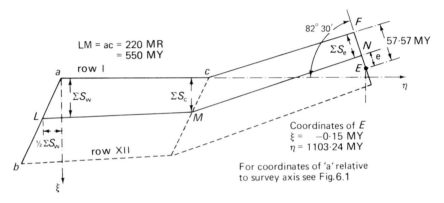

FIG. 6.5. Specification of the geometry of the alignments at Le Ménec.

Take the $\eta$ axis along the first part of row I and the $\xi$ axis towards the south through $a$. The normal distances of any line $LMN$ (Fig. 6.5) from the row I are $\Sigma S_w$, $\Sigma S_c$, and $\Sigma S_e$, where $S_w$, $S_c$, and $S_e$ are given above, and the summation is taken up to the line considered. The line extends $\frac{1}{2}\Sigma S_w$, that is $\frac{1}{2}\xi_w$ to the west of the $\xi$-axis and is straight for a distance of 550 MY to $M$ where it is $\Sigma S_c$ from row I. It is again straight to $N$ on the cross-line where it is $\Sigma S_e$ (that is $FN$) from row I. The distance $FE$ (57·57 MY) is considered to give on our survey a reasonably good fit to the stones shown on Fig. 6.2. The coordinates of $E$ (Fig. 6.5) come from our survey, and point $a$ has been found by the statistical analysis (see Fig. 6.1).

We have seen that $L$ is a node, and since $LM$ is an integral number of rods, $M$ is also a node. It follows that if we calculate the length $MN$ we find the position of the node adjacent to $N$. This can be compared with what we find on the ground.

Since the locus of $M$ is not necessarily a straight line, the coordinates of $M$ have been found for each line. Using Megalithic yards the calculation proceeds thus:

$$\xi_M = \Sigma S_c, \qquad (6.2)$$

$$\eta_M{}^2 = (550 - \tfrac{1}{2}\xi_L)^2 - (\xi_L - \xi_M)^2, \qquad (6.3)$$

$$e = NE = 57{\cdot}57 - \Sigma S_e, \qquad (6.4)$$

$$\xi_N = -e \sin 82°{\cdot}5 - 0{\cdot}15, \qquad (6.5)$$

$$\eta_N = 1103{\cdot}24 - e \cos 82°{\cdot}5, \qquad (6.6)$$

$$l^2 = (MN)^2 = (\xi_N - \xi_M)^2 + (\eta_N - \eta_M)^2. \qquad (6.7)$$

The results are given in skeleton in Table 6.1. By subtracting the length $l$ *in rods* from the next integer we get the distance from $EF$ to the first node to the east, column (c). Column (b) gives the position of the node as found from the rows near the east cromlech.

A comparison of the two sets of nodes is shown in Fig. 6.6. It will be seen how remarkably the two 'curves' follow one another. It is unnecessary to attempt to make a mathematical assessment of the probability of this happening accidentally; the result would obviously be a minute fraction. We can in fact say with certainty that the nodes were carried through from end to end with remarkable accuracy. The mean difference between the 'curves' is only 0·11 MR or about 9 inches. This is so small that in order to reduce it to zero we need only use 6·8017 ft as the value for the Megalithic rod instead of 6·800 ft.

It has been mentioned that we cannot be certain of the position of the knee. Consideration of the geometrical fit of the assumed lines when drawn on the large-scale survey indicates that we cannot move $M$ by more than 2 or 3 MR. But a movement of 3 MR has the effect of changing the calculated node (c) at $N$ by only 0·03 MR and so would have no effect on the general conclusions to be drawn from Fig. 6.6.

The subject was considered to be so important that when we returned to Carnac in 1971 a remeasurement of the overall length of the site was made with a 100-ft steel tape supported at five points, the end rods being provided with a spirit bubble so that they could be made accurately vertical. The result differed by only 6 inches from the original chaining. Longitudinal spacings of the stones in all the rows at the east end were remeasured to make sure that the values there were correct. These are given in Table 6.2.

A change in one of the transverse spaces *at the west* by 1 MY will move the node *at the east* end by about 0·5 MY or 0·2 MR. It can be seen from Fig. 6.6 that this is an unacceptable amount in the first eight rows. Examination of the spacings of the last four rows on the survey in Figs 6.1, 6.2, and 6.3 taken together indicates the difficulty of finding any improvement.

Position of nodes relative to cross
line EF at East End.

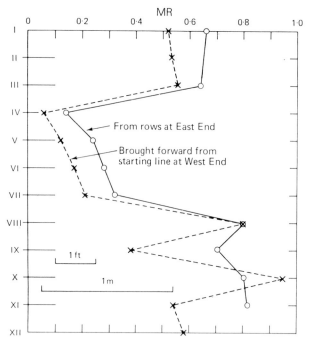

FIG. 6.6. Comparison of nodes: calculation versus survey.

**Table 6.2.** *Result of the analysis of the remnants of rows at the east cromlech shown in Fig. 6.2*

| Row | $n$ | Node (MY) | Node (MR) | $s^2/\delta^2$ | p.l. (%) | |
|---|---|---|---|---|---|---|
| I | 5 | 1·65 | 0·66 | 0·030 | — | |
| II | — | — | — | — | — | Too few stones to give a p.l. |
| III | 5 | 1·61 | 0·64 | 0·226 | — | |
| IV | 7 | 0·36 | 0·14 | 0·247 | — | |
| V | 11 | 0·64 | 0·24 | 0·237 | 11 | |
| VI | 10 | 0·71 | 0·28 | 0·091 | < 1 | |
| VII | 19 | 0·79 | 0·32 | 0·223 | 6 | |
| VIII | 13 | 2·00 | 0·80 | 0·270 | 13 | |
| IX | 24 | 1·75 | 0·70 | 0·270 | 11 | |
| X | 13 | 2·00 | 0·80 | 0·253 | 11 | |
| XI | 16 | 2·05 | 0·82 | 0·299 | 15 | |
| XII | — | — | — | — | — | |

The positions of the nodes given here are relative to line *EF* (see Fig. 6.2). p.l. = probability level.

**6.8.** Some statisticians have criticized our treatment of Le Ménec alignments and have claimed that using the alignments alone it is not possible to show conclusively the use of the Megalithic rod in its construction. Perhaps if they had started by visiting and studying the site they would never have attempted an analysis of this kind which ignores the evidence coming from the Le Ménec cromlechs, from Kermario (Chapter 7) and from the cromlechs at Kerlescan (Chapter 8). To combine the evidence and draw a conclusion needs a philosophical approach; even the most advanced statistical theories do not help. Twenty years ago statisticians were much more ready to listen to a reasoned argument without resorting to elaborate mathematical theories. Had we in the first place waited for statistical theories to develop we should never have been able to proceed.

To our mind one of the most convincing arguments is to plot on a large scale the nodes along each line of the alignments and to see for oneself that there is only one set of crosslines which pick these up, namely that at 2 in 1 to the lines. Any one with an open mind will not need much further evidence.

Patrick and Butler (1974) have criticized our solution to the geometry of Le Ménec. In our reply, however, we were able to point out that in fact their recalculation of the values on which our Fig. 6.6 is based improves the agreement considerably. This is shown in Fig. 6.7.

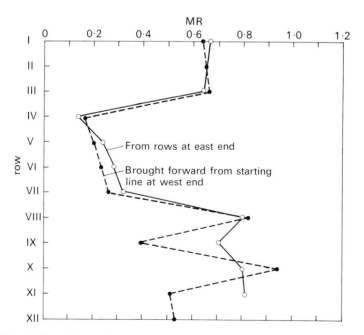

Fig. 6.7. As Fig. 6.6 but calculated on an assumption suggested by Patrick and Butler.

## 6.9. Megalithic yard

It seems that the best value we can get for the Megalithic yard from Le
Ménec is obtained by using the nodes obtained from the stones at the two
ends along with the overall chained length. The statistical mean values of the
positions of these nodes are unlikely to be in error by more than a few inches
and so the error produced is of the same order as the inaccuracy of the overall
chaining. It follows that the final value for the Megalithic rod is $6\cdot802\pm0\cdot002$
ft or $2\cdot073\pm0\cdot001$ m. This makes the Megalithic yard $2\cdot721\pm0\cdot001$ ft or
$0\cdot8293\pm0\cdot0004$ m which is comparable with the value found from the
Kermario alignments, from Avebury and from Brogar in Orkney.

We believe that we have reconstructed the design to which the Le Ménec
cromlechs and rows was set out. This belief is based on the following:

   (a) only one line of nodes could be found at the west end and this crossed
       the rows at an angle of 1 in 2 to the normal;
   (b) we found that a quantum of 1 MR suited at both ends;
   (c) we found how the bend at the knee is given by the juxtaposition of two
       Pythagorean triangles; and
   (d) we found almost perfect agreement between the positions of the nodes
       found at the east end with that brought forward along the individual
       rows with a quantum of $6\cdot802$ ft.

## 6.10. The heights of the stones

Anyone visiting Le Ménec or Kermario is immediately struck by the manner
in which the largest stones in both alignments are concentrated at the west
ends. But there is also some increase in size at the east end of Le Ménec as
can be seen in Fig. 6.8 which shows how the mean height varies from end to

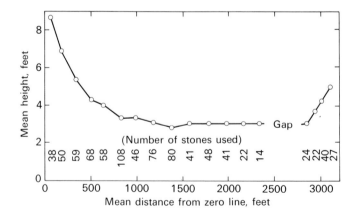

FIG. 6.8. The mean height of the stones along the rows at Le Ménec.

end. The figures given are based on measurements or estimates of a large percentage of the stones, the numbers below the graph showing how many stones were used to form each average. In so far as the general shape of the stones does not vary greatly the mass of the stones at the west end must be nearly 27 (that is $3^3$) times greater than that of those in the middle where, for about 2000 ft, the average height is not much different from 3 ft.

An attempt was made to see how the height falls off in the rows taken two at a time. Each point shown in Fig. 6.9 is the mean height of groups of contiguous stones, each group containing from 3 to 12 stones. The distances are taken from the zero or inclined starting line and, with this presentation, the 5 graphs are pulled together (above 150 ft) rather better than when the distances are measured from a line normal to the rows. But it will be seen that below 150 ft the rows which abut on the cromlech tend to be high and would fit better into the general picture if the distances had been measured from the cromlech. In other words we may say that roughly the size of the stone used depended on the distance from the first stone in the row and went on decreasing for about 800 ft. Thereafter the height remained at an average of about 3 ft till within about 300 ft of the east cromlech, when it rose gradually to about 5 ft.

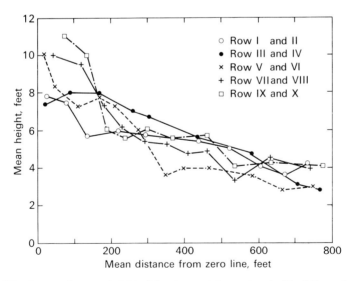

FIG. 6.9. The decrease in mean height of the stones at the west end of Le Ménec shown in greater detail.

# 7

## THE KERMARIO ALIGNMENTS

**7.1.** THIS set of stone rows is slightly longer than that at Le Ménec, and stretches over the pond which now fills the Ravin de Kerloquet. Like Le Ménec, Kermario probably had a cromlech at each end but all traces of these are gone.

We made an accurate survey in 1972 to a scale of 1 in 500. In 1973 the survey was checked at the site and carried further east into the woods where we surveyed a number of fallen stones. Still further on we included an upright 6-ft menhir *E* (see Fig. 7.1) which perhaps belongs to the alignments. This single stone is on the field boundary just before the high ground in the wood where according to M. Jacq, son-in-law of Le Rouzic, there may have been a cromlech.

In 1972 much of the ground was covered by thick whin which made accurate surveying difficult, but the whole site has since been almost completely cleared. The fact that our two open traverses run from end to end agree to within a few inches in length and azimuth gives us complete confidence in the backbone on which our survey is based. The original survey sheet is about 8 ft long and so a large-scale reproduction cannot be given here, but an accurate small-scale copy with our geometrical interpretation is shown in Fig. 7.1 and details of parts in a larger scale will be found in Figs 7.2, 7.3, and 7.4. A key plan is shown in Fig. 7.5, divided into seven sections so that each section can be analysed and discussed separately.

It will be seen that the main part of the alignments consists of seven rows (I–VII) which are today about 3700 ft long. To the south of these there are various other lines, but discussion of these will have to wait till later. At the west end it is seen that the rows are curved to a radius of about 1000 MR. Throughout sections 1, 2, and 3 the rows are parallel and spaced 12 MY apart.

**7.2.** At Le Ménec the angle of the bend at the knee in the middle of the rows was decided by the juxtaposition of two almost exact Pythagorean triangles. In Kermario there are three such bends each based again on coupled right-angled triangles. The geometry is shown in the insets (a), (b), and (c) on Fig. 7.1. The first bend (a) is produced by two right-angled triangles, one with short sides of 12 and 21 and the other of 10 and 22. Now $12^2 + 21^2 = 585$, and $10^2 + 22^2 = 584$, which shows how accurately these two triangles will fit

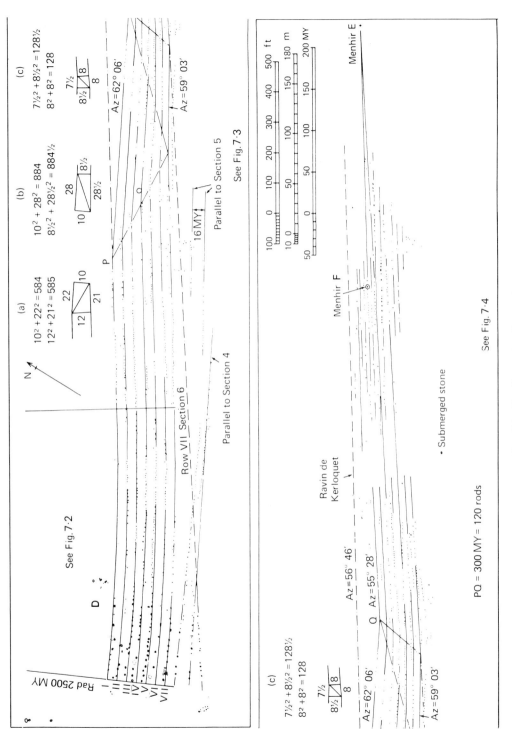

FIG. 7.1. The Kermario alignments.

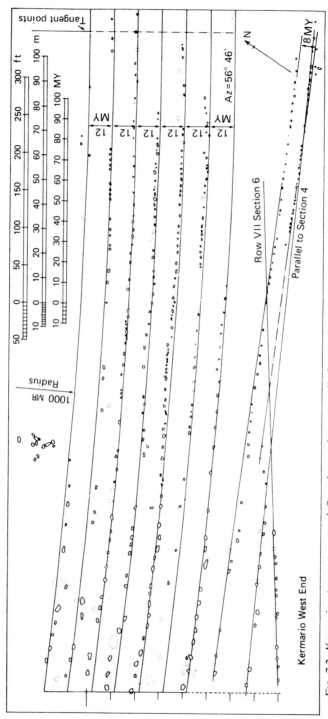

FIG. 7.2. Kermario, stones at west end. Superimposed are arcs, all of 1000 MR (2500 MY) radius. These arcs form extensions of the parallel rows at 12-MY spacing that run from the tangent point eastwards, all at an azimuth of 56° 46'.

[80]

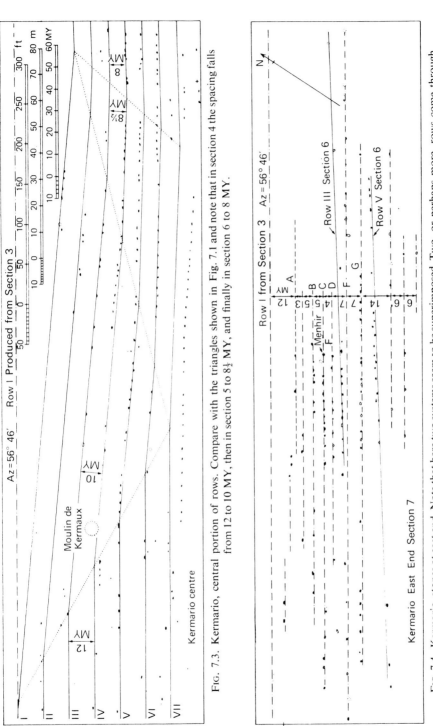

FIG. 7.3. Kermario, central portion of rows. Compare with the triangles shown in Fig. 7.1 and note that in section 4 the spacing falls from 12 to 10 MY, then in section 5 to 8½ MY, and finally in section 6 to 8 MY.

FIG. 7.4. Kermario, stones at east end. Note that here two systems seem to be superimposed. Two, or perhaps more, rows come through from section 6 and the others are parallel to section 3.

together on the common hypotenuse. The emerging rows have been turned through $+5°\,20'$ and at the same time the spacing is reduced from 12 MY to 10 MY. The second bend (b) is effected in the same way but here the sum of the squares is 884 for the one triangle and $884\frac{1}{2}$ for the other. The row spacing is reduced from 10 MY to $8\frac{1}{2}$ MY and rows II to VII emerge at $+2°\,17'$ to the original direction. The next bend (c) is effected by two triangles which are not quite so exact, the sum of the squares being $128\frac{1}{2}$ and 128. These triangles have the effect of reducing the spacing from $8\frac{1}{2}$ MY to 8 MY and bending the rows so that the final angle to the original direction is only $-1°\,18'$. Owing to the slight inexactitude of the various triangles, slightly different theoretical values are possible for the calculated angles, but the permissible range is small and the final direction of the rows on the ground differs by only a few minutes from the theoretical value. Considering that the ground is anything but level and that the lines have come through three bends this must be regarded as a remarkable achievement.

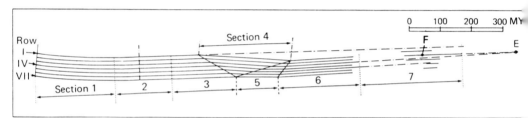

FIG. 7.5. Kermario: key plan showing sections for analysis.

**7.3.** It will be seen that at the east end (section 7) there are remains of two different systems. Indeed, it seems probable that the original erectors were making some alteration here or substituting one system for another. At the end of section 6 the alignments come to the Ravin de Kerloquet. This has now been artificially flooded and it may well be that there are stones under the water. We did in fact survey one which was below the water in 1972 but whose top was allowed to show above the surface in the dry spring of 1973. From our point of view this steep-sided ravine is interesting because it may be possible, by analysis of the rows on the two sides, to find out if the original erectors succeeded in carrying their chainage across the ravine accurately. Unfortunately the disturbance of the rows has made this difficult but it seems likely that the error was at most less than a foot (see below, Fig. 7.11).

It must again be emphasized that disturbance in nearly all the rows has been very great. Large numbers of stones have been re-erected; many of them carry the re-erection mark. The destruction is still going on; two stones which were upright in 1972 we found pushed over in 1973. It is therefore hardly surprising that we had difficulty in fitting lines to the stones and analyzing the spacing. One can picture the stones lying down at all sorts of angles before the re-erectors came along and tried to put them up in rows without any guidance as to where the original lines had been. The various slight bends in the lines probably deceived them in several places when they tried to straighten the rows.

The statistical analysis which was undertaken assumes that there are enough of the stones in their original positions to allow some sort of result to be obtained. After many months of work a definite pattern did in fact appear; a pattern which cannot have been apparent to the re-erectors and so can owe nothing to them. For the first six sections there can be little doubt about the suggested geometry. It is inconceivable that the three pairs of triangles shown in Fig. 7.1 can have appeared by accident, and further proof of their reality appears in the statistical analysis of the stone spacing to be given shortly. There is evidence that rows III and V continued across the ravine to reappear among the stones in section 7 which otherwise are in rows parallel to the rows in sections 2 and 3, some 2000 ft away. To demonstrate this, row I from section 3 has been produced by calculation and drawn on Figs 7.3 and 7.4.

### 7.4. Theory of the statistical analysis

Figure 7.6 shows three stones forming part of a long row. The distances of these, $y_1$, $y_2$, and $y_3$ have been measured from an arbitrary zero. Assume that the quantum to which the stones were originally set out was $2\delta$ and imagine marks (nodes) on the ground equally spaced at $2\delta$. It need not be assumed that there was a stone at every node; certainly where big stones were used there might be several quanta between each pair. We do not know how the first node ($A$) stands in relation to the zero; in fact we have to find the position of the nodes (given by $b$) which makes the average residual equal to zero. We have

$$y = b + 2m\delta + \epsilon, \tag{7.1}$$

where $m$ is an integer, $b$ is to be found, and $\epsilon$ is the residual.

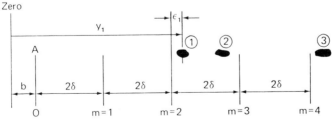

FIG. 7.6.

If the stones had not been much disturbed so that the residuals could be small it would be easy to assume a value for $b$, calculate the residuals, take the mean and adjust $b$ to make this zero. But even when the best value has been found for $b$ some of the residuals may still be large, and frequently during the work a small change in $b$ will make a residual numerically greater than $\delta$ so that the stone has to be allotted to the next node. For example, if $b$ in the figure is tentatively increased, stone 2 will become nearer to node 2 (that is $m = 2$) than to node 3 and the value of $m$ will have to be decreased by unity. When we have found the value of $b$ which makes the sum of the residuals zero, the sum of the squares $\epsilon^2$ will be a minimum, and it avoids confusion if this property is used. In fact, the method adopted on all the Kermario rows was to try five or six values of $b$ and for each to find $\Sigma\epsilon^2$. These were plotted to find the value of $b$ giving a minimum. At every change of $b$, values of $\epsilon$ which became greater than $\delta$ had to be subtracted numerically from $2\delta$. Instead of plotting $\Sigma\epsilon^2$ it is more instructive to plot $s^2/\delta^2$ where $s^2$, which Broadbent calls the 'lumped variance', is $(1/n)\Sigma\epsilon^2$, $n$ being the number of stones. If $n$ is large and the stones are really randomly placed, $s^2/\delta^2$ will remain close to one-third as $b$ is changed. If, on the other hand, the stones are not random but still show some trace of a quantum of $2\delta$ then, when $s^2/\delta^2$ is plotted on $b$, there will appear a kind of sinusoidal curve with roughly as much above one-third as below it. The more stones there are, the smoother and more regular will be the curve. The further the maximum and minimum values of $s^2/\delta^2$ are above and below one-third, the more confident we can be that we are dealing with stones set out with the assumed quantum.

Broadbent's relation between the probability level and $s^2/\delta^2$ and $n$ will be found in Thom 1967, Fig. 2.1. We shall use this figure to determine a probability level corresponding to the *minimum* value of $s^2/\delta^2$. This may not be theoretically correct, but at least it gives a good criterion whereby results can be compared.

The stones in most parts of the alignments have been so much displaced that it is necessary to have a large number in a row if a reliable value of $b_m$ (the value of $b$ making $s^2/\delta^2$ a minimum) is to be obtained. But it is not safe to use a very long row because then any systematic error produced by a slight difference between the quantum actually used by the erectors and that assumed by us might begin to have an effect large enough to upset the whole process. For this reason all preliminary work has been done with lengths of under an arbitrarily chosen length of 300 MY.

If we could find a straight line crossing the rows and passing through a node on each, it would make the analysis much easier because all the rows in a section could then be taken together. In the Le Ménec alignments such a line was found at an angle of 1 in 2 to the normal. But in the Kermario alignments the nodes for all seven rows in sections 1, 2, and 3 seem to lie on the normal: in other words, the nodes appear opposite one another.

An examination of the old cadastral maps shows how several of the rows were used last century as field boundaries and in some of these rows the spaces have evidently been filled by stones from the neighbouring rows. If we have identified the original nodes correctly, it might be possible to identify the intrusive stones and so to improve the analysis, but this has not yet been attempted and all the stones near the line being analyzed have been retained.

To the east of the ravine the stones have suffered less but a solution here was delayed for several months because it was not realized (a) that here there were remains of two systems, and (b) that the rows belonging to the second system probably had a quantum of 2 MY, but that running through the area two rows, namely III and V from the west system, retained the $2\frac{1}{2}$ MY quantum.

We found that if the setting out is perfect with a quantum of $2\frac{1}{2}$ MY then on a long row $s^2/\delta^2$ for the quantum of 2 MY will be 0·3125. The converse shows 0·320. Since these are both less than one-third this shows that if we attempt to analyze a very long row with the wrong quantum significance will appear.

It seems that in some rows in Kermario, when both quanta are tested, we get values of $s^2/\delta^2$ not greatly different from those just quoted. But row G, section 7 shows an unexplained result, as can be seen in Fig. 7.7. Here the $2\frac{1}{2}$-MY quantum shows $s^2/\delta^2 = 0·20$, and yet the 2 MY quantum has $s^2/\delta^2$ as low as 0·27. Other considerations, as we shall see, indicate that here we should expect a quantum of 2 MY.

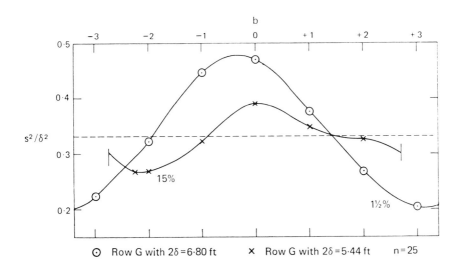

FIG. 7.7. Comparison of two quanta for row G.

## 7.5. Details of the analysis

Marks were established accurately by using the basic traverse on the 1:500 survey in each section on row I, each mark being an integral number of Megalithic rods apart measured *along* this row. (Here the Megalithic rod was taken as 6·80 ft.) Fiducial lines were drawn through each of these marks at right-angles to the portion of row I *in the section*. The distance, $y$, of the apparent centre of each stone considered to belong to the row was scaled from the fiducial line with the easterly direction taken as positive. A few stones more than 4 or 5 ft from the assumed line were neglected as being unreliable. Assuming a quantum of $2\delta = 6·80$ ft we formed for each row in every section the residuals $\epsilon = y - 6·8m - b$ (see (7.1)) for six or seven values of $b$, taking care that a value of $m$ was used on every stone which would keep $\epsilon$ numerically less than $\delta$, that is less than 3·40. These residuals were then squared and summed for each row, and so the values of $s^2/\delta^2$ were found. From these we could find the probability levels.

Ultimately we should like answers to the following questions:

(1) Was the $2\frac{1}{2}$-MY quantum really used?
(2) How were the initial nodes placed?
(3) Were the nodes carried through from end to end or was a new system started at each break in direction?
(4) Did the measurements follow round the arcs at the west end?

Owing to the disturbances and/or the small number of stones in some rows, these questions could not be considered independently, but a start had to be made somewhere.

The method used for the detailed analysis of the various sections will be found in Thom and Thom 1974 and here we propose to give only a few examples and the results. At Kermario, as in Le Ménec, we do not believe it is possible to deduce from first principles a value for the quantum used. The disturbances have been too great for this but we can apply Broadbent's first method and find out what probability level results from trying various quanta. In spite of criticisms which have been made of this method, it seems perfectly sound provided we use quanta which have been demonstrated to exist elsewhere. This restricts us to multiples of 1 MY or of $2\frac{1}{2}$ MY.

For the first five sections the $2\frac{1}{2}$-MY quantum proved to be better than 2 MY. Section 3 in fact showed a probability level of $1-1\frac{1}{2}$ per cent for the $2\frac{1}{2}$-MY quantum, but sections 1 and 2 were poorer.

## 7.6. Analysis of the sections

*Sections 1, 2, and 3.* In sections 1, 2, and 3 we were also able to show that originally the nodes lay on a normal line and not, as at Le Ménec, on a line at 2 in 1.

In section 1 the rows are curved to a radius of about 1000 MR but it does not seem possible to determine if the arcs are concentric or if each has exactly this radius; nor is it possible to be certain of the exact position of the tangent points (Fig. 7.2). There is little doubt about the spacing; this seems to be 12 MY and remains at this value in sections 2 and 3, the rows, as elsewhere at Kermario, being parallel.

*Section 4.* This section follows the first bend or knee. We have seen that the nodes in each row approached the bend from section 3 uniformly spaced and opposite one another. Were they carried on round the bend without a break or was a new start made so that the nodes were again opposite one another? In Fig. 7.8 we show a comparison of the two assumptions. The values of $s^2/\delta^2$ are plotted assuming that the nodes continue round the bend and show a probability level of 4 per cent whereas the assertion that they are on normal lines shows 30 per cent. An examination of the inset (a) in Fig. 7.1 shows that the side of the lower triangle (21 MY) is 1 MY shorter than that of the upper (22 MY) and this means that the nodes in row $(r+1)$ should be 1 MY ahead of those in row $r$ and this is what we find they are.

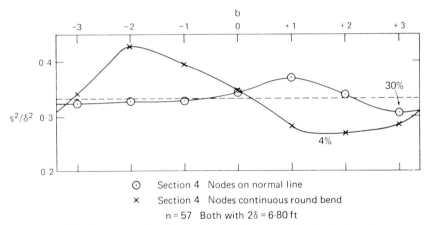

FIG. 7.8. Analysis to find the position of the nodes after the first bend.

*Sections 5 and 6.* The inset (b) in Fig. 7.1 shows that crossing from section 4 to section 5 causes the row $r$ to 'catch up' on row $(r+1)$ by $28\frac{1}{2}$ less 28, that is $\frac{1}{2}$ MY, and inset (c) shows that crossing to section 6 produces another $\frac{1}{2}$ MY. Thus in section 6 we expect that the nodes will be again opposite one another and furthermore the rows will be parallel or nearly parallel to those in section 3. This is what we find, but section 6 is difficult and shows a probability level of 15 per cent, whereas sections 4 and 5 show $4\frac{1}{2}$ and $2\frac{1}{2}$ per cent. The reason may be that one or two intrusive lines here come back from section 7 where, as we shall see, two systems are superimposed.

*Section 7.* Weeks of work were spent on analyzing this section. It would not respond to bringing the nodes through from section 6 and in fact we found that only rows III and V showed a reasonable probability level (2 per cent together) when analyzed in this way. The values of $s^2/\delta^2$ are shown in Fig. 7.9 for these two rows. There are perhaps remnants of other lines which have come through from section 6, but it seems that, excluding rows III and V, the most satisfactory explanation is to use a quantum of 2 MY.

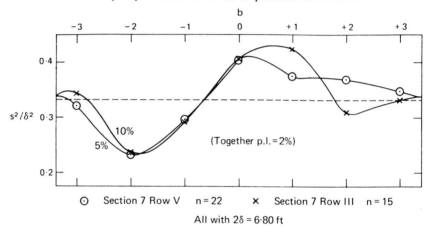

FIG. 7.9. Analysis of section 7, rows III and V.

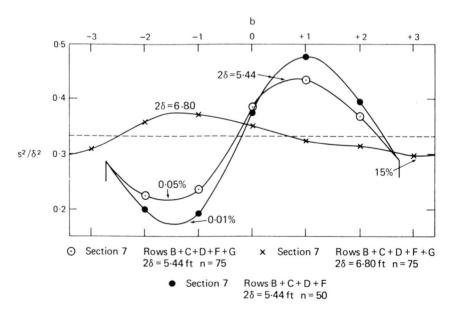

FIG. 7.10. Analysis showing superiority of a quantum of 2 MY in section 7.

Thus taking rows $B+C+D+F+G$, Fig. 7.10, with a $2\frac{1}{2}$ MY quantum gives a probability level of 15 per cent, whereas with a 2 MY quantum we obtain a level of 0·05 per cent and if we exclude row G we find 0·01 per cent. This is by far and away the lowest value given by any section. The reason is certainly because this end of the alignments has suffered very little *recent* disturbance.

All the small-scale surveys reproduced here have been very carefully reduced from our large-scale plan and in Figs 7.3 and 7.4 we show row I brought through from section 3 at an azimuth of 56° 46′. It will be found that rows A, B, C, D, F, and G are at the same azimuth, whereas rows III and V stand out as belonging to section 6.

Thus there is evidence of the most convincing kind that there are two systems of lines in this section. Perhaps they served two purposes and were both in use at the same time but it seems possible that a change of plan was in progress, one system being replaced by another. The argument against this last suggestion is the manner in which the two systems are interlaced. There was no complete removal of one before the other was built. One must also bear in mind that both systems are linked to the rows further west. Rows III and V come from section 6 and the others are accurately parallel to the rows in section 3.

## 7.7. Position of nodes

The statistical analysis gave us the position of the nodes in each section. These positions were referred to points set out along row I uniformly spaced at 1 MR where we took 1 rod to be 6·800 ft. It has been found that starting at section 1 the nodal positions advanced progressively as we moved east thus indicating that the length of the rod used by the builders was slightly greater than 6·800 ft.

This is seen in Fig. 7.11, which shows the amount of the nodal advance at each section. Rectangles have been used instead of points to remind us that there is uncertainty in the values given. Sections 3, 4, 5, and rows III and V of section 7 have low probability levels of the stones being random and these have been used to control the straight line drawn through the rectangles in Fig. 7.11. It will be seen that the nodal positions in section 7 are as shown, less than 1 ft above the line; that is they are further to the east than might be expected. This agreement is interesting because the Ravin de Kerloquet comes between sections 6 and 7. The ravine is now partly filled by an artificial pond but it has steep sides 5–10 m high, making it difficult to measure accurately across the hollow. It is not clear how the erectors crossed this obstacle using rods. Had they used a measured rope without allowing for its sag and stretch, the nodes in section 7 might have been anywhere (depending on the properties of the rope and how it was used) whereas as we have seen they seem to be less than 1 ft to the east. Methods of allowing for sag and stretch

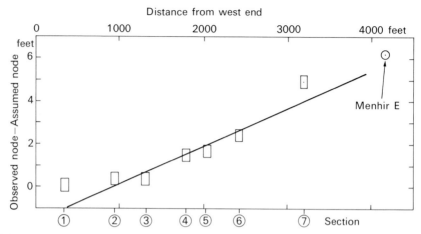

FIG. 7.11. The nodal positions along the Kermario alignments compared with nodes equally spaced at 6·800 ft.

are well understood today but would not have been readily available to these people and it seems most likely that they crossed the ravine using rods, plumbing down or up at the ends, and so an overall error of a foot can perhaps be considered reasonable.

If we accept the straight line drawn in Fig. 7.11 an increase in the length of the Megalithic yard of about 0·17 per cent is indicated, making it about 2·724 ft and the rod 6·810 ft.

### 7.8. The rows on the south side

It seems, from what has gone before, that the main body of the alignments consists of seven rows of stones, but external to these on the south side there are other rows which at first sight do not fit into the scheme. Most of them have, however, some connection with the main seven rows. This will be seen in Figs 7.1 and 7.2 where (for example) row VII in section 6, when produced westwards, picks up a line of a dozen stones at the extreme west. Also at the west there is a row exactly parallel to the rows in section 4. In addition, there will be found in Fig. 7.1 the remains of two rows 16 MY apart parallel to section 5. Perhaps we should not be disappointed that the long row immediately south of section 4 (see Fig. 7.3) seems to have no relation to anything. It lies very close to the edge of the wide road which has been built in recent years, and so these stones may have been moved. The stones south of section 6 seem to form part of some other system.

We do not know the position or direction of the closing line at the west end. In Fig. 7.2 this has been drawn at right-angles to sections 2 and 3 and so is parallel to lines joining the nodes on these sections. But in Fig. 7.1 the closing line is assumed to be a radius from the centre of the arcs. It may be noticed that there is an otherwise unexplained row of stones which will be found to be exactly at right-angles to this radius and so would be tangential to row VIII had this ever been set out.

Professor Atkinson has pointed out that menhir $F$ (section 7 and Fig. 7.4) is probably much older than the alignments.

In Le Ménec it is clear that the setting out began at the west end because at this end the nodes lay on straight lines. The geometry forced the nodes out of step so that at the east end they zigzagged across the rows, exactly as the theory dictates. In Kermario, however, we cannot use this criterion to decide where erection started, because the rows are parallel and in each section are equally spaced, with the result that the nodes, though out of step in sections 4 and 5, start and end by being opposite one another. The size of the stones at the west end does however indicate that the start was probably there.

The peculiar mix-up of rows in section 7 leaves us with the question: were these two systems part of some scheme which used both sets of rows or, when the civilization collapsed *circa* 1500 B.C., were the builders in process of replacing one system by another?

## 7.9. Possible use of the alignments

It is most unlikely that seven rows over 3000 ft long were set out merely to demonstrate the properties of three pairs of triangles but we cannot give any convincing explanation of any use for the Kermario alignments. In Thom and Thom 1974 we show how the distance of the circular arcs in sections 1 and 2 from the straights in sections 2 and 3, being approximately quadratic in form, could have been used to find the extrapolation distance for the backsights at Kerran, Kervilor, St. Pierre, and Quiberon. But there are obvious objections to this use which, in any case, would explain less than half the site.

Like Le Ménec, the stones at the west end are much larger than the average size. It may be that at an earlier date these formed a simple extrapolating sector like that at St. Pierre, Quiberon, and afterwards were rearranged to form part of the seven arcs that we now find. This may explain the large size, which certainly must have been an embarrassment if these arcs were really meant to represent the quadratic function necessary for even simple extrapolation.

One cannot help being impressed by the great accuracy with which the lines were laid out. After passing through three bends the azimuth of the rows is still within a few arc minutes of the theoretical direction deduced from the geometry of the six triangles involved. The ground is by no means level, and, for example, the high ground in sections 3 and 4 near the Moulin de Kermaux cuts off any attempt to sight right through; and yet the rows in section 7 are placed accurately parallel to those in section 3.

# 8

## KERLESCAN AND PETIT MÉNEC

**8.1.** IT is usual to think of the site at Kerlescan and that at Petit Ménec as being entirely separate, with the farm and the road between them. An examination of Fig. 8.1 shows, however, that they were probably constructed to form one design. Our traverse connecting the two surveys went a long way round, but we have no reason to doubt that Fig. 8.1 shows them in their correct relative positions.

**8.2.** There are the remains of two cromlechs at Kerlescan. At the west end lies the barrel-shaped cromlech of which we give a larger plan in Fig. 8.2. On the plan we have superimposed the geometrical outline to which it was undoubtedly set out. It will be seen how accurately the menhirs stand on this outline. Today there are no stones on the north arc but the small-scale survey made by Hülle shows that he saw some trace of this arc in 1947.

The geometrical outline (Figs 8.2 and 8.3) assumes that the radius of each of the three arcs was 60 MR and that $ER = 19$ MR, $RF = 20$ MR, and $AR = RB = 22$ MR. This seems to be a very simple construction but when we look into it we find that like many of Megalithic man's designs it embodies several peculiar properties. To set it out we must make $RP = 38$ and $RQ = 41$, where $P$ and $Q$ are the centres for the arcs (Fig. 8.3). Then $PQ = (38^2 + 41^2)^{\frac{1}{2}} = 55 \cdot 90$. Bisect $PQ$ at $T$ so that $TQ = 27 \cdot 95$ or practically 28, and since $SQ = SP = $ the radii $= 60$ MR, then $ST = (SQ^2 - TQ^2)^{\frac{1}{2}} = 53 \cdot 09$. It is now easy to calculate the total perimeter and this is found to be 150·1 MR. A little further trigonometrical calculation shows that the diagonals are 52·44 MY, or practically 21 MR. It thus appears that all the dimensions including the diagonals and the perimeter are practically integral in Megalithic rods.

**8.3.** The remains of what has been a very large cromlech lie in the woods to the north of the Kerlescan alignments. Most of the stones are fairly large but some are difficult to find because of the dense undergrowth. Surveying was difficult, but we believe that we have succeeded in making a plan which is accurate to a few inches. A much reduced copy is shown in Fig. 8.4. In order to connect this up with the Kerlescan alignments the northern row of these is shown on the figure.

Le Rouzic mentions 7 upright and 36 fallen menhirs, but our count shows

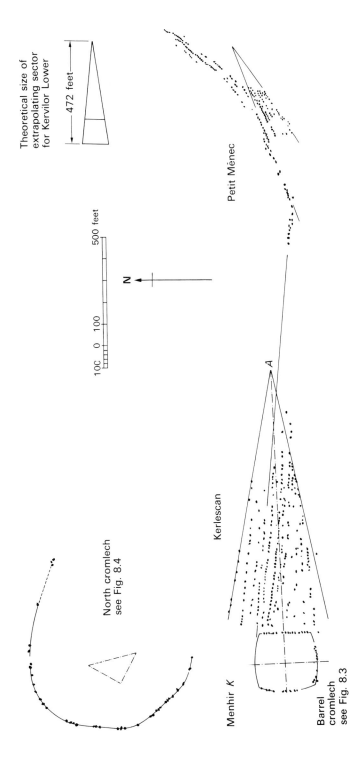

Theoretical size of
extrapolating sector
for Kervilor Lower

472 feet

100 0 100
500 feet

N

Petit Ménec

Kerlescan

A

North cromlech
see Fig. 8.4

Menhir *K*

Barrel
cromlech
see Fig. 8.3

Fig. 8.1. Kerlescan and Petit Ménec.

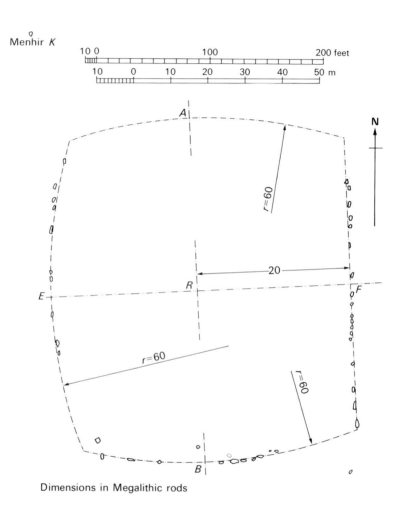

Dimensions in Megalithic rods

FIG. 8.2. The barrel-shaped cromlech, Kerlescan.

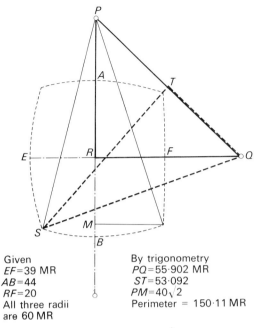

Given
EF=39 MR
AB=44
RF=20
All three radii
are 60 MR

By trigonometry
PQ=55·902 MR
ST=53·092
PM=40√2
Perimeter = 150·11 MR

FIG. 8.3. The geometry of the barrel-shaped cromlech, Kerlescan.

that in or near the ring there are 36 upright and 6 fallen. If the upright menhirs have been re-erected then Fig. 8.4 shows that the work was done with accuracy.

This construction is based on a triangle with sides 23, 25, and 34 MR. Since $34^2 = 1156$ and $25^2 + 23^2 = 1154$, the triangle is demonstrated to be very nearly right-angled. Centred on the vertices of this triangle there have been described three arcs of radii 40, 30, and 38 MR. These arcs are joined by straight lines as shown. This construction was made with the greatest care on tracing paper, and slid about on the large-scale survey until the best fit was found. This demonstration was most impressive, showing as it did that the line passes through the majority of the stones and misses the others by only a narrow margin. We have attempted to continue the outline in the north to $B$ by an arc of radius 111 MR and then on by a straight line to $D$, but this part of the construction is uncertain.

It is to be hoped that our partial reconstruction will allow future workers to discover more evidence regarding the missing part of the ring, but it is doubtful if the complete geometry can ever be established.

The accuracy with which this cromlech has been set out is comparable to that found at Avebury. Kerlescan is, however, smaller and has no ditch and bank. It was nevertheless a huge undertaking and we are left with the question

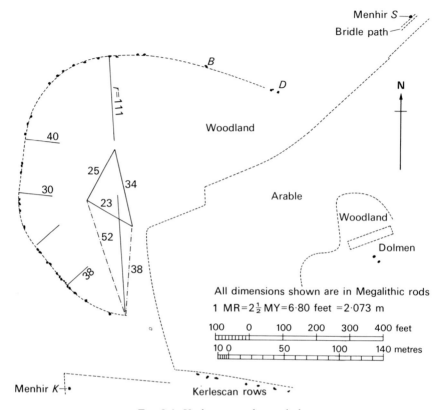

FIG. 8.4. Kerlescan north cromlech.

why was it ever built. That the Megalithic builders used the 23, 25, 34 triangle instead of the simple, 3, 4, 5 as at Avebury shows that there must have been some other stringent conditions to be met. What were they?

**8.4.** The two cromlechs, the alignments, and Petit Ménec are shown in Fig. 8.1. There is perhaps some slight evidence that there is an apex at *A* on the axis of the barrel cromlech and it seems that row IV is tangent to the barrel cromlech and is identical with the west row at Petit Ménec.

The stones in the alignments are not randomly placed. There is some indication of a quantum of 6·8 ft and the rows do fall into groups. Further than that we are not at present prepared to go. This is a much more complicated site than Le Ménec or Kermario, and it is to be hoped that a detailed examination of the whole area will bring to light some clues to the riddle of its overall geometry.

## 8.5. The extrapolating sector

We have shown (Thom 1971) that the necessary width of an extrapolating sector is

$$G_0 = KD \, \partial Az/\partial \delta,$$

where $Az$ = azimuth, $\delta$ = declination, and the radius is $4G_0$. If $D$, the distance to the foresight, is in kilometres and $G_0$ is in Megalithic yards, then $K = 4.79$ and $2.91$ at the major and minor standstills respectively.

The radius vector of the moon in its orbit varies between $r_0(1-e)$ and $r_0(1+e)$, where $e$ = eccentricity of the orbit = $0.0549$. The speed of the moon in its orbit is controlled by the length of the radius vector and this affects $G$ in such a manner that $G = G_0(1\pm e)^4$. Since $(1+e)^4 = 1.238$ and $(1-e)^4 = 0.798$ it follows that on any given night $K$, instead of being exactly $4.79$ as above, may have any value from $K = 4.79 \times 1.238 = 5.93$, to $K = 4.79 \times 0.798 = 3.82$.

It follows that for accuracy it would have been necessary to measure $G$ at each standstill (see Thom 1971, Fig. 9.11). A sector would then need to provide for the greatest value of $G$ encountered.

The line for the moon rising behind the Grand Menhir Brisé at the minor standstill passes from Le Moustoir over Petit Ménec to Kervilor. For Kervilor Lower $D = 7.10$ km, and the maximum value of $G$ is $43.5$ MY = $118$ ft, giving $4G = 472$ ft. For Upper Kervilor these values need to be increased slightly and for Le Moustoir, which is much further away, they need to be increased still more.

In the inset in Fig. 8.1 we show the size of the theoretical sector for Kervilor Lower. It will be seen that this is not greatly different from the sector at Petit Ménec.

We published a detailed survey of this sector in Thom and Thom 1971, and we were criticized for claiming that this could be an extrapolating sector because the lines did not radiate exactly from a common centre. In this connection it should be pointed out that we do not know how these sectors were built to give the extrapolation values. It is easy for us today to show that there should be a true sector of radiating lines, but the original designers may have found them in the first place by some empirical method; and even if they realized that a sector was the correct shape, how did they find the radius? What we find may be simply the remains of the early experiments.

# 9

# THE TWO MEGALITHIC OBSERVATORIES IN CARNAC

**9.1.** THE largest artificially cut stone in Europe is that commonly called Le Grand Menhir Brisé or sometimes Er Grah. The name Er Grah refers to the tumulus which started at Le Grand Menhir and ran through what is now the car park.

The total length of the menhir was about 70 ft (21 m) and from its cubic content it is estimated to weigh over 300 tons. It is now broken into four pieces. A plan of these as they lie today is shown in Fig. 9.1. It will be seen in the photographs of the ends of the two bottom sections (Fig. 9.2) how perfectly these parts fitted together although the stone probably fell about 700 years ago. We agree with Atkinson that the only explanation (short of Cyclopean intervention) for the present position of the sections is that the lower break, or at least the separation, occurred while the stone was still upright and that a possible explanation of its present position is that it was shaken down by an earthquake.

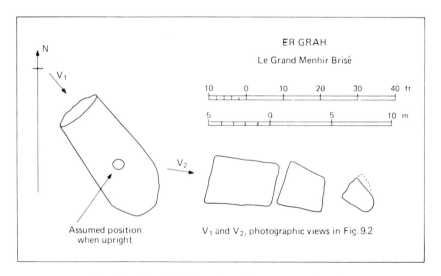

FIG. 9.1. Plan of Le Grand Menhir Brisé as it lies today.

FIG. 9.2. Le Grand Menhir Brisé. *Top*, from the north-west ($V_1$ in Fig. 9.1), the end of the base section. *Bottom*, from the west ($V_2$ in Fig. 9.1), inverted mirror-image of the end of the next section.

In Britain we generally find that the tallest stones are lunar backsights, but there seems no need to use a stone of this size as a backsight. If on the other hand it was a lunar foresight the reason for its position and height becomes clear, especially if it was intended as a universal foresight to be used from several directions (Fig. 9.3). There are eight main values to be considered. These correspond to the rising and setting of the moon at the standstills when the declination is $\pm(\epsilon \pm i)$ (Chapter 2). Since the stone now lies flat there is no possibility of seeing it today directly except from the south-west. Accordingly it was necessary to construct from contours on the French maps a profile of the ground along each line. Four of these are shown in Figs. 9.4 and 9.5 in which the line of zero height is shown curved to the mean curvature of the earth's surface decreased by the curvature of the refracted ray. This arrangement allows a line of sight to be represented by a straight line. We can thus assess the possibility that Le Grand Menhir Brisé was, in its upright position, visible from any point under consideration. It also makes it easy to see if any suggested backsight position is so high that Er Grah would appear below the horizon *behind*. There is a water tower not far from Er Grah and this is visible from all round. Accordingly the next step was to

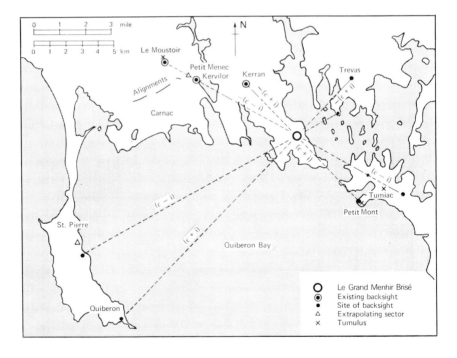

FIG. 9.3. Le Grand Menhir Brisé as a universal lunar foresight.

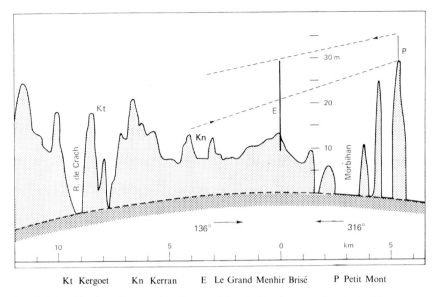

Kt Kergoet     Kn Kerran     E  Le Grand Menhir Brisé     P  Petit Mont

FIG. 9.4.  Profile along line at azimuth = 136° for declination = $\pm(\epsilon + i)$, Earth's curvature being decreased by curvature of refracted ray.

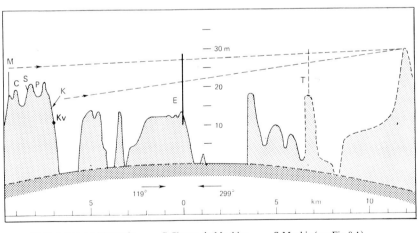

M Tumulus, Le Moustoir     C Champ de Menhirs     S Menhir (see Fig. 8·4)
P Petit Ménec     K Kervilor     E Le Grand Menhir Brisé
T Tumulus, Tumiac (off line)     Kv  Kervilor lower

FIG. 9.5.  Profile along line at azimuth + 119° for declination = $\pm(\epsilon - i)$, Earth's curvature being decreased by curvature of refracted ray.

determine the exact coordinates of the tower relative to Er Grah. In the absence of any definite information as to where the stone originally stood we have measured to the point marked by a ring in Fig. 9.1. We ran a traverse along the road so that the water tower could be sighted from several points sufficiently far apart and so found that the centre of the tower lies 635 m distant at an azimuth of 335° 09′. With this information it is possible to obtain closely the azimuth of Er Grah from distant positions by first observing that of the tower. The top edge of the tower is about 27 m above the ground under Er Grah.

**9.2.** In order to examine the observatory which we believe to be centred on the large Menhir $M$ near Le Manio we found it necessary to make extensive surveys in the district. These are shown on Fig. 9.6. One of the lines to Er Grah runs through this survey as will be seen on the right of the figure.

We had already made accurate surveys of the alignments at Le Ménec, Kermario, Kerlescan, and Petit Ménec. We then proceeded to run a number of long traverses to connect up the various menhirs in the area. The open traverses have mostly been checked by independent tacheometric measurements and the greatest error in the long, closed traverses was about 3 ft. Over 30 astronomical determinations of azimuth were made at various points along the traverses. Some of the sections were very difficult, for example, the part $MU$ ran through almost impenetrable woodland and after an unfortunate experience with an irate peasant (whereby we practically lost a part of our traverse) we tried to keep to the roads. It will be realized that in an area of this size it was necessary to take into account the convergence of the meridians. Since we wished to use the astronomically determined azimuths we used a conical projection, otherwise a survey of this size would have been distorted and the traverses would not have closed. The origin is near Le Ménec, approximately at latitude 47° 35′·5. Short traverses were run at various points to examine the places where it appeared that the sight line between the backsight and the foresight might not clear the ground. These parts of the rays have been shown by doubling the line. For example, the ray from $R_1$, the stone on top of the Le Moustoir tumulus, grazes the ground at three points: (1) at Champ de Menhirs, (2) just after stone $S$, and (3) between Petit Ménec and Kervilor. We think it clears the ground at all three but in any case this stone is perhaps not in its original position and was probably not intended as a backsight. The ray from the stone near the west end of Le Moustoir Tumulus ($R_2$) seems to clear all along. From station 15 on our traverse above Kervilor we were able to see the water tower near Le Grand Menhir. We determined the azimuth carefully and so we were able to obtain the azimuth of Le Grand Menhir with sufficient accuracy from all points on these lines. M. Eric Bonnet drew our attention to a site which was being removed to make way for a house at Kv (Fig. 9.6) below Kervilor. A plan of the site is

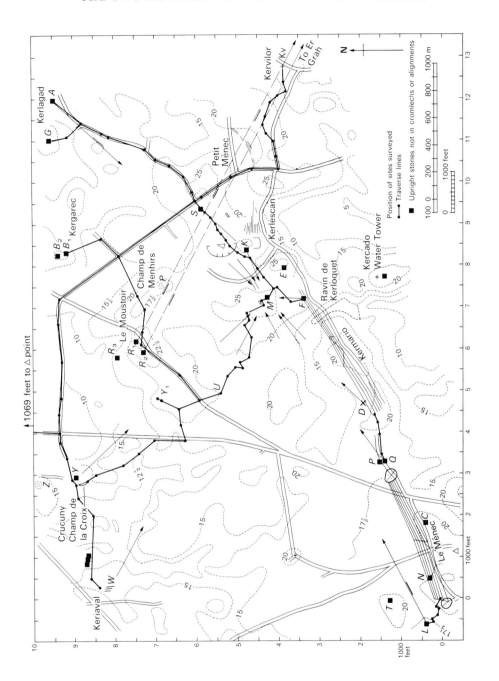

FIG. 9.6. Sites near the Carnac alignments.

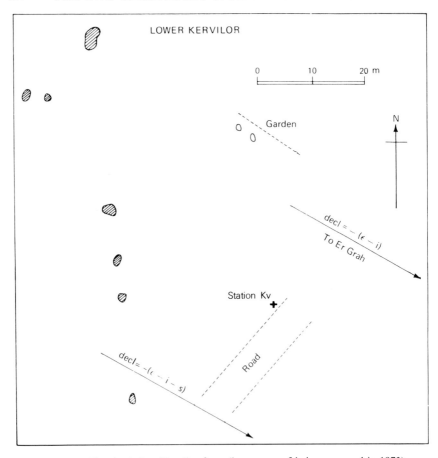

Fig. 9.7. The site below Kervilor farm (in process of being removed in 1973).

given in Fig. 9.7. From here the top of Er Grah would have been visible (see Fig. 9.5). There is a small unimpressive stone *C* in the field above Kervilor just through the gate near the dolmen and a fallen stone in the lane that runs behind the farm.

### 9.3. Backsights for Le Grand Menhir Brisé

We shall now consider each of the possible lines on which the menhir could have been used as a foresight.

*The line for* $-(\epsilon + i)$. Between the road junction at Le Chat Noir and Kerran there is a dolmen. Some 80 ft west-south-west from the dolmen there is a small menhir leaning over at about 45°. By careful solar observations, the azimuth of the water tower from this stone was found to be 132° 52'·4. The distance to the water tower was taken from the map, and so by calculation we found that the azimuth of Er Grah is 116° 13'·3. On the map this line beyond the menhir seems to pass just to the left of the tumulus on Petit Mont (Fig. 9.4) where the ground level is perhaps 31 m. Taking eye level as 16·5 m, we estimate the altitude to be 3'. Applying mean refraction and parallax 57', we find the declination to be −28° 46'. It has been shown that $i$, the inclination of the lunar orbit, had the same mean value in Megalithic times as today, namely 5° 08'·7; and so, if we assume that the upper limb was being observed, we find that the corresponding value of the obliquity of the ecliptic is about 23° 53'.

Before we try to read too much into this result the azimuth ought to be checked by direct measurement to a pole erected at Er Grah, and by some method the horizon altitude should be measured. It is possible that the small menhir which we used may be the last of a ring of stones round the dolmen but that does not seem likely.

The declination from the Kerran dolmen is 8' or 9' lower than that from the stone. As the dolmen may be much older than Le Grand Menhir, the fact that this is close to the value of the perturbation can only be accidental, unless indeed this site was one of the controlling points fixing the position of Er Grah. The fact remains that we have, at Kerran, whether by accident or design, backsights which show very closely declinations of $-(\epsilon+i)$ and $-(\epsilon+i+\Delta)$.

*The line for* $-(\epsilon-i)$. There are several places on this line which are possible and indeed are marked by stones. Although the stone on the top of the tumulus at Le Moustoir is in the correct position, this is probably by chance; and in any case the line from here to the menhir passes through the Champ de Menhirs and the backsight may have been there. The ground *at* the tumulus at Le Moustoir seemed at first to be too low but on examination it becomes apparent that from the menhir $R_2$ near the south-west end of the tumulus the sight line is probably clear over the lower ground to the right of Champ de Menhirs.

The site Champ de Menhirs is situated on a low flat-topped hill. The stones look like boulders, but while some are half buried others are undoubtedly upright. We made a survey (Fig. 9.8) of all that shows and connected it up with our main traverse. Among the stones there is a peculiar trapezium consisting of low slabs set on edge and it appears that from here the declination of Le Grand Menhir Brisé, or rather of the horizon behind it, is near $-(\epsilon-i)$. After passing stone $S$ the line runs very close to the ground, so close that if the observer moved much to his left Er Grah would probably not be visible.

The site just below Kervilor was being bulldozed to make way for a house when we made a survey of what remained at Easter 1973 (Fig. 9.7). We

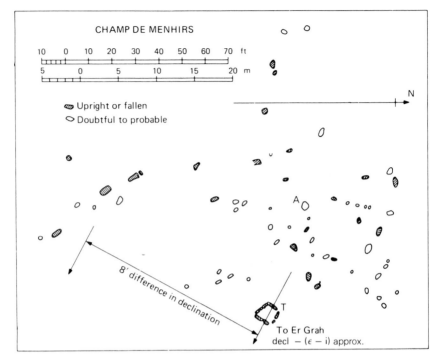

FIG. 9.8. Champ de Menhirs, near Le Moustoir. Some of the stones shown may be outcrops but those shown hatched are considered to be either upright or fallen menhirs. The site is on a low flat-topped hill; the highest point is near A.

connected this survey to station 15 by a tacheometric traverse. Although this site is low, the top half of Le Grand Menhir would have been visible (see Fig. 9.5), and as it is in the correct position the stones are probably the remains of a backsight for this menhir. They are now piled in a meaningless heap.

*The line for moon rising with declination*$+(\epsilon-i)$. The observing site for this declination must have been between Rohu and the sea, about a kilometre south of St. Pierre. It could not have been much above the 10-m contour or Er Grah would have appeared below the distant hills. The area is now occupied by gardens, houses, etc., and no traces of stones have been found on the plateau, but this is being eroded by the sea. There are hundreds of stones scattered on the beach, but one of these looks like a large menhir. It may have slipped out from the high ground when this was eroded. In St. Pierre, however, there is a part of a sector (Fig. 9.9) of which there is enough left to fix the radius as being at least 700 ft, and this is very close to the theoretical value required for extrapolation at this site, namely $4G = 720$ ft.

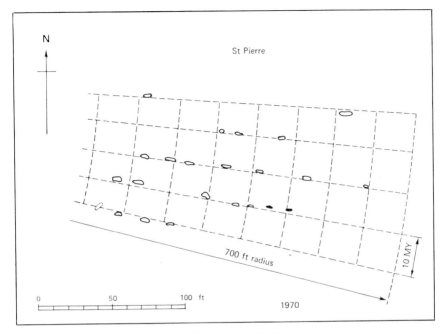

FIG. 9.9. The sector at St. Pierre.

*The line for* $+(\epsilon+i)$. The observing site here was at the end of the main Quiberon peninsula. Near it is the impressive menhir called Goulvarh, and this is orientated in the required direction: north-east/south-west. Off the north end of Belle Isle there is a reef, now submerged, but it would have been an island in Megalithic times. As seen from Goulvarh the sun at the winter solstice set over the reef and there may have been a clearly defined projection to use as a foresight; it thus seems likely that Goulvarh was a solstitial backsight. With the theodolite placed at Goulvarh, a number of accurate azimuth sets was taken to the sun and Venus. A lamp placed on the higher part of Er Grah (15 km distant) then enabled the azimuth of the line joining the stones to be found. This is 46° 02′; with a hill horizon altitude of 2′ this gives the declination of 28° 20′, which is too low for $+(\epsilon+i)$. There is another menhir in a garden quite near but M. Jean-Luc Quinio assures us that this stone has been put there recently.

*The four lines for the setting moon.* No definite stone backsights have so far been found for the four positions from which the moon was observed to *set* with declination $\pm(\epsilon\pm i)$ but the locations of the sites are fairly definite.

   On the hilltop just to the west of Trevas there is a stretch of high ground of sufficient width to accommodate all the necessary cases of $-(\epsilon+i\pm s\pm\Delta)$.

This was checked by actual measurements to the water tower beside Er Grah. There are irregularities on the ground which do not seem natural, and these may indicate that this ideal site, with Er Grah showing against the distant Belle Isle, had in fact been used. The backsight for $-(\epsilon-i)$ may have been at Pointe de Locmiquel in what is now a cultivated field. The line for $(\epsilon-i)$ passes over the centre of Arzon and just to the north of the huge tumulus at Tumiac. The backsights could have been either at Arzon or past the tumulus. On the assumption that the observing site for $(\epsilon+i)$ was on the south side of the Gulf of Morbihan, the only position providing the necessary side move-ment is on the high ground in front of the tumulus on Petit Mont. The gorse cover is so deep and thick that the ground could not be examined in detail and in any case the whole site was occupied by the Germans as a gun emplace-ment during the Second World War.

It has now been shown that there is at least one site on each of the eight lines which has the necessary room for side movement. The results obtained at those sites where there are menhirs or stones are summarized in Table 9.1.

## 9.4. Finding the site for Le Grand Menhir

We must now try to think of how a position was found for Er Grah which would have satisfied the requirements. It must be emphasized that this was a very difficult problem. Increasingly careful observations of the moon had probably been made for hundreds of years. These would have revealed unexplained anomalies due to variations in parallax and refraction, and so it may have been considered desirable to observe at the major and minor standstills at both rising and setting. At each standstill there were 10 or 12 lunations when the monthly declination maximum and minimum could have been used. At each maximum or minimum, parties would have been out at all possible places trying to see the moon rise or set behind high trial poles. At night these poles would have needed torches at the tops because any other marks would not be visible until actually silhouetted on the moon's disc. In the meantime some earlier existing observatory must have been in use so that the erectors could be kept informed about the kind of maximum which was being observed; they would have needed to know the state of the perturbation.

Then there would have ensued the nine years of waiting till the next stand-still when the other four sites were being sought. The magnitude of the task was enhanced by the decision to make the same foresight serve both stand-stills. We can understand why this was considered necessary when we think of the decades of work involved in cutting, shaping, transporting, and erecting *one* suitable foresight. It is evident that whereas some of the sites, such as Quiberon, used the top of the foresight Er Grah, others, such as Kerran, used the lower portion. This militated against the use of a mound with a smaller menhir on the top. Much has rightly been written about the labour of

**Table 9.1.** *Sites which may be backsights for Le Grand Menhir Brisé*

| | Azimuth | Altitude | Parallax | Declination observed | Compare | | |
|---|---|---|---|---|---|---|---|
| Le Moustoir, $R_2$ | 118° 17′ | −2′ | 57′·7 | −18° 22′ | $-(\epsilon - i - s - \Delta)$ | = | −18° 22′ |
| Kervilor, stone C | 119° 09′ | −1′ | 57′·7 | −18° 53′ | $-(\epsilon - i + \Delta)$ | = | −18° 53′ |
| Kervilor, stone D | 118° 27′ | 0′ | 57′·4 | −18° 27′ | $-(\epsilon - i - s)$ | = | −18° 29′ |
| Kerran, small menhir | 136° 13′ | +3′ | 57′·4 | −28° 46′ | $-(\epsilon + i - s)$ | = | −28° 46′ |

putting Er Grah in position, but a full consideration of the labour of finding the site shows that this may have been a comparable task.

We now know that for a stone 60 ft high the siting is perfect. We do not know that all the backsights were completed. But the fact that we have not yet found any trace of a sector to the east does not prove that the eastern sites were not used, because the small stones may have been removed; or perhaps the extrapolation was done by the simpler triangle method or perhaps it was done at a central site at the Carnac alignments.

No one who sees Le Grand Menhir Brisé can fail to be impressed, or to ask the reason for its being there. Many explanations have been advanced but they all fail to account for the sheer size of the stone or, indeed, for its position. The explanation we have given covers both size and position. In use, both the height of the top and the vertical length were needed: the top for backsights where the hills appeared behind the stone and the bottom for the nearer backsights when the horizon was lower. The reasons for the choice of the position have already been given.

It will be seen in Table 9.1 that the backsights at Le Moustoir, Kervilor, and Kerran seem to give accurately the required declinations. In our opinion an equally important point is that there are eight possible positions from which all the cases could have been observed and at all of these there was room for the necessary side movement. Evidently the observers wanted long lines and this made the task of finding a suitable position difficult in the extreme. If anyone doubts the difficulty let him try to plan in terrain of this kind a lunar observatory with long lines for all eight cases. Let him then think of what was involved when no convenient maps were available.

For this project the erectors must have had the use of an existing observatory. This was almost certainly the observatory which was centred on the menhir at Le Manio. We shall now show that the evidence from Le Manio is much fuller than that from Er Grah.

### 9.5. The Le Manio foresight

It has been mentioned above that before the erectors of Er Grah could have succeeded in the complicated and difficult task of finding a suitable site they must have had the use of an earlier observatory. There is now no doubt that this was centred on the menhir on the hilltop at Le Manio. The smaller observatory with its shorter sight line would have been easier to arrange. We have found 6 lunar backsights for this hilltop in addition to two calendar backsights. The stone is the tallest in the district and stands at $M$ on the highest hill in the neighbourhood (Figs 9.6 and 9.10).

### 9.6. The hill near Le Manio

We show in Fig. 9.11 a small-scale reproduction of a survey of the menhir $M$ and the enclosure which stand practically on the top of the hill. The enclosure

FIG. 9.10. The menhir at Le Manio.

is described in Le Rouzic's inventory (1965) as an 'enceinte rectangulaire formée de petits menhirs, acquise et restaurée par l'Etat. Ce monument était primitivement enfoui dans un tertre tumulaire allongé, qui a été complètement enlevé'. If all the stones were formerly covered as suggested by Le Rouzic, there must have been a large mound and we tentatively suggest that this was originally an elongated mound retained by the 'petits menhirs' which we see today but that these became covered as the mound subsided and spread. The approximate contours we give suggest that some of the material from inside the enclosure has been deposited on its south side. The remainder is probably now built into the dry stone walls, of which there are several on the hill. At the menhir the ground is some 6 ft lower than the general level round the quadrilateral. The menhir seems to have been re-erected by Le Rouzic, who admits that it was scarred during the process.

When the hill was viewed from the surrounding country (except perhaps from the north) there would have been two projections on the skyline: the tumulus and the menhir. It is to be noted that the north wall of the enclosure

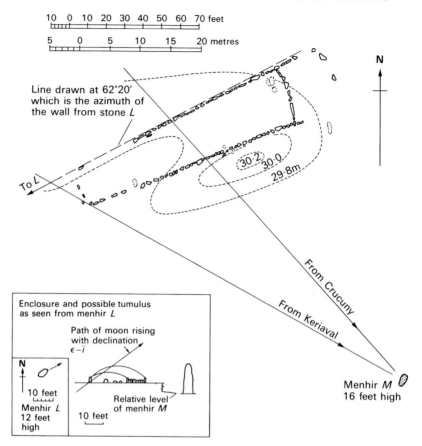

FIG. 9.11. The enclosure and menhir at Le Manio with inset showing the ground plan of menhir L. The datum of the contours is uncertain by ±1 m.

as it stands today has an azimuth of about 63°, while the azimuth of the wall from the stone L is 62° 21′ (see Fig. 9.11).

The particulars given in Table 9.2 show that the use from L of the north side of the enclosure as a foresight gives a declination of 18° 44′ or almost exactly $(\epsilon - i)$, and the inset in Fig. 9.11 shows that the tumulus we have imagined as filling the enclosure provides the necessary foresight for the rising moon. Two observers would be necessary, one bringing the upper limb and the other the lower limb into the corner of sky provided by the north wall of the tumulus and the ground.

In assessing the probability that L is really a lunar backsight, we may note that the menhir might be said to be orientated on the hilltop and that the wall is on the exact azimuth (see Fig. 9.11).

**Table 9.2.** *Sites which may be backsights for the hilltop at Le Manio*

| | Distance (ft) | Azimuth | Altitude | Parallax | Declination observed | Compare | |
|---|---|---|---|---|---|---|---|
| Kerlagad, stone A to menhir M | 7032 | 222° 39' | 14' | 57'·7 | −29° 09'·5 | −(ε+i+s−Δ) | −29° 09' |
| Menhir S to menhir M | 2652 | 233° 42' | 21' | 0' | −23° 39' ±6' | −(ε−s) | −23° 39' |
| Menhir L to 'tumulus' wall | 8700 | 62° 17' | 13' | 57' | +18° 46' | +(ε−i) | +18° 45' |
| Boulder Q to menhir M | 4894 | 53° 30' | 25± | 0' | +23° 35'± | +(ε−s) | −23° 39' |
| Menhir K to menhir M | 1240 | 246° 08' | 4± | 0' | −16° 13'±15' | Sun at Martinmas and Candlemas | |
| Crucuny, menhir Y to menhir M | 6366 | 137° 24' | 32' | 57'·7 | −28° 53' | −(ε+i−Δ) | −28° 54' |
| Keriaval (§9.8) | | | | | | | |
| Stone D near Kermario (§9.7) | | 0° 00' | | | | | |
| Menhir F (§9.7) | | | | | | | |

**9.7.** We shall now look at the other sites in the area which may have been placed to use the hilltop as a foresight (see Table 9.2).

*Stone A at Kerlagad.* The large menhir $G$ is not intervisible with $M$ and in any case it is not on the correct azimuth, but there is a small menhir $A$ visible from $G$ and we believe this to be a backsight for $M$. We ran (and checked) a traverse to both stones and then examined the line of sight from $A$ where it seems to graze the hillside. Because of trees and scrub it is difficult to be sure but the line appears to clear and gives a declination of $-(\epsilon+i+s-\Delta)$, or what is practically the same value, $-(\epsilon+i+\Delta)$. Moving to the position for $-(\epsilon+i)$ would definitely make the menhir $M$ visible from near $A$.

*Stones S and K.* Menhir $S$ stands on the edge of the bridle path about 300 ft from the main road, opposite the road to Kerlagad (Fig. 8.4). It is about 9 ft high with sides 3 ft × 3 ft orientated north-west and south-west, and so might be said to be orientated on $M$. $K$ is the large well-known stone near the south cromlech at Kerlescan. From $S$ the upper limb of the midwinter setting sun appeared to graze the bottom of $M$ and in an exactly similar way the moon with declination $-(\epsilon-i)$ grazed the bottom of $K$. $SK$ is a very short ray but the low ground in the valley prevented $K$ from being put farther away and this declination is in any case given by the line from $A$ to menhir $M$. From $K$ in its present position the sun set behind $M$ at the important calendar dates, Martinmas and Candlemas (see tables in Thom 1967, Ch. 9).

*Stones P and Q.* These stones lie one on each side of the road between the east cromlech at Le Ménec and Kermario. $Q$ is a large 8-ft egg-shaped boulder and from it the south limb of the midsummer sun would have been seen to rise close to the menhir $M$. From stone $P$ the upper limb of the solstitial sun would have risen over the mound, but since we do not know the shape of the tumulus no accurate value of the declination can be given. Neither of these stones can be accepted as a well-established backsight.

*The Stones at D.* This collection of stones (see Fig. 7.2) perhaps formed a backsight now in a ruinous condition. It *may* be the remains of a lunar backsight because from the southerly stones the moon at the major standstill would have appeared to rise near to menhir $M$.

*Stone F.* This is the stone which Atkinson (1973) described as belonging to a long barrow that was older than the alignments. From $F$, $M$ bears due north. In fact the two stones are within a foot or two of being on the same meridian.

*The Stone at C.* This menhir stands near the south side of Le Ménec alignments. Seen from it, the solstitial sun rose with its centre near the top of the tumulus covering the enclosure. There seem to have been three stones in all near *C*, and so perhaps an accurate backsight existed here.

### 9.8. The alignments at Keriaval

This site is in a depleted condition, but from our survey (Fig. 9.12) it is evident that these upright stones are remains of alignments. We did not have time in 1973 to run a traverse to the site, but from a position near the alignments we were able to see the water tower at Kercado and we know the coordinates of this relative to *M*. Accurate solar observation gave us the azimuth of the water tower, and so we were able to calculate the approximate azimuth from the site to stone *M*.

In 1976 we connected the site to our main traverses and obtained verification of the 1973 results. We also made a completely new survey of the upright

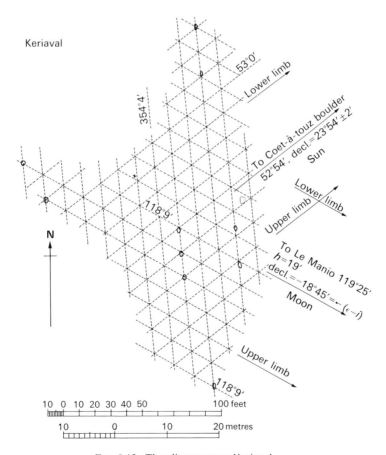

FIG. 9.12. The alignments at Keriaval.

stones. The rock shows through the ground at various places but there were two places where what looked like the stump of a broken stone was seen. Only excavation can show if these have been stones but we have put them on the survey. The large boulder on the east side may be a fallen stone.

It is evident that there have been rows of stones running at an azimuth of 354°·4 spaced 11·71 ft apart. We found we were able to superimpose a set of equally spaced lines crossing these which pick up every stone except one and since we again know the overall width (188·4 ft) the spacing is 12·53 ft. The angle between the rows is 55°·5. These two spacings and two angles completely define the geometry and allow us to calculate trigonometrically that the diagonals run at 53°·0 with a spacing of 14·21 ft. We have based the calculation on the two spacings because we can determine these accurately and hence know the azimuth of the diagonals accurately.

On the figure we have drawn arrows which show approximately where an observer would have stood to see the moon (centre, upper, and lower limb) rise behind the menhir at Le Manio when the declination was $-(\epsilon - i)$.

It will be seen that from the central arrow the azimuth of the Le Manio menhir is 119° 25' and the azimuth of the cross lines is 118°·9. Evidently these cross lines indicated the rising point of the moon at the minor standstill. Before moonrise they would obviously have assisted in finding the stone at Manio, which would at this site be only some 2 arc minutes wide, past the corner of the enclosure.

On the top of the hill at Coët-à-touz there is today a church which can be seen from far and near and just to the north of the church is a large boulder roughly 7 ft × 4½ ft × 4 ft. We ran an open traverse to this boulder and so are able to show that the sun rising at the summer solstice would appear behind it. Three arrows in Fig. 9.12 show the particulars. It will be seen that from the central arrow the azimuth of the Coët-à-touz boulder is 52° 54' and the azimuth of the diagonal lines is 53°·0.

It must be pointed out that there is no indication of the position which an observer should occupy in order to see sunrise at Coët-à-touz unless indeed it be the large boulder immediately to the east of the alignments. In this connection we have to take into account the uncertainty of the positions of all the arrows shown on Fig. 9.13. We consider that this uncertainty, which is largely produced by the uncertainty in our knowledge of the level of the site, may amount to ±10 ft. This makes the altitude of the foresights uncertain by a few arc minutes and so affects the values for the declinations. It will be realized that it is only here and there that one can now get a view through the woods and so we have to depend on our traverses for azimuths and on map spot levels for altitudes.

When we first surveyed this field we were surprised to notice that none of the spacings was an integral number of Megalithic yards, but the reason for the spacing is now apparent.

It will be seen that Keriaval forms the backsight for two foresights namely the stone at Le Manio and the boulder at Coët-à-touz and both of these foresights are indicated by the direction of the rows. Furthermore, as will be shown, the rows provide a method of extrapolating to the lunar maximum declination from two nights' observations.

It will also be noticed that the diagonals of the diamonds formed by the rows lie at an azimuth of about 87°, which is not very far from the sunrising position at the equinox but this has not been checked.

When we worked out the exact geometry of the rows and published it (Thom, Thom, and Gorrie 1976) we did not know about Coët-à-touz and were agreeably surprised to find from our later traverse that one set of cross rows pointed accurately at this outstanding feature.

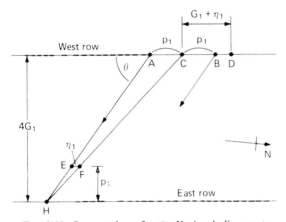

FIG. 9.13. Suggested use for the Keriaval alignments.

## 9.9. Possible use of the rows

The perpendicular distance between the east and west rows, or what remains of them, is 124 ft. It is interesting to note that this is the necessary length $4G$ for an extrapolating sector for use with the moon rising at $M$, provided that the line of movement of the observer is at right-angles to the sight line.

We might speculate that observers, instead of moving at right-angles, moved along the west row of stones. Let $A$, Fig. 9.13 be the position from which the moon was seen to graze the foresight $M$. Points $A$ and $H$ were marked. The next night the observer had to place himself at $B$. $AB$ was bisected at $C$ and the distance $AC$, which we shall call $p_1$, was set out from the east row. Now measure $EF$ parallel to the rows and note that by similar triangles $EF = p_1^2/4G_1$ which we shall call $\eta_1$ (c.f. Thom 1971). We must now set out a distance $(G_1 + \eta_1)$ from $C$; $D$ is then the extrapolated position, that is the position the observer would have occupied if it so happened that the maximum negative declination had occurred at the instant when the moon was rising.

The procedure just described is, however, theoretically correct only if the fundamental distance $G_1$ had been measured (Thom 1971, §9.6) by moving *along* the rows. It is indeed possible that there were other rows, now destroyed, which made the width greater than 124 ft; but until the site is properly excavated we cannot assume this with any certainty. Excavation of the area is obviously desirable.

There are other sites, for example, at the Communion stones in Dumfries-shire and at a site near Dounreay in Caithness, where there are parallel rows, and these should be examined to see if perhaps they were associated with a lunar foresight.

### 9.10. The hill at Le Manio as a universal foresight

We have now described ten possible backsights, namely $A$, $S$, $K$, $F$, $L$, $D$, $P$, $Q$, $W$, and $Y$. The uses of $A$, $S$, $K$, $F$, $W$, and $L$ seem to us to be well established and these alone allow us to conclude that this complex was a solar and lunar observatory (see Table 9.2).

We assume that Le Rouzic re-erected the menhir $M$ in its original position. Why then is this position so far to the south and not on a slightly higher position near the enclosure? In examining what we find it is necessary to remember that Megalithic activity of the kind we are considering was spread over perhaps a thousand years and so we must not be surprised to find one system superimposed on another. We suggest that $M$ was erected at a later date than the tumulus to fit into a new pattern being developed for the backsights. The ray from $A$ grazes the hillside, which slopes down to the south-east, where shown. We found that taking levels here was difficult because of trees and scrub, but the graze seems to be close; so close that it may have been considered necessary to site $M$ in its present position instead of at the enclosure. Perhaps also $M$ was sited well away from the tumulus to avoid confusion and to allow it to be seen from Kerisval.

M. Jacq, son-in-law of Le Rouzic and, before he died, curator of the Miln–Le Rouzic museum in Carnac, told us that there had been a cromlech at the east end of the Kermario alignments on the high ground immediately to the east of $E$. Perhaps there were backsights for $M$ on this hill, but the site seems to be very near $M$ and so the backsights may have been further away, near Kerdreneven.

Once $M$ was erected, the backsights $S$, $K$, $A$, and perhaps $W$ and $Y$ were built where we now find them. This is entirely speculative, but if it is correct then we suggest that at this stage work on this observatory was dropped (including the re-siting of the 12-ft menhir at $L$) and activity was diverted to the much larger scheme involving the erection of the huge foresight known as Le Grand Menhir Brisé.

## 9.11. Crucuny

In Fig. 9.14 we show all that is left of this cromlech known locally as Le Champ de la Croix. The stone cross leaning in the wall outside the cottage is badly broken and needs repair. The part of the ring remaining has survived because it now forms a wall along the cart track that runs along its west side. It is difficult to know which stones are in their original positions and which ones have been built in recently. Perhaps the menhir Y formed part of the cromlech but this seems most unlikely because it is higher and more rectangular in plan than the others.

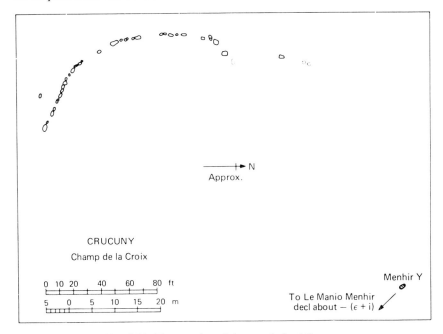

FIG. 9.14. The remains of the cromlech at Crucuny.

Our survey in 1976 showed that from this menhir the declination given by the line from the stone to Le Manio is $-28° 53'$, which could be a relevant lunar declination, but Le Manio menhir seems to be 3 or 4 ft too low to enable the observer to see over the intermediate ridge at the point marked $Y1$ on Fig. 9.6. One of our traverse lines passed over this ridge and we made a tacheometric survey of the position where we calculated the line from Crucuny would pass. Our somewhat rough levelling showed that the ridge was just too high, but more accurate work might give a different result. On the ridge there are two stones among the trees, one of which might be Mega-lithic. These stones are 190 ft apart and the line passes between them showing that this is a possible position for a backsight. Perhaps it was considered to be too near to Le Manio and an attempt was made to use a backsight at the stone *Y*; but this is, as we have just shown, somewhat doubtful.

### 9.12. The three stones near Keriaval

In the woods some 300 m east of the dolmen at Keriaval there is an alignment of three menhirs each about 4 ft high. The line is straight, orientated 99°·7 and the spacing is 15 MY and 13 MY, going east.

From the centre stone the azimuth of the large boulder on the summit at Coët-à-touz is 52° 53'·5. Taking the difference in level to be 13 m, the declination is 23° 42'. The distance is small (4106 ft) and the declination is thus very sensitive to position and height, but this is perhaps the lower limb of the sun at the summer solstice.

The line passes about 170 ft from the menhir *Z* on top of the tumulus at Crucuny and so presumably clears the tumulus which otherwise would block the view.

However, the reason for having these three stones is not clear; the line is not at right-angles to the line of sight to Coët-à-touz and its azimuth does not give accurately a pertinent declination. The declination of the north-east end of the tumulus at Le Moustoir is about $-8°·3$, and this is the declination of the sun at one of the calendar dates; but the azimuth would need to be about 102° and the line of the stones is 99°·7.

### 9.13. Checking the traverse by connecting to French triangulation points

There is a triangulation point on the south edge of Fig. 9.6 on the site that once had a water tower, and another just to the north of the northern edge of the same figure at the church on the high ground at Coët-à-touz. The French authorities provided us with the grid coordinates of these points in metres:

| | | |
|---|---|---|
| (1) Granite block at old water tower | E 192889·0 | N 301944·0 |
| (2) Church spire at Coët-à-touz | E 194056·4 | N 305368·1 |
| | $\Delta E = 1167·4$ | $\Delta N = 3424·1$ |

From these the distance is $(\Delta E^2 + \Delta N^2)^{\frac{1}{2}} = 3617$ m $= 11\,869$ ft, and the grid bearing of (2) from (1) is arc tan $\Delta E/\Delta N = 18° 49'·6$. To reduce that to an azimuth we apply the correction calculated as $-3° 58'·3$ in Appendix A, giving 14° 51'·3 for the azimuth of (2) from (1). We connected these two points on to our traverse and found their coordinates on our grid to be (in feet):

| | | |
|---|---|---|
| (1) | E 1134 | N −395 |
| (2) | E 4179 | N 11 069 |
| | 3045 | 11 464 |

Hence we arrive at the following values: distance, 11 862 ft; grid bearing, 14° 52'·3; correction, 0'·2; and azimuth, 14° 52'·5. It will be seen that the error in our survey is 7 ft in distance and 1'·2 in azimuth.

The distance along our traverse was about $3\frac{1}{2}$ miles, most of it being in difficult country, so we had good reason to be satisfied and to believe that the points we tabulate in Table 9.3 are probably correct to $\pm 4$ ft.

**Table 9.3.** *Coordinates of key points in the area covered by Fig. 9.6*

| Point | E | N | Point | E | N |
|---|---|---|---|---|---|
| L | −634 | +374 | Y | 2894 | 8973 |
| M | +7203 | 4288 | Keriaval 3 stones | 900 | 8693 |
| $R_1$ | 6149 | 7480 | Kercado Water Tower | 7685 | 1593 |
| $R_2$ | 5912 | 7304 | P | 7512+ | 6846+ |
| G | 11 015 | 9595 | Boulder at Coët-à-touz | 4205 | 11 130 |
| A | 11 964 | 9462 | a in Fig. 6.1 | −27 | 218 |
| S | 9338 | 5858 | | | |
| 15 | 11 421 | 4276 | Le Grand Menhir Brisé | 33 270± | −7420± |
| Kv | 12 859 | 3761 | | | |
| K | 8338 | 4790 | | | |
| E | 7909 | 3861 | | | |
| F | 7204 | 3398 | | | |

The origin is near Le Ménec and the north axis is in the meridian there. Any bearing $AB$ calculated from these coordinates should have $1.78\ E_A \times 10^{-4}$ arc minutes added to it to give the azimuth of $AB$ from the $A$ end.

The coordinates of Le Grand Menhir Brisé are not intended for direct calculation of its azimuth, but are for obtaining its approximate distance when an azimuth has been measured to the Locmariaquer water tower.

# 10

## BROGAR

**10.1.** THE main island of Orkney (Pomona) contains many archaeological surprises, among them Maes Howe and Skara Brae, and the adjacent mountainous island of Hoy has the Dwarfie Stane, which is a large boulder with a chamber excavated inside it. One of the islands of the archipelago, Eday, still has three large menhirs and there are menhirs on some other smaller islands.

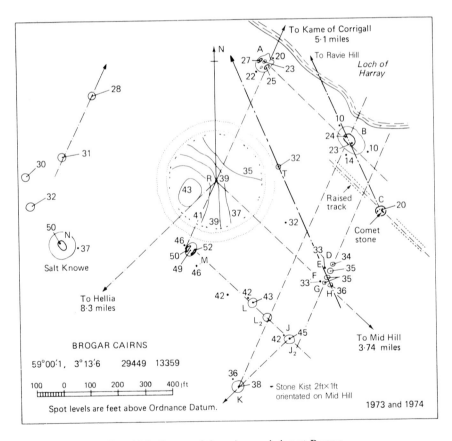

FIG. 10.1. Survey of the cairns and ring at Brogar.

The largest Megalithic site is the Ring of Brogar. In Chapter 3 we have seen how the ring itself gives an accurate value for the Megalithic yard, but more important is the fact that the mounds in the adjacent fields form the most complete Megalithic observatory remaining in Britain. We shall accordingly describe and discuss the site in detail.

The contours inside of the Ring (Fig. 10.1) show that the ground is not level. Why was a more level site not chosen? Almost certainly it was because from this site it is possible to see at least four lunar foresights. In general, given two natural foresights, a position can be found for a backsight from which the foresights can be used to show the setting or rising points of two celestial bodies. Consider observing the sun setting behind the top of a hill. The locus of all points from which we can see the phenomenon is a line across country. Suppose there is another hill and another body then there will be another cross-country line. *Provided that the terrain permits*, a backsight can be placed where the lines cross and this will serve both foresights. But it will be only by chance that this backsight can serve for a third foresight. Apparently the Ring of Brogar is in such a position that the required backsights for all four foresights could be placed in its immediate neighbourhood.

The four definite foresights are:

the high cliffs at Hellia (Fig. 10.2);
a small clean-cut notch on Mid Hill (Fig. 10.3);
two slopes on Kame of Corrigal (Fig. 10.4); and
a small dip 8 miles away which we shall call Ravie Hill (Fig. 10.5).

Referring to Fig. 10.1 it will be seen that the mounds can be used to identify all four. A survey of the area was made in 1849 by Lt. F. W. L. Thomas and, in Fig. 10.6, we show a part of this remarkable work. It will be seen that at the spot on our survey which we have marked $T$, Thomas has written the words 'a very small tumulus'; but no care has been taken of this tumulus and there is now only an area of slightly raised stony ground which has been levelled recently. Some yards from $T$ on the line to $G$ there is a trace of what may have been another small cairn of stones.

We have made a tacheometric survey of the area (Fig. 10.1) with levels and this shows that all the other tumuli shown by Thomas can be identified today. Mound $L_2$ has almost been ploughed away but it can be seen when the grass is short by looking from the lower ground so that it appears in profile. The Ordnance Survey large-scale map shows it by a broken ring.

Provided we have a profile from one point, by making use of the coordinates and levels from Fig. 10.1, we can calculate it from any other, but this is accurate only if the foresight is two-dimensional, that is, if it can be treated simply as a silhouette at a known distance. We have visited Mid Hill, Kame of Corrigal, and Ravie Hill and consider that this assumption is sufficiently accurate at these foresights, but it is obvious from an inspection of the

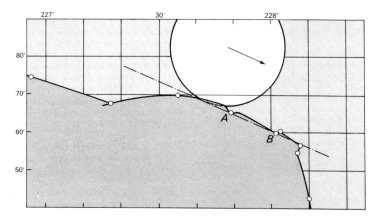

FIG. 10.2. Moon setting on the cliffs at Hellia at the minor standstill.

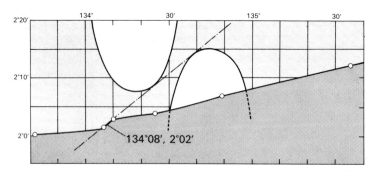

FIG. 10.3. Moon rising on Mid Hill, 3·74 miles distant, at the minor standstill.

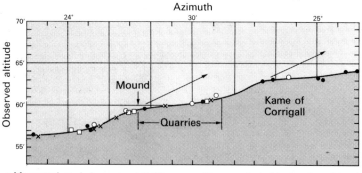

○ Measured at $J_2$ in poor visibility      × Measured at $J$ but reduced to $J_2$

● Measured at centre but reduced to $J_2$   □ Measured at $L_2$ but reduced to $J_2$

FIG. 10.4. Composite profile of Kame of Corrigall.

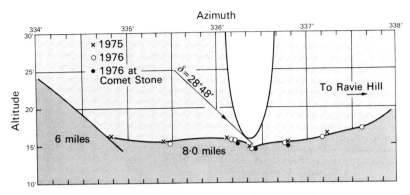

FIG. 10.5. Moon setting near Ravie Hill with declination ($\epsilon + i$). Measurements made at centre of ring and at $H$ have been reduced to Comet Stone.

contours at Hellia that the observed profile there will change as we move about the site. Accordingly, we measured the Hellia profile from $R$ and $J$. Similarly for Kame we measured the profile from $R$, $J$, $J_2$ and $L_2$; the collected coordinates are shown in Fig. 10.4, all having been reduced to $J_2$. At each of these points we used the sun/time method of determining azimuth, and all were referred to a common referring object a known distance away. This enabled us to compare one azimuth with another and so all have been checked.

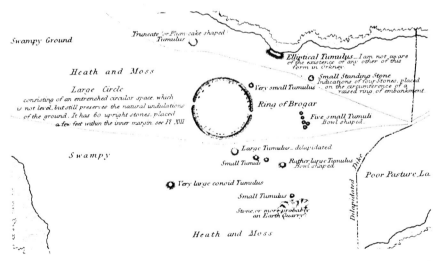

FIG. 10.6. Part of the survey made in 1849 by F. W. L. Thomas, taken from his Account of some of the Celtic antiquities of Orkney, *Archeologia, or Miscellaneous tracts relating to Antiquity*, xxxiv (1851), 88–136.

### 10.2. Kame of Corrigal

When we visited the position of the foresights at Kame of Corrigal we found over an area about 50 yards by 50 yards a number of holes from which slabs of stone had been quarried. The debris from each hole lay beside it and may have raised the ground profile by perhaps 2 ft in the part indicated in Fig. 10.4, but this will not appreciably affect the declination. An artificial mound about 5 ft high exists in the position shown in Fig. 10.4. The coordinates of this seen from the centre $R$ are 25° 21′, 61′·2, determined, when the visibility was too poor to use any other method, by placing a car headlamp on the top of the mound after sunset. This mound is on the western edge of the quarried region and may have been raised when the quarry holes were dug, but the reason for its construction is not obvious. Since its declination from Brogar is within 0′·5 of that of the slope to the west, it is tempting to think that it has been the position for an artificial foresight. Perhaps archaeologists can establish the age of the quarries and of this mound. There does not seem to be any road leading to the area of the pits, but not far away are the remains of a track along the hillside perhaps for hauling peat.

### 10.3. The Comet Stone

This stands on a low mound as shown in Figs 10.1 and 10.7. The mean azimuths of the two flat faces of the slab called the Comet Stone are about 133° 30′ and 134° 30′, and from here the Mid Hill notch is at 135° 07′·8. The stone has evidently maintained its position for over three thousand years. We found an interesting feature near the Comet Stone, namely a causeway or low ridge of slightly higher ground running towards the north-west. It appears again to the south-east of the raised platform round the stones (see Fig. 10.7). In 1849 Thomas showed a track following this ridge so far, but skirting round the Comet Stone and not rejoining the ridge on the other side. It seems likely that this was originally a Megalithic construction but over the centuries it was perhaps used as a cart track across low ground. A careful survey (Fig. 10.7) was made of the edges and centre line of the causeway enabling its azimuth to be determined. The mean direction of the centre line of the portion of the causeway that is visible is 134° 30′ ± 30′ and it passes about 9 ft to the north-east of the Comet stone. The declinations of the Mid Hill foresight from points on the line of the track are:

| | |
|---|---|
| opposite Cairn $A$ | − 18° 54′; |
| opposite Comet Stone | − 18° 49′; |
| at apparent south end | − 18° 47′. |

Of these declinations, that at the Comet Stone is the only one which is definite, but the track was probably long enough to allow it to be used as a line of movement to permit extrapolation to be carried out. In Temple Wood

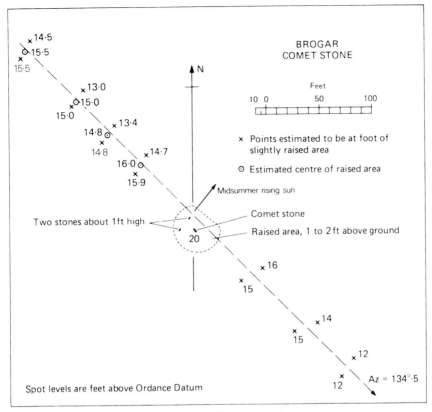

FIG. 10.7. The Comet Stone and raised ridge.

the line of movement is at about 67° to the sight line, but, provided the fore-sight is high enough, there is no reason why the observer should not move along the line of sight itself. In fact at Campbeltown, where the foresight is on the meridian, there is no other possible direction as movement across the line of sight would not affect the declination. At Campbeltown the ground slopes down towards the foresight and so shortens the necessary movement and makes the operation practicable.

## 10.4. Remains of cairns

The field immediately to the north-west of the area enclosed by the Ministry is under cultivation. We noticed in this field three or four places where the ground was slightly above the surrounding level. These mounds may be natural or may have been deposited recently. Nevertheless, we have marked their positions on our survey (Fig. 10.1). It will be seen that a line joining two of the mounds points to Kame and gives a declination of about 28° 54′, which is $(\epsilon + i - \Delta)$. We consider that it would be wrong to include this in any statistical analysis unless some more substantial evidence is found to show that these very low mounds are prehistoric remains.

## 10.5. The position of the Brogar site

We believe that we can explain the position chosen for the Brogar observatory. The rugged cliffs at Hellia in Hoy form an attractive foresight because the slope at the top of the cliff is parallel to the path of the setting moon at the minor standstill, but the upper limb could not have been used since this would have forced the Ring south-eastwards and down on to the lower ground. The ridge on which the cairns $M$, $L$, and $J$ stand formed a perfect platform along which the observer could move as he watched the setting moon. Looking from this ridge in the other direction there are the less impressive foresights on Kame of Corrigal, and so this same ridge could have been used as an operating platform for viewing both foresights. Perhaps to avoid ambiguity, $J_2$ is not marked in any way apparent today but the position is easily found by standing so that the small cairns $D$, $E$, $F$, and $G$ appear below Kame. From the same general area it was possible to watch the moon rising at the minor standstill on the almost perfect foresight provided by the small notch on Mid Hill. At the time when the moon was expected to rise it was necessary to have some warning so that observers placed along the line of movement could be prepared for the emergence of the upper limb. Since the horizon at Mid Hill rises to the south, this meant that the man watching should have been stationed to the north-east. But here the site is limited by Loch Harray. To compensate it was necessary to raise the watcher's eye level. This explains the large mound $A$, placed as far to the north-east as possible and as high as necessary. In partial darkness it was desirable to have an indication of the direction in which the small notch lay on Mid Hill. There could have been poles on both mounds $A$ and $B$ on the line of sight. We shall see shortly that the height of $B$ was limited because it was necessary to see over it from the Comet Stone to Ravie Hill.

For Kame, Salt Knowe served the same purpose placed, as it was, well to the left—but not too far to the left, or it would then have been on lower ground: as we shall see later other considerations probably fixed its exact position. For the setting moon no warning was necessary. The foresights at Kame may seem unimpressive but there was no other natural foresight available in this direction, and if the builders wanted to keep the backsights grouped in one compact unit they were indeed lucky to find, in the right place, these two steeper slopes on the horizon. While they are unimpressive to look at they would have been perfectly satisfactory to use.

## 10.6. Hellia and Kame

There are two notches on the Hellia profile marked $A$ and $B$ on Fig. 10.2.

Since both of these give identical declinations it seems safe to take them as being the foresights used by the builders of the cairns. At an earlier date, when the Ring of Brogar was built, the general line of the slope above the cliff was probably sufficient with the lower limb of the moon. From $J$ over $K$, the declination corresponds to $-(\epsilon-i)$ and from $L$ the same notches show $-(\epsilon-i+\Delta)$ or $-(\epsilon-i+s-\Delta)$. This perhaps rules out $J$ and $L$ as backsights for Kame, which indeed is indicated by the line $KL_2B$. The lower foresight at Kame from $K$ or $L_2$ shows $(\epsilon+i+s+\Delta)$ and the upper with $J_2GFED$ shows an identical value.

## 10.7. Ravie Hill

The foresight here lies on the track from Rose View farm to the east-south-east. The sites of two cairns are marked on the large-scale Ordnance Survey map and these seem to nave been one on each side of the shallow valley which runs through the ridge. This slight depression forms the foresight that we measured at Brogar (Fig. 10.5). Although unimpressive it is unambiguous and is quite visible to the naked eye. It is indicated in Fig. 10.5 by the line $HFT$ and by the line from the Comet Stone over cairn $B$. The altitude is low $(14'$ from $G)$ and this makes the refraction somewhat uncertain, but the graze with the ground is not unduly long.

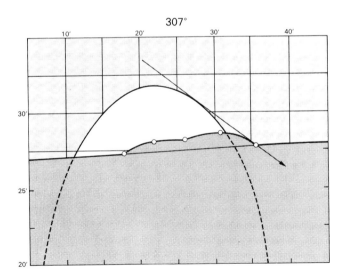

FIG. 10.8. Moon setting at minor standstill on cairn as seen from Stenness Circle with declination $(\epsilon-i+\Delta)$.

### 10.8. Foresight for $(\epsilon - i)$ from the Stenness Ring

The Ring of Bookan is not visible from Brogar, but on the horizon in this direction there are some mounds made by the debris taken out of the adjacent quarries, now disused. On the horizon there is also a prehistoric cairn among the mounds (Fig. 10.8). We measured its azimuth and altitude from the centre of the Stenness Ring and deduced its declination. The azimuth of the bottom of the right-hand side of the cairn was found to be 307° 35′; the altitude was 27′·8. Using the appropriate values of parallax, $s$, and $\Delta$ we find that the declination is 19° 08′·4 and that this gives $\epsilon = 23° 52′·4$. This is almost identical with the value obtained from the north declinations at the Brogar cairns (see §10.12).

The reason for using Stenness instead of Brogar was that there was no natural foresight at Brogar and no position where an artificial foresight could have been erected, whereas from Stenness the cairn is on the horizon.

### 10.9. Visibility of the moon

The moon can be seen in the brightest sunshine but we do not yet know how low it could have been and yet remain clear enough for observation in daylight. We are doubtful about the possibility of seeing the moon setting on Ravie Hill at 10 a.m. in December but in thinking about this, we bear in mind how very low the sun was. At that time of year it attained a meridian altitude of only $7\frac{1}{2}°$. Observation at 10 p.m. in June would also have been difficult. All the other foresights have a reasonable altitude of 1° or over and seem to be satisfactory.

### 10.10. Lines for $\pm(\epsilon \pm i)$

We find at several of the observatories lines for one or other of these declinations, that is declinations with no $\Delta$, and so we were not surprised to find one at Brogar. Before we can admit the existence of these lines we must show how they could have been established and how they might have been used. For example, consider the Hellia line from $J$ over $K$. In the autumn two observers, one using the upper limb of the moon and one the lower, could establish a stake for the centre at the autumnal equinox at $-(\epsilon - i - \Delta)$; and similarly near midwinter for $-(\epsilon - i + \Delta)$. Midway between the two would be approximately the required position for $-(\epsilon - i)$.

What probably happened was that the observers placed a stake for every observable monthly maximum (or minimum) near the standstill and from these the midpoint would be deduced. An examination of Fig. 2.1 makes this clearer. We tend to assume that only the extreme declination maxima were observed. It is, however, unlikely that the observers would have had more than a general idea of the date of the expected maximum, and so they would have begun work long before and tried to observe every monthly maximum before and after the extreme. This could also have had the advantage of training assistants in the technique of observing.

A method of extrapolating to each *monthly* maximum was essential and had been developed (Appendix B). Every month's work would have left an extrapolated stake on the ground, and so if bad weather interfered at the extreme maximum there would not have been much difficulty in estimating the ground position. The solution of the case of a missing monthly maximum involved only small movements corresponding to 2 or 3 arc minutes and would not have been so difficult as extrapolating to the monthly maximum from two days' work, which is dealt with elsewhere (Thom 1971). We suggest that a method of using the backsights might be as follows. Consider one for $(\epsilon + i)$ and refer to Fig. 2.1. Stakes would be placed as above for the points marked on this figure $B$, $C$, $E$, and $F$. Stakes $B$ and $C$ would be those for $Q$, that is, one on each side of the permanent mark for $(\epsilon + i)$. The dates of $B$ and $C$ would be known and so the date could be found when the rising declination was $(\epsilon + i)$. Similarly for $E$ and $F$ the date could be found when the falling declination was $(\epsilon + i)$. The date midway between these two was approximately the time of the maximum and we have suggested that, knowing the date of one of the maxima, multiples of the period 173·3 days could be added to predict the 'danger times' for eclipses. It is true that within limits any mark would serve instead of that for $(\epsilon + i)$, but the latter gives the most accurate interpolation.

This may sound a long method of finding the date of the maximum but it was short compared with the years which must have been spent on the erection of the Ring and later of the cairns; and it would have been quite possible for a people who could place the backsights and who were capable of building the Avebury Ring and of setting out the complicated geometry of the Carnac alignments.

The above assumes that the length of the 173-day period was known. Somewhere and at some time it must have been discovered, but to find the period is not quite so easy as it appears. In Thom 1971 it is shown that the time interval between two apparent maxima is 2·2 per cent too short, whereas the interval between two minima is too long by the same amount. The most accurate method available was to use two maxima, one in one standstill and the other in the next, but this would necessitate keeping track of the eclipses in between so that the number of periods was known.

### 10.11. Reducing the measurements

In Table 10.1 we give the particulars for those lines with indications on the ground, such as two or more cairns pointing to the foresight. To show how the calculations were made we shall illustrate by giving full details for the line to Hellia from $J$ looking over $K$. With the latitude $(\phi = 59° 00'·1)$, the azimuth, and altitude, we found that the declination was close to $-(\epsilon - i)$. As already explained, this could not be observed directly by Megalithic man and we assume it was found by a method like that described in §10.10.

We shall assume that there were two observations made 3 months apart when the nominal values of declination were $-(\epsilon-i+\Delta)$ and $-(\epsilon-i-\Delta)$. In the first of these, since $\Delta$ and $i$ are of opposite sign, we try June or December and calculate the time when the moon was on the foresight from (Hour angle of foresight)+(Longitude of moon)−(Longitude of sun) and take June at 3 a.m. as giving the better time. Similarly for $-(\epsilon-i-\Delta)$ the possible months were March and September, and September at 9 p.m. is the more likely. The temperature is not very critical and we take the modern mean values at Kirkwall for these two times. According to the *Nautical Almanac* tables the refraction corresponding to the altitude, temperature, and mean barometric pressure is $-23'\cdot7$. We take the mean parallax for the two cases from Chapter 2 and so find the geocentric altitude. From this we can find the declination, using

$$\sin \delta = \sin \phi \sin h + \cos \phi \cos h \cos Az. \qquad (10.1)$$

All the values in Table 10.1 have been worked in a similar manner but as we do not know whether to use, for example, $(\epsilon+i+s-\Delta)$ or $(\epsilon+i+\Delta)$, we have calculated in these cases for both assumptions and have used the mean.

In this table we have included only two lines which have no indication on the ground, namely Hellia from $L$ and from $M$. Our reason for including them is explained in §10.5. Perhaps mound $M$ was made large because it served as backsight for two lines. By applying the appropriate values of $i$, $s$, and $\Delta$ we obtain the obliquity of the ecliptic.

### 10.12. Effect of graze

The mean value of $\epsilon$ obtained from the lines giving north declinations is $23° 53'\cdot7$ and that from the lines giving south declinations is $23° 50'\cdot7$. The difference of $3'\cdot0$ may be due to the refraction we used being too small. An increase in the numerical value of the refraction in the above calculation would decrease all geocentric altitudes; this would decrease the north declination but would increase the south declination numerically. Since $d\delta/dh$ is slightly less than unity the increase in refraction required to make the obliquity from the north declination equal to that from the south is only slightly greater than $1\frac{1}{2}'$.

We first showed in Thom 1969 that when reducing measurements made of Megalithic remains more consistent results are obtained by using slightly increased values for refraction, but we did not then realize that this was the effect of the graze. It now appears that this is exactly what we should expect from a ray grazing the ground at the foresights, namely an increase of an arc minute or so in the refraction. The overall mean obliquity is $23° 52'\cdot2$, which corresponds to 1460 B.C. but a reference to §10.15 shows that this cannot be accurate to any nearer than $\pm150$ years.

## 10.13. The histogram

For any one of the four values of $\pm(\epsilon \pm i)$ there are seven possible nominal declinations of which we might possibly find traces. There are, for example, the nominal values:

(1) $\epsilon + i + s + \Delta$;
(2) $\epsilon + i + s$;
(3) $\epsilon + i + s - \Delta$, or $\epsilon + i + \Delta$;
(4) $\epsilon + i$;
(5) $\epsilon + i - s + \Delta$, or $(\epsilon + i - \Delta)$;
(6) $\epsilon + i - s$;
(7) $\epsilon + i - s - \Delta$.

For (3) and (5) the two values obtained in either case are so close that it is impossible to differentiate between them.

If we find a mark on the horizon which gives a declination within the limits $\epsilon + i \pm \frac{1}{2}°$, it might appear that we can always find a nominal value for the declinations which will suit. This might be true if we were satisfied with an agreement between observed and nominal values of 3 or 4 arc minutes, but our declinations are measured to $\pm 1'$ and so a real test is possible. This is why we have gone back to Brogar five or six times and measured and remeasured the notches from the various backsights until we were sure of the azimuths and altitudes.

If we subtract $\epsilon + i$ from each of the values above we are left with $\pm(s + \Delta)$, $\pm(s)$, $\pm(s - \Delta)$, and $\pm 0$. We therefore plot a histogram of the difference between $\pm(\epsilon \pm i)$ and the observed declinations. As in Fig. 8.1 of Thom 1967 we have done this by plotting at each value an area of Gaussian shape and adding the ordinates together.

In Table 10.1 we give results from nine lines. On the histograms in Fig. 10.9 these nine values are distinguished by shading the Gaussian areas. In the upper histogram we took the values of declinations straight from Table 10.1 but in the lower we have used values for the refraction increased by $1\frac{1}{2}'$ (see §10.12). There are eight other values taken from the various cairns, etc. at the site, but only two of these could be said to have any indication as to which foresight we ought to use. The eight values are:

(1) Hellia from ground level at Salt Knowe;
(2) Mid Hill from ground level at $A$ over $B$;
(3) Mid Hill from $G$;
(4) Mid Hill from Thomas's cairn $T$;
(5) Kame upper from top of Salt Knowe;
(6) Kame upper from ridge near $M$ looking over the ring centre $R$ and cairn $A$;
(7) Kame lower from Salt Knowe ground level;
(8) Kame upper from Thomas's cairn $T$.

**Table 10.1.** *Determination of the declination and obliquity of ecliptic from the Brogar backsights*

| Foresight | Backsight | Azimuth | Altitude | Hour Angle | Nominal Value | Date Time | Declination | $\epsilon$ | $\epsilon_{mean}$ |
|---|---|---|---|---|---|---|---|---|---|
| Hellia | $J$ over $K$ | 227° 50' | 65'·2 | 51° | $-(\epsilon-i)$ | June 3 a.m. / Sept. 9 p.m. | −18° 43'·3 | 23° 52'·0 | 23° 52'·0 |
| Hellia | $L$ | 227° 36' | 64'·6 | 51° | $-(\epsilon-i+s-\Delta)$ / $-(\epsilon-i+\Delta)$ | Sept. 9 p.m. / Dec. 3 p.m. | −18° 50'·0 / −18° 49'·9 | 23° 50'·4 / 23° 49'·5 | 23° 49'·9 |
| Hellia | $M$, ground level | 227° 13' | 65'·0 | 51° | $-(\epsilon-i+s)$ | June 3 a.m. / Sept. 9 p.m. | −18° 58'·4 | 23° 51'·6 | 23° 51'·6 |
| Mid Hill | Comet stone | 135° 07'·8 | 128'·8 | 311° | $-(\epsilon-i+s-\Delta)$ / $-(\epsilon-i+\Delta)$ | Mar. 3 a.m. / June 9 p.m. | −18° 50'·0 / −18° 48'·7 | 23° 50'·4 / 23° 48'·4 | 23° 49'·4 |
| Mid Hill | $M$, ground level over $LJ$ | 133° 27'·8 | 120'·1 | 311° | $-(\epsilon-i-s-\Delta)$ | Mar. 3 a.m. | −18° 19'·5 | 23° 50'·7 | 23° 50'·7 |
| Kame Lower | $L_2$ over $B$ | 24° 27'·5 | 58'·4 | 208° | $+(\epsilon+i+s+\Delta)$ | Sept. 9 p.m. | +29° 25'·4 | 23° 54'·2 | 23° 54'·2 |
| Kame Upper | $J_2$ over $GFED$ | 24° 40'·0 | 61'·5 | 208° | $+(\epsilon+i+s+\Delta)$ | Sept. 9 p.m. | 29° 25'·1 | 23° 54'·5 | 23° 54'·5 |
| Ravie Hill | $HF$ over $T$ | 336° 47' | 14' | 153° | $(\epsilon+i-s+\Delta)$ / $(\epsilon+i-\Delta)$ | Mar. 4 a.m. / June 10 p.m. | 28° 52'·0 / 28° 54'·0 | 23° 51'·6 / 23° 52'·4 | 23° 52'·0 |
| Ravie Hill | Comet Stone over $B$ | 336° 23' | 15' | 153° | $(\epsilon+i-s)$ | Mar. 4 a.m. / Dec. 10 a.m. | 28° 47'·8 | 23° 54'·6 | 23° 54'·6 |

There is always a choice of dates 6 months apart. We choose the date that gives the best seeing conditions.

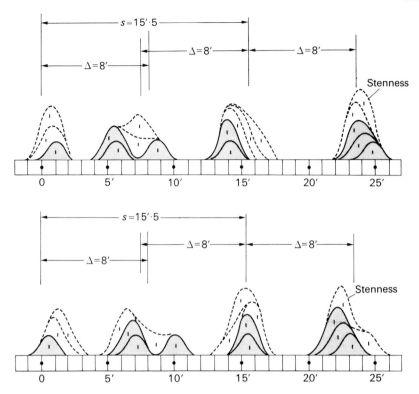

FIG. 10.9. Histogram of difference between observed declination and $\pm(\epsilon \pm i)$. The lower histogram shows the effect of increasing the refraction by $1\frac{1}{2}'$. The shaded areas are from Table 10.1.

All these give declinations near one of the values $\pm(\epsilon \pm i)$ and we do not know of any others that suit except the cairn on the ridge from the Stenness Ring, and that has been indicated on the histogram. They are all shown in both histograms by unshaded areas. It is worthy of note that all these nine aggregate into the clumps on the histogram in as convincing a manner as do those from Table 10.1. It is shown in Chapter 2 that $s$ and $\Delta$ vary through a small range. Taking $s$ as $15'\cdot5$ and $\Delta$ as $8'$, we have marked what might be called the expected values above the histograms. We consider that the manner in which the areas group themselves round these values is in itself a convincing demonstration that we are dealing with a genuine lunar observatory. Note particularly that there is a clear space between the heaps and note that, especially on the lower histogram, no point comes further than $2'$ from one or other at the nodes. The probability that the values could come together by accident in the manner shown is obviously almost vanishingly small, as is shown in the next section.

**10.14. Probability level at which we can accept the values shown on the histogram on Fig. 10.9**

We shall assume that the peaks on the histogram in Fig. 10.9 should be spaced 7'·8 apart, that is that there is a quantum of $2\delta = 7'·8$. This makes peaks at 0', 7'·8, 15'·6, 23'·4, and these values are very close to the expected value. We can now apply Broadbent's first method.

From the values given in Table 10.1 we deduce

$$\Sigma\epsilon^2 = 23·55 \quad \text{for} \quad n = 18,$$

where $\epsilon = |\text{decl} - (\epsilon \pm i)| - 7·8\,m$, and $m$ is 0, 1, 2, or 3; $s^2 = (1/n)\Sigma\epsilon^2$, and since $\delta = 7·8/2$, $s^2/\delta^2 = 0·086$.

When we try to use Fig. 2.1, Thom 1967, we find that the lowest value of $n$ given is 20, and the lowest value of $s^2/\delta^2$ is 0·18 but if we sketch in the value for $n = 18$ and extrapolate it we find that the probability level cannot be far from 0·2 per cent.

This is a most important conclusion and there does not seem to be any way of avoiding it. We have explained how we went back to Orkney year after year to make sure that the azimuths and altitudes were correct, and we have given full details as to how the values used above were deduced.

An examination of Fig. 10.1 (the Brogar survey) shows that the four foresights are indicated thus:

Mid Hill by four lines; Kame of Corrigal by three lines; Hellia by one line; and Ravie Hill by two lines. This in itself proves that we are here dealing with a carefully laid out lunar observatory. The histograms show that it was arranged to deal with various cases of $\pm(\epsilon \pm i \pm s \pm \Delta)$ and we have just shown that the probability level for acceptance is about 1 in 500.

In §10.15 we shall show that it is difficult to understand how Megalithic man succeeded in placing the backsights so accurately.

**10.15. Comparison with the Greenwich values of declination**

In Fig. 2.3 will be found values deduced from the actual lunar declinations as supplied by Greenwich for the era 2100–1300 B.C. They have been modified as described in §2.6 so that they are ready for comparison with observed values of declination that have been obtained by taking the parallax as 57'. The measured values of the declinations are shown in the figure for some of the foresights by a band instead of a line to draw attention to the uncertainty of the effect of graze, etc.

Bearing in mind that the actual declinations of the moon are shown by triangles and rings, and the bands are from site measurements, the difficulties of explaining the good fit of the values in the histogram Fig. 10.9 are evident.

The slow fall in obliquity of 38" per century is almost obscured by the scatter of the points and this makes it impossible to infer an exact date for the site. It would make dating easier if we knew that the lines were established during a short period or if the work was spread over a century or more. If we assume that the cairns were erected as a result of observations made during two or three standstills, Fig. 2.3 shows that prior to 1300 B.C. there are only three dates that suit approximately all five cases shown, namely *c.* 1700, *c.* 1500, and *c.* 1400 B.C.

In looking at Fig. 2.3 it is to be remembered that in several cases the declinations, as shown by both the triangles and the rings, were available so that a mean could often have been used. Of these three dates the best is 1700 B.C., say from 1750 to 1650 B.C., but the shorter period of 1500–1480 B.C. is also reasonably good if we can be sure that the work was done at two standstills.

If, however, we accept that the activity was spread over a time interval of duration comparable to the parallax period of 178 years, then the era from 1600 to 1400 B.C. is slightly preferable because the bands seem to pass through the average of the points slightly better in these centuries. It will be remembered from §10.12 that the date corresponding to the obliquity found was 1460 B.C. This is simply the date where the mean sloping line drawn through all the points in Fig. 2.3 cuts the bands.

What we cannot explain is the method used by the erectors to get the cairns in positions that give the small residuals that we see in Table 10.1. How could they obtain an average position from the points in Fig. 2.3?

It is interesting to speculate that during the period from perhaps 2000 B.C. onward the builders had found the parallax cycle of 178 years and so, by 1600 or 1500 B.C., could allow for parallax changes. If archaeologists can show that the Brogar *ring* was built in the third millenium this idea does not seem impossible, but it means that there was a very long period of uniformity of effort with systematic recording of results. This may not at present seem likely, but it is necessary to guard against the tendency to underestimate the knowledge of Megalithic people and their ability to keep records.

Looking at the histogram it does not seem possible to overcome the difficulty by assuming that the lines got into place accidentally, and we cannot dismiss as accidental the manner in which the foresights are indicated by the arrangement of the cairns.

# 11

## STONEHENGE

**11.1.** STONEHENGE, in Wiltshire in the south of England, is in many respects unique among Megalithic remains: most of its stones have been shaped and dressed in a manner which we find in no other stone circle; the large upright menhirs are capped by lintels, and the main central part of the monument is an architectural entity carefully designed by an engineer–architect who seems to have had a well-developed sense of proportion and a sound grasp of the relevant mechanical principles. We must also realize that the total time interval throughout which work went on at Stonehenge was greater than the nine centuries which have elapsed since the Norman Conquest. The site is not on a hilltop or in a valley, but on a broad shoulder sloping gently down to the east-north-east. Just below the surface of the ground lies the chalk into which the foundations were cut. Avebury is larger than Stonehenge, but the more complicated design used there spread the ring over such a wide area that its appeal now depends on its size rather than (as at Stonehenge) on the feeling of perfection induced when one views Stonehenge from almost any position. An authoritative description of Stonehenge is given by Atkinson (1960).

The earliest parts of the monument, probably constructed about 2800 B.C., are the ditch and bank, the Aubrey holes, the Heel stone, and perhaps the 'stations' (see Fig. 11.1). The Aubrey holes cut down into the chalk (so called because John Aubrey in the seventeenth century noticed depressions and this clue, when followed up by R. S. Newall, led to their discovery) seem to have been filled and excavated several times and today we can see only the concrete discs which have been placed flush with the ground to mark their positions. On the Aubrey ring there are (or were) two so-called stations, each of which consisted of a stone in the middle of a mound, the whole being surrounded by a ditch. The rectangle is completed by the two station stones; both are still to be seen, one upright and one almost prostrate. There are indications in the underlying chalk that two other stones existed between the Aubrey circle and the bank. Placed off-centre in the beginning of the avenue is the Heel stone, a large undressed menhir with a surrounding ditch. Some trace of the banks which bounded the avenue are still to be seen in the field on the other side of the highway. We do not know what was inside the Aubrey ring when it was constructed, but from the very large number of holes which have been found in the chalk we know that at a later date the centre part was occupied by a ring or rings which were rebuilt more than once. An aerial view of the monument is shown in Fig. 11.2.

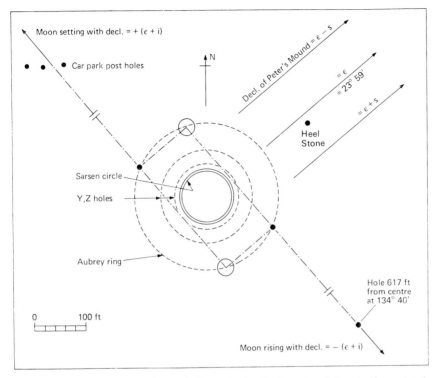

Moon setting with decl. = + (ε + i)

Car park post holes

N

Decl. of Peter's Mound = ε − s

= ε
= 23° 59'

= ε + s

Heel
Stone

Sarsen circle

Y,Z holes

Aubrey ring

Hole 617 ft
from centre
at 134° 40'

0        100 ft

Moon rising with decl. = − (ε + i)

FIG. 11.1. Stonehenge car park post-holes and other features in relation to the rectangle
formed by the two 'stations' and the two stones on the Aubrey ring.

When people think of Stonehenge they probably think of the two impressive rings which were eventually built in the centre of the monument about
2100 B.C. The outer of these rings is the sarsen circle, which originally
consisted of 30 huge stones, capped by a complete ring of lintels. These lintels
were cut to the curve of the circle in plan and were all at the same level. The
method of attaching these to the uprights is shown in Fig. 11.3. It is evident
that so long as the tenons do not fail, the ends of neighbouring lintels are
held together so that distortion in a horizontal plane is prevented. We know
that some of the uprights were longer than others and so go deeper into the
ground. Any tendency of a shorter upright to tilt was prevented by the two
lintels which rested on it. No serious study has ever been made of the stresses
induced in the tenons in the event of the failure of one of the foundations. It
is evident that the shear stress in the tenon might be considerable and might
have produced failure.

Inside this circle stands the ring of trilithons. There are five pairs, and each
pair originally carried a lintel attached in the same way as the lintels in the
sarsen ring. Only one member of the south-west trilithon is today upright;

Fig. 11.2. Aerial view of Stonehenge (Cambridge University Collection, copyright reserved).

it may be the tallest standing stone in Britain, but it is not the most massive. Between these two rings there are remains of the bluestone circle of shaped but smaller stones cut from an entirely different material. There are also remains of another bluestone ring inside the trilithons. Atkinson has excavated enough of this area down to the chalk to show the complexity of the remains. Outside the sarsen circle there are two rings of holes, the Y and Z holes, said by archaeologists never to have held posts or stones. These are not marked in any way, but some of them can be detected in dry weather by stamping on the surface. When the car park on the other side of the highway was being excavated, three post-holes were found; their positions are marked by white concrete discs in the tarmac. These had definitely contained tree trunks about $2\frac{1}{2}$ ft in diameter, and their presence suggests that much more may be hidden under the soil if only we knew where to look.

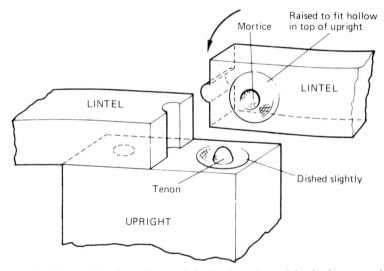

Fig. 11.3. The method of attachment of the lintels to the uprights in the sarsen ring.

## 11.2. The geometry

Before one can study the geometry to which the various rings were laid out, it is necessary to have an accurate survey. Existing surveys all seemed to have some distortion, and accordingly in 1973 we undertook the survey of everything which was showing on the surface. Atkinson made available to us details of his recent excavations inside the sarsen circle, but we have made use of only part of this material. We made a plan of the main ring and everything showing inside it to a scale of 1 in 84, and another to a scale of 1 in 250 extended to the ditch and including the Heel stone. The contours on this at 6-inch intervals were surveyed by several staff members of the Survey Branch,

Royal School of Artillery. Altitudes all round the visible horizon as seen from the monument were also measured. It is not possible to give the full surveys here, but we show small-scale copies which illustrate our conclusions and the material on which these are based (Figs 11.4, 11.5, and 11.6).

Figure 11.4 shows the survey of the inner part. Measurements to the upright stones were made at heights of 6 inches and 2 ft above the present ground. (Atkinson states that originally the ground level was considerably higher than it is today.) Some of the stones have been re-erected in recent years and several full-sized stones and some broken stones still remain prostrate.

STONEHENGE

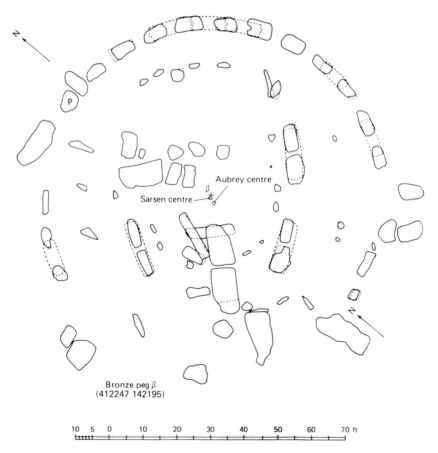

Fig. 11.4. The sarsen ring and its interior, based on the 1:84 plan.

Figure 11.5 shows the same survey, but with the fallen stones omitted. Stone *P* (Fig. 11.4) has also been left out as it seems to have been inserted recently. The stones in the sarsen circle and in the trilithon ring have been divided into three classes. First, those which are considered to be in their original position; secondly, those which have been 'straightened' in recent

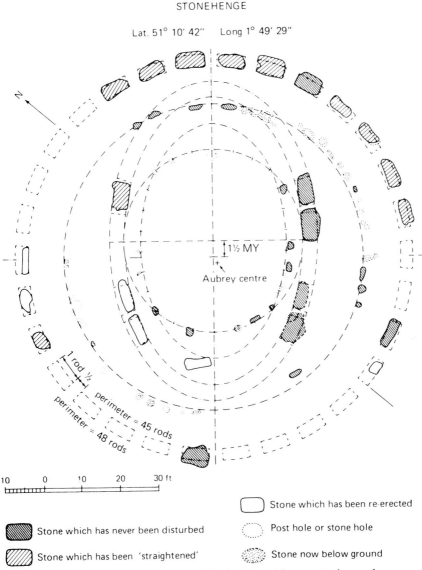

STONEHENGE

Lat. 51° 10' 42"     Long 1° 49' 29"

1½ MY

Aubrey centre

1 rod ½

perimeter = 45 rods

perimeter = 48 rods

10     0     10     20     30 ft

Stone which has been re-erected

Stone which has never been disturbed

Post hole or stone hole

Stone which has been 'straightened'

Stone now below ground

FIG. 11.5. The sarsen ring and its interior, with geometry imposed.

years; and lastly, those which have been re-erected. The necessary information came from Atkinson. He suggested to us that as the south trilithon is inclined inwards and tapered, we ought to displace the outline slightly outwards to compensate. The amount was small, only three inches, but nevertheless we have shown these two stones in dotted outline. Details of the bluestone stumps now below ground were also provided by Atkinson. Much of the area has at one time or another been excavated down to the chalk.

Post-holes in the chalk are shown in dotted outline, but it should be pointed out that the whole area seems to have many such holes. To avoid confusion we have shown on Fig. 11.5 only those which lie near one or other of the hypothetical rings that we have superimposed on the survey. Some of these perhaps did not belong to any ring but may have served other purposes. We would remind the reader that authorities are agreed that the best interpretation of the complicated evidence is that at different times there have been several rings or systems of rings in this area.

Atkinson has pointed out that the inner faces of the sarsens and trilithons were mostly worked flat and had been polished, whereas most of the outer faces had been left rough or even rugged. Accordingly we decided to be guided primarily by the inner surfaces of these stones in determining the geometry to which the rings had been set. From Fig. 11.5 it will be seen that it is a tenable hypothesis to assume that the intention was to contain the stones of the sarsen circle between concentric circles with circumferences of 45 and 48 MR, the difference in radius being 0·48 MR. The 45-MR dimension is built up by allowing exactly one rod for each of the 30 stones and exactly half a rod for each gap. On this basis, therefore, the theoretical diameter of the inside circle is $45/\pi$ rods or 97·41 ft (taking 1 Megalithic rod = $2\frac{1}{2}$ Megalithic yards = 6·806 ft).

## 11.3. The trilithons

It is shown in Fig. 11.5 that four of the trilithons are accurately contained between two ellipses, $30 \times 20$ and $27 \times 17$ MY. The inner of these ellipses is based on a triangle which nearly satisfies the Pythagorean condition in integers: $2a = 27$, $2b = 17$ and $2c = 21$. The square of the hypotenuse is 729 and the sum of the other two squares is 730. Since this is such an important site we shall examine the geometry in some detail by calculating the perimeter accurately. We assume that $2a$ is exactly integral in Megalithic rods and then take the two cases when either $2b$ or $2c$ is integral (Table 11.1).

**Table 11.1.**

| $2a$ | $2b$ | $2c$ | Perimeter (MR) | Error |
|------|------|------|----------------|-------|
| 27 | 17 | 20·98 | 28·03 | 0·03 MR or $2\frac{1}{2}$ inches |
| 27 | 16·97 | 21 | 27·99 | 0·014 MR or 1 inch |

In either method the residual from the whole number 28 is so small that we may well ask how it was possible to measure round a perimeter about 200 ft long with an error of only an inch or two. Only one closer approximation is known and that is in the ellipse at Penmaen-Mawr.

After experiments on the survey plan it was decided that the centre of the ellipses was on the axis $1\frac{1}{2}$ MY from the sarsen centre. A precise representation of the suggested geometry of the sarsens and trilithons could then be drawn on tracing paper and placed over the survey. In deciding on the final exact position, the greatest weight was given to the stones which are known to be in their original positions. The only stones which do not fit perfectly (radially and circumferentially) are those which have been 'straightened'.

The above procedure automatically gives the position of the centre and the azimuth of the axis. It appears that the latter is very close to 50°, perhaps 49° 57′ ± 3′. If it is assumed to be exactly 50° then the north–south line through the centre touches the edges of two of the 'boxes' or sections into which the sarsen stones were originally placed (see Fig. 11.5).

The intended width of the eight uprights in the trilithon ring seems to have been 1 rod and the spaces $\frac{1}{4}$ rod and 4 MY, all measured on the inside ellipse. One stone edge is on the minor axis. These have been carefully set out in Fig. 11.5, and when both sides are considered the 'boxes' so provided fit the stones very well.

It will be seen that the four spaces between the five trilithons are all about 4 MY, while the other dimensions are in rods. Other considerations, perhaps the aesthetics of the final result, probably decided these mixed dimensions.

### 11.4. The Bluestone rings

Atkinson suggests that there were 60 stones in the larger ring, with the stone on the axis necessarily omitted. Like many stone circles in Britain the spacing is not uniform, but if we take a mean interval of $1\frac{1}{2}$ MY the diameter becomes 28·65 MY. A circle of this size has accordingly been drawn on the survey.

For the inner ring a circle is also shown, with an ellipse that is based on a triangle having sides 22, 14, and 17 MY. The sums of the squares are satisfactory, being 485 versus 484. It will be noticed that the inner circle and inner ellipse produce a kind of oval with 'corners'. It has a calculated perimeter of 51·06 MY which, when divided into 26 parts, produces a spacing of 1·96 MY. (It is seen that two existing stones and one hole are in corners.) The 26 evenly spaced ticks marked round the ring on the survey appear to show approximately the positions of all the stones and holes near the ring. From the evidence we possess we cannot, however, be sure that we have correctly interpreted the designers' intentions in this ring. Here, as in the bluestone ring, things do not fit with the precision we found for the sarsens and trilithons. Reference should be made to Atkinson 1960 to appreciate the real complexity of the various rings which seem to have existed here.

## 11.5. The Great Trilithon

One of the members of the great south-west trilithon is fallen and broken. The other stone has been re-erected and so we cannot be certain of its exact original position. Atkinson points out that both faces of these two stones were finished and polished, perhaps because the position for observing the solstitial sunrise was here. This trilithon must have stood at right-angles to the axis, possibly touching the inner ellipse. The upright member is about one Megalithic rod wide, and it is rather surprising to find that its fallen neighbour is considerably wider.

## 11.6. The Aubrey holes

In 1973 Atkinson and Vatcher, by laborious prodding, located accurately the outlines of all the Aubrey holes which were accessible. The centres of the shapes so marked out on the ground were indicated by metal stakes or by holes drilled in the discs of concrete previously placed to mark some of the holes, and these stakes and drilled holes were surveyed accurately by us (Fig. 11.6). The statistical centre and radius of the Aubrey ring was then found by the method given in Thom 1967. The standard deviation of the radii to the holes is 0·56 ft and the mean radius is $141·80 \pm 0·08$ ft.

We might define the position of a hole in azimuth from the Aubrey centre as $\theta = Km + L$ degrees, where $m$ takes all values from 1 to 56, and $K$ is $360°/56$. We find that $L = 3°·7$ and the standard deviation of the individual values is $\pm 0°·56$, which corresponds to $\pm 1·4$ ft. It thus appears that the holes were more accurately placed radially than circumferentially.

The value of the radius quoted above gives a figure for the circumference of 891·0 ft, that is almost precisely 131 MR. If we assume that the intention was to make the circumference *exactly* 131 rods, then we obtain a value for the Megalithic rod of 6·802 ft, which can be compared with the value of 2·722 ft found for the Megalithic yard at Avebury.

Since the position of the first Aubrey hole is $L = 3°·7$ from geographical north, and the mean spacing is $K = 6°·429$, the north point is very nearly midway between two holes; and since there are $8 \times 7$ holes then all the cardinal points and the four intermediate points (north-east, south-east, etc.) lie midway between holes.

## 11.7. The Y and Z holes

These holes in the underlying chalk are not visible but we have added them to Fig. 11.6 as accurately as possible from a plan provided by Atkinson. Obviously they were never intended to be on complete circles, but Fig. 11.7 shows that they lie on two spirals, each consisting of two semicircles. Spirals of this kind with several whorls are found on petroglyphs or 'cup and ring' marks in other parts of Britain (Chapter 5). The radii of the dotted semicircles shown on the western half are $9\frac{1}{2}$ and 13 MR and since the separation of the centres is $\frac{1}{2}$ MR, it follows that the other two radii are 9 and $12\frac{1}{2}$ MR. The best fit seems to be obtained by arranging to have the line of the centres, that is the line on which the two halves meet, at an azimuth of about 130°. It is evident that the position we have chosen for the centres cannot be substantially different from that used by the designers.

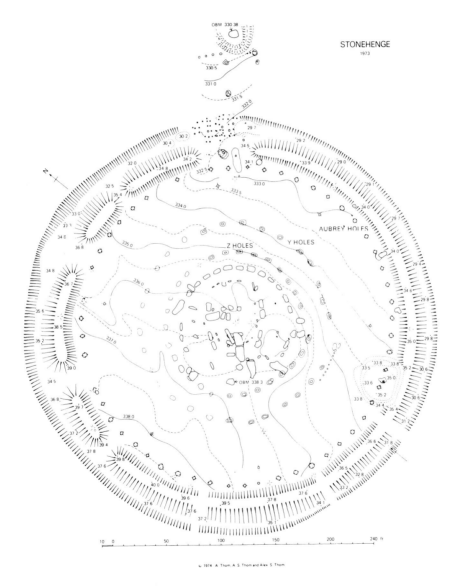

FIG. 11.6. Stonehenge, based on the 1:250 plan. Latitude of centre = 51° 10′ 42″.

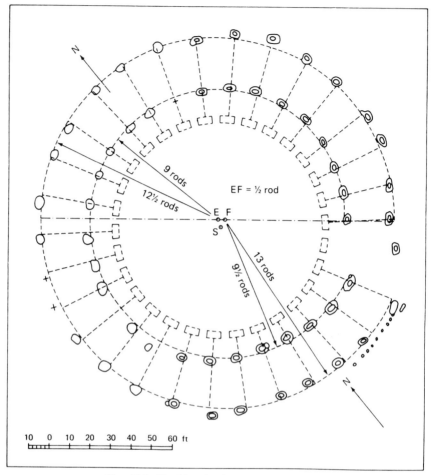

Fig. 11.7. The Y and Z holes at Stonehenge.

Figure 11.8 shows the central region to a larger scale. On it we see the relative positions of the seven centres, namely

(1) the bronze underground pin $\beta$ on which our whole survey was based;
(2) the centre ($S$) of the sarsen circle;
(3) a centre ($D$) found approximately from the intersections of lines joining opposite pairs of Y and Z holes;
(4, 5) the chosen positions ($E$ and $F$) of the centres of the semicircles drawn dotted in Fig. 11.7;
(6) the Aubrey centre ($A$); and
(7) the position of the trilithon centre is shown by the small ellipse $TR$ at $1\frac{1}{2}$ MY from $S$.

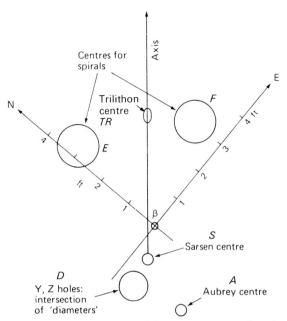

FIG. 11.8. The relative positions of the seven centres at Stonehenge.

The positions of $S$ and $A$ are known relative to $\beta$ to within an inch or two, but the exact positions of $D$, $E$, and $F$ are less certain. The diameters of the circles showing the various centres are indicative of the uncertainty of the exact positions.

It might be an interesting exercise to find by a least squares method the most likely position for the spirals, but in view of the uncertainty of the exact positions of the intended hole centres this is not worth while attempting at present.

The fact that the Y and Z holes lie on radial lines drawn through the centres of the sarsen stones in the main ring shows how closely these holes were intended to be related to the ring. Did they carry a helical stair to give access to the lintels? It seems that for some reason or another the intention was to place them radially with the sarsen stones, on two spirals, in such a position that the distance of the holes from the sarsens would not vary greatly round the ring.

### The Astronomy of Stonehenge

### 11.8. The solstitial line

It is universally admitted that the axis of Stonehenge pointed to the rising solstitial sun, but which part of the sun's disc was intended? To settle this we need to know the altitude of the horizon and the azimuth of the axis. The altitude of the horizon from $5\frac{1}{2}$ ft above the ground level in the centre of the

monument was measured and found to be about 36 arc minutes, with an
uncertainty of perhaps 0′·5 because of bushes, trees, and vegetation. In 1901
Sir Norman Lockyer found 35′ 30″ when perhaps there were fewer trees.

We have seen that the azimuth of the axis is about 49° 57′. When we take
the refraction to be 27′·0 and the parallax 0′·1, the declination becomes
23° 54′·4 ± 2′, which is the obliquity of the ecliptic at the date 1800 ± 300 B.C.
Thus it would seem possible that the axis was orientated on the sun when half
of the orb was above the horizon at about the date of the erection of the
sarsens.

C. A. Newham drew our attention to a little mound, Peter's Mound, on the
top of the high ground which forms the horizon from the centre of the rings.
As this mound may well be of importance despite its small size, we made a
contour plan of the ground; this is shown in Fig. 11.9.

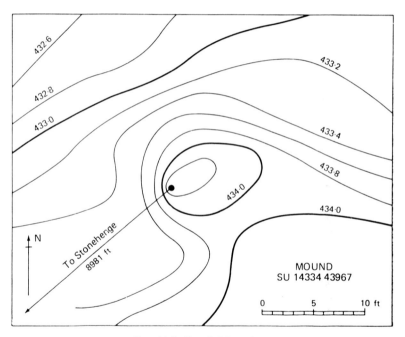

Fɪɢ. 11.9. Peter's Mound.

The azimuth of the mound was measured by us and found to be 49° 47′·6.
The Royal School of Artillery surveyors provided us with the grid coordinates
of the mound (14334, 43967) and of the bronze pin at Stonehenge (12247·43,
42195·20), and from the differences we find that the grid bearing is 49° 40′
and the azimuth 49° 48′, which agrees with the measured value. With the above
values for refraction and parallax we find the following particulars:

| From | Azimuth | Altitude | Declination | Date |
|------|---------|----------|-------------|------|
| Aubrey centre | 49° 47 ·3 | 36′·0 | 24° 00′·2 | 2700 B.C. ±300 |
| Heel stone | 49° 45 ·5 | 38′·4 | 24° 03′·2 | 3380 B.C. ±300 |

These dates happen to be close to the date now being given to the Aubrey ring but it will be noticed that the declination is that of the sun's centre. It is not possible to judge when the sun's centre is on the horizon, but if a mound were there then the method would be to have two observers, one for the 'upper' limb and one for the 'lower', where the terms refer to declination and not to altitude. One of the observers gets into such a position that the upper limb grazes the mound and the other similarly uses the lower limb. The point on the ground midway between these positions would be found for each morning as the solstice approached. The turning point could be marked on the ground and would show the solstice.

Taking the above determinations at their face value we might say that, if the mound is Megalithic, it belongs to the same era as the Aubrey ring. Some 600 years later, when the sarsens and trilithons were being erected, the rising point of the mid-orb had moved to the right and so the axis was put as we find it today, at an azimuth of 50° or slightly less. We are perhaps attaching too much importance to a few cubic feet of earth, but whether it is Megalithic or modern it has an important lesson for us: all this part of the ridge ought to be fully examined by competent archaeologists before the young trees recently planted grow and break up any relevant traces which may perchance still exist. Sergeant-Major Bowden searched the Army records of buildings, etc. that had been on that ridge and found that the position of Peter's Mound had always been kept clear.

### 11.9. The lunar lines

Early in 1963 C. A. Newham drew attention to the fact that the long sides of the station rectangle (Fig. 11.1) indicated the moon setting in its extreme north position.[1] It is reasonable to conclude that Stonehenge was a lunar as well as a solar observatory, but no accuracy could have been possible if the backsights and foresights were confined to the monument itself.

### 11.10. The lunar hypothesis

The hypothesis that the site of the monument is a lunar observatory invites us to examine eight sight-lines to find out if any of these could have carried distant foresights on the apparent horizon. The human eye can resolve two

[1] The only documentary evidence of 'Peter' Newham's work is an article in the *Yorkshire Post* of 16 March 1963. An earlier paper he had written was destroyed in a fire at the printer's office. In 1973, however, he did publish a pamphlet, *The astronomical significance of Stonehenge*.

points about 20 arc seconds apart and so a foresight of 1 arc minute width would have been sufficient, that is, $1\frac{1}{2}$ ft for every mile. For the longer lines the foresight could well have been of brushwood, but as it was to be used only every nineteen years, its site would need to be marked in a permanent manner by a stone or a mound of earth. We had hoped that some trace of these mounds might still exist and indeed it might be claimed that there is evidence of this; but only extensive digging by archaeologists can settle the matter.

We set out to seek foresights for the eight limiting lunar rising and setting positions with declinations $\delta = \pm(\epsilon \pm i)$ where $\delta$ is the declination, $\epsilon$ the obliquity of the ecliptic, and $i$ the inclination of the lunar orbit. We believe that the positions for four of these may have been located, if not accurately pinpointed: (1) Gibbet Knoll above Market Lavington; (2) near the mound inside Figsbury Ring; (3) near Hanging Langford camp; and (4) on Chain Hill. In addition there was probably a foresight at the position now occupied by the Coneybury tumulus.

It will be shown that, for each of the first three lines above, the ray grazes a ridge near Stonehenge; so perhaps only at night with cooling ground would the foresight be easily seen down to its base at ground level. During the day all three would have been visible (a) from the level of the lintels on the sarsen circle, or (b) if the foresights had been reasonably high.

Yet the monument could have been raised by moving it slightly to the north-west and there does not seem to be anything to have prevented the foresights being similarly moved. Why was this not done? It seems that it was of prime importance to use an artificial foresight for the rising solstitial sun; and as Newham pointed out to us, if Stonehenge had been raised even by a few feet, the distant hills to the north-east would have come into view, thus destroying the usefulness of the foresight that we have called Peter's Mound.

**11.11.** We shall now discuss the various possible foresights in detail

*Gibbet Knoll* (9·16 miles). Scattered over the Wiltshire Downs we find numerous mysterious markings. There are ditches, banks without any apparent use, and peculiar shapes set in various places, some on the hilltops. Gibbet Knoll above Market Lavington may be merely another one of these and it is not a very impressive one (see Fig. 11.10). It consists of what might be described as a long step in the otherwise flat ground; a step about four feet in height, with the ground raised on the east side. Its importance for us is that it is in exactly the position that a lunar foresight for Stonehenge ought to occupy.

In some conditions it is difficult or impossible to see the ground at Gibbet Knoll from eye level at Stonehenge during the day. This could most easily be tested by heliograph. We mounted a spot-lamp near $C$ on the top section of a surveying staff so that it could be slid up and down from 5 ft to 14 ft above the ground. The total length of the ray was about nine miles, and a mile and a quarter from Stonehenge it grazed a field of growing wheat at the end

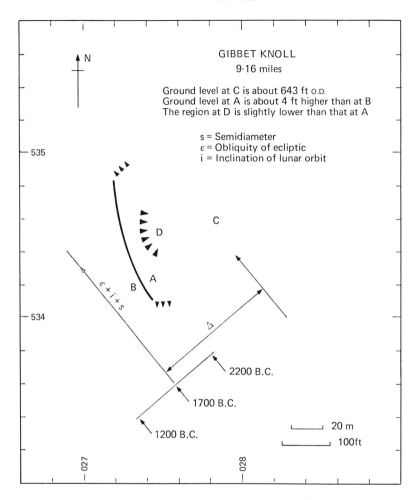

Fig. 11.10. Gibbet Knoll, near Market Lavington, showing the approximate positions for the moon's upper limb setting at 2200, 1700, and 1200 B.C. at the major standstill. The movement necessary for the pertubation Δ is also shown.

of Fargo plantation. Shortly after sunset the light was switched on at a height of 14 ft and it was immediately visible from eye level at Stonehenge. There we measured its azimuth and altitude and by Morse code requested that the light be lowered. When it was 9 ft above the ground the altitude was again measured, but when it was lowered to 5 ft it could not be seen. Probably the ray was then in the wheat or hidden by trees.

The Royal Artillery surveyors measured, in the field, the exact grid coordinates of the two ends of the Gibbet Knoll. As we know the altitude and therefore the height above the theodolite level at Stonehenge, we could calculate the refraction coefficient defined as

$$K = Bt^2/LP,$$

where $B$ = refraction (arc seconds), $P$ = barometric pressure (inches of mercury), $t$ = absolute temperature °R (that is °F + 460), and $L$ = length of ray (feet).

It will be seen in Fig. 3.2 of Thom 1971 how this refraction coefficient increases at sunset; but, during the experiments on which that figure was based, the coefficient seldom exceeded 12. On the Gibbet Knoll ray we found a coefficient of about 24 when the lamp was 14 ft above ground level and 27 when it was 9 ft above ground level. These very high values of refraction were almost certainly produced as the ray grazed over the cornfield. The ground was cooling rapidly by radiation to the sky, and producing a temperature gradient in the air immediately above it. This gradient is affected by a number of factors, such as the state of the sky, what has happened earlier in the day, and the amount of cloud and wind. A high wind, by reducing the temperature gradient, reduces the coefficient. This indicates how difficult it is to see a *low* foresight at Gibbet Knoll, but it would presumably always be visible from the level of the lintels. It will be seen that the same critical condition also applies to the Figsbury Ring and Hanging Langford foresights. Details of the measurements will be found in Table 11.2 which also gives the calculated declinations.

Gibbet Knoll represents the furthest possible north setting point of the Moon's upper limb. We do not know what type of foresight was used; perhaps it was a pile of brushwood on a mound of earth. This would be visible silhouetted on the moon's disc provided it was some 12 ft wide, by no means an impossible size.

*Figsbury Ring (6·6 miles).* This large fortification is much more modern than Stonehenge, but in the middle of the flat area inside there is a clear indication of what has been an earth mound and we used this as a reference point (Fig. 11.11). The grid coordinates are about 18838 33835. Using these and the known coordinates of Stonehenge we obtain a grid bearing of 141° 46′ and so an azimuth of 141° 54′. Unfortunately there is a wood about 3000 ft from Stonehenge which prevents this azimuth being checked directly and behind the wood is a ridge which is grazed by the ray to Figsbury Ring. We could not find the Ordnance Survey bench mark at Figsbury Ring but, by using several of the spot levels on the Ordnance Survey maps, we estimate the level of the mound to be 484 ± 2 ft O.D. and so the altitude from eye level at Stonehenge must be about 12′·0.

By reciprocal levelling from the bench marks at Stonehenge we found the level of the top of the tumulus at Coneybury to be 386 ft (not 389 as shown on

**Table 11.2.** *Details of lunar foresights at Stonehenge*

| Foresight | Distance (miles) | Azimuth | Altitude | Declination | Compare value for 2000 B.C. | |
|---|---|---|---|---|---|---|
| Gibbet Knoll | 9·2 | 319° 56′ | 20′ | +29° 20′ | $+(\epsilon+i+s)$ | $= 29° 20′$ |
| Figsbury Ring, mound | 6·6 | 141° 54′ | 12′ | −29° 01′ | $-(\epsilon+i)$ | $= -29° 04′$ |
| Hanging Langford Camp, mound | 8·0 | 237° 47′ | 21′ | −18° 52′ | $-(\epsilon-i)$ | $= -18° 47′$ |
| Chain Hill | 3·7 | 216° 30′ ± | 22′ | −29° 30′ ± | $-(\epsilon+i+s+\Delta)$ | $= -29° 28′$ |

The mound at Hanging Langford Camp is given simply as a reference point.

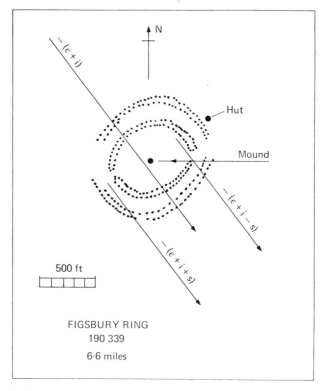

FIG. 11.11. Figsbury Ring, showing the position of the low mound and the estimated positions of possible foresights.

the Ordnance map). From there we ran a tacheometric traverse along the ridge and so found that the highest point on the line from Stonehenge to Figsbury is at a level of about 362 ft, 5430 ft from Stonehenge.

This implies that the altitude of the ridge where the ray crosses is about 11′·7. (We assume that in Megalithic times eye-level at the centre of Stonehenge was about 343 ft.) Thus a foresight placed near the position of the mound would be seen from Stonehenge silhouetted on the sky. Using the above values (and taking refraction as 32′·0) we obtain a lunar declination of $-29°\ 00'$ which is within 2′ of $-(\epsilon+i)$ at 1600 B.C.

*Hanging Langford Camp* (*8·0 miles*). Figure 11.12 shows how the banks and ditches of this peculiar construction wind upwards to the crest of the long ridge along which runs the Roman road from Salisbury to the west. The figure also carries lines showing where on the ridge, as seen from Stonehenge, the lower and upper limb of the moon would have set at the minor standstill about 2000 B.C. Growing wheat prevented a complete examination of the

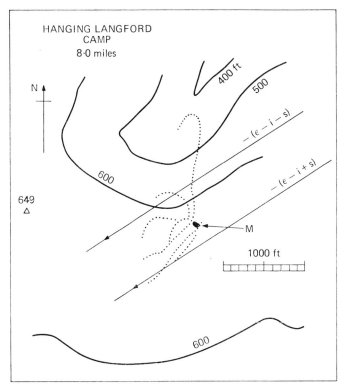

Fɪɢ. 11.12. Hanging Langford Camp. The grid coordinates of the trigonometric station on the left are 400698·6, 135321·6. The dotted lines show the banks and ditches. The declinations are estimated values from Stonehenge centre. The positions of the arrows are considered correct to ±100 ft.

ridge and so we do not know exactly the height of the highest points on the rays, but we assume them to graze at a height of 640 ft. From this we calculate that the altitude from eye level at Stonehenge is about 21′·2. For this ray there is again an intervening ridge rather less than a mile from Stonehenge. The measured altitude of this ridge at the appropriate point, reduced to an assumed eye level of 343 ft, is about 22′·2. Accordingly it seems likely that in daylight conditions the ridge at Hanging Langford is just hidden by the nearer ground, but anything more than about 8 or 10 ft high would come into view. We have not had an opportunity of testing this ray at night with a lamp, but conditions seem almost identical with those at Gibbet Knoll. The Ordnance map contours indicate that at Hanging Langford the ray is near the ground for perhaps 2000 ft; one might consequently expect night-time astronomical refraction under certain conditions to be raised considerably, thus raising the numerical value of the calculated declination. The effect would be that the arrows on Fig. 11.12 would be slightly displaced to the north.

There is at or near the point marked $M$ in the figure a mound about 50 ft long, but this may be merely a part of the system of banks and ditches. We ran a traverse from the trigonometrical station to this mound and found its grid coordinates to be 401313 135270. With an altitude of 22′ this gives a declination of $-18°$ 52′. We do not consider it likely that this mound ever carried a foresight for Stonehenge, but it gives a convenient point to use in any future work.

*Chain Hill* (*3·7 miles*). An ideal position for a foresight for $-(\epsilon+i)$ would be on the top of Chain Hill. All this area is cultivated which makes it unlikely that anything will be found here, but Fig. 11.13 shows where one might look. The plantation known as Stapleford Clump has been superficially examined without result. It is interesting that one of the old tracks which radiate from Stonehenge leads towards Chain Hill. It has slight deviations but it was probably straight at one time. Its general direction is about 216°·5, and this with the altitude of the ridge behind, at Chain Hill, gives a declination of about $-29°·5$, which is close to $-(\epsilon+i+s+\Delta)$, the most southerly position.

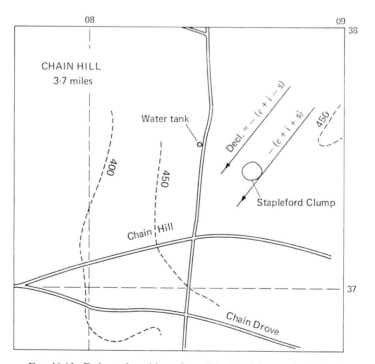

FIG. 11.13. Estimated position of possible foresights on Chain Hill.

*Coneybury tumulus (5000 ft).* We give a sketch (Fig. 11.14) showing the appearance of this tumulus from Stonehenge. It will be seen that if there ever was a Megalithic foresight here it could not have been very far from the position now occupied by the tumulus. The observed altitudes are such that there is no possibility of anything being seen further away than this ridge.

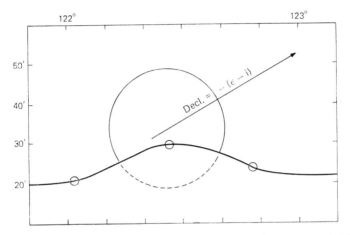

FIG. 11.14. Tumulus on Coneybury Hill. Sketch showing where the moon rose in 2000 B.C. with declination $-(\epsilon-i)$, in relation to the position now occupied by the tumulus, distance 5000 ft.

*Medieval road.* In the fields across the road from Stonehenge there are remains of two parallel banks running west-south-west and so cutting across the avenue. Professor Atkinson is convinced that these are the remains of a medieval road. If this is correct then the road was never completed because there is a bell barrow that straddles it and has not been cut through. We became interested in this track when, on making a careful survey, we found that it was at such an azimuth that the moon at the minor standstill would set on the west end as viewed from the east end. This reminded us of the track at the Comet Stone at Brogar and the manner in which it indicates the Mid Hill notch. It seems, however, that it is only by chance that this track indicates the setting moon at the minor standstill.

*The remaining lines.* We have discussed five of the eight lines which would make a complete set. Two of those remaining are more difficult to examine— those for the moon rising in the north-east. The foresight for $(\epsilon+i)$ could only have been on the relatively near high ground now built up at Durrington. The other, for $(\epsilon-i)$, probably grazes the ridge among the houses and runs to the high ground at Dunch Hill. The difficulty that has to be overcome is that the ridge has a side slope so that accuracy is needed and somewhat difficult surveying through gardens and roads is required. But scrutiny of the contours on the existing 1:25 000 Ordnance map indicates that a graze is very likely.

## 11.12. The position of the backsights

In what has gone before we have assumed that the foresights were viewed from the centre of Stonehenge, but we must now consider if this was really so. If Stonehenge merely provided a backsight from which to make the simple kind of observations which must have preceded anything more elaborate, then perhaps after many decades of watching the observers would have been able to place foresights showing roughly the limits of the moon's movement.

But now consider what would happen if Stonehenge was to be used as one, perhaps the principal one, of the accurate observatories. The observer had to be able to move rapidly transversely to get into such a position that the edge of the moon's disc appeared to graze the foresight. He then marked his position by a stake in the ground. After two or three nights' observations straddling the time of the maximum declination he had the data necessary to enable him to extrapolate to the stake position for the maximum declination (which would in general have happened between two observing times).

Consider the conditions for observing Gibbet Knoll, for which a clear movement of several hundred feet was required. If the observer had to move further to his right than the Heel Stone, his eye level would have fallen more than 3 ft and Gibbet Knoll might have been hidden. Now suppose that a point $M$ is the extreme left point on the line of movement, corresponding to the greatest possible numerical declination. Then all stake positions must lie to the *right* of $M$. This is true whether we are thinking of Gibbet Knoll in the north-west or Figsbury in the south-east; each will have its own $M$ and it is desirable that each $M$ should lie some distance to the left of the centre of the monument. The range of operations will then be kept at such a level that Gibbet Knoll will not be obscured. This perhaps explains the arrangement shown in Fig. 11.1, where we see that if we stand on the mound of the south 'station' and look over the station stone to the north-west our line of sight is displaced to the left of the sarsen circle; and, similarly, if we use the other station and look towards Figsbury, the line is again displaced to the left.

The line to the north-west passes through the car-park post-holes and these we suggest may have contained posts tall enough to carry a platform on which temporary foresights could be placed. Shortly before he died in April 1974, C. A. Newham drew our attention to a hole or small depression in the ground near the Figsbury line which might have held a similar post for the south-east line. Until this hole is properly excavated there can of course be no proof that there ever was a post here.

If a raised platform was necessary for the Gibbet Knoll and Figsbury rays, then it was also necessary for the ray to the north-east for $(\epsilon - i)$, because here also the ground falls for the first several hundred yards. The position would, however, have been in land which has since been so much cultivated that there is little chance of finding anything by superficial examination.

We do not wish to say that Stonehenge *must* have been used in this way; but notice that the sides of the station rectangle do indicate the two foresights, Figsbury Ring and Gibbet Knoll, and remember that the accuracy attainable by the use of the station rectangle itself is not nearly sufficient to allow any scientific study of the lunar movements.

The long rays present two more problems. Why was it necessary to use a ray 9 miles long when a shorter one was available? And how was the correct position for the distant foresight determined? In the fifteen or twenty seconds of available observing time there does not seem to be any direct method by which these people could have signalled to a party at the foresight to move right or move left. An intermediate pole would have helped because when the moon was on the horizon this could have been placed exactly in position. The distant foresight could then have been ranged into place the next day with plenty of time available. This may explain why grazing rays were desirable. But the ridge which produces the graze is, in all important cases, at a distance of about a mile. This is beyond shouting distance, but one can think of ways whereby this could have been overcome. With an intermediate foresight on a platform on the top of, for example, the car-park posts the work would have been simplified.

### 11.13. The roads radiating from Stonehenge

We have already described the road running towards Chain Hill. There are, however, two other roads radiating from Stonehenge. A particularly straight track is that which runs off at an azimuth of 194°·6 towards the horizon where the altitude is about 20'·2. This gives a declination of $-37°\ 30'$, which is that of Alpha Centauri about 2640 B.C. This star is one of the three brightest in the sky.

The track which radiated from the monument at an azimuth of 9°·1 gives a declination of about $+38°·5$, but there does not seem to be any astronomical significance to this value.

### 11.14. Conclusion

We have shown that Stonehenge may have been the central point of a lunar observatory of a size comparable to the observatory which we believe was centred on Le Grand Menhir Brisé in Brittany. In the Breton observatory there was a central foresight to be observed from the surrounding backsights, whereas at Stonehenge the observations were made from the monument to distant foresights.

An interesting fact about the Stonehenge lines is that certainly three, and possibly four, of them graze the nearer ground 1–2 miles distant before reaching the foresight position. If this was intentional, perhaps it was to make it easier to establish the far-off foresight. Or was it to impress the populace by appearing to bring into view in the evening, foresights which during daylight may have been invisible? Or was it pure chance that when the site was chosen so that the solstitial ray to Peter's Mound was a grazing ray there were four other grazing rays for the moon? Whatever the explanation, our work has shown that much research is necessary before we shall know exactly what really was visible from Stonehenge in different conditions. This will entail measuring the refraction of the grazing rays (as we did once only for Gibbet Knoll) at different times of day and under a variety of meteorological conditions.

# 12

## SHETLAND

**12.1.** THE Shetland Islands are altogether about 70 miles long, stretching from Sumburgh in latitude 59° 51'·2 to Herma Ness in latitude 60° 50'·7. A visit to the buildings and remains of buildings of all kinds at Jarlshof on the southern tip of the islands makes one realize, as nothing else can, that the area has been inhabited almost continuously from the second millenium B.C. to modern times. Where else in the world can one find a place like Jarlshof so far north?

Remains of many Megalithic sites exist throughout the whole length of the islands. In many places today we find only a single standing stone but often the presence of other stones lying nearby shows that the sites had been much more complex. Even on Unst, the most northerly island, Megalithic remains are to be found.

### 12.2. Lund, Island of Unst, HY 578034

At Lund on Unst there is a megalith about 13 ft high with at least one other stone beside it. The particulars that follow depend entirely on azimuths obtained by prismatic compass, corrected for the magnetic variation and compass error. It may be noted, however, that an error of 1° in azimuth produces in this latitude a declination error of only about 0°·3. To the north-west there is a particularly prominent lump on the horizon. The azimuth of the dip to the right of the lump is 324°·0 and the altitude 47'. The corresponding declination is 24°·1 and so the upper limb of the midsummer setting sun would have appeared momentarily in the dip. On a hilltop about a quarter of a mile distant there is a menhir on the horizon. The azimuth is 218·6° and the altitude 3° 43'; with lunar parallax these yield a declination of −18° 17', which is nearly −(ε−i−s−Δ); so this menhir is perhaps a foresight for the moon setting at the minor standstill. A fallen stone lies at a lower level than the main stone at an azimuth of about 44° and so the three stones are nearly in line.

The flat face of the main menhir is orientated on a flat lump on the horizon to the south-east. Unfortunately we did not have time to visit this but the particulars are: azimuth, 154°·2; altitude, 2° 18'; and declination, −24°·2. This is so close to the declination of the lower limb of the sun at midwinter that we may assume it to be intentional.

We see, therefore, that this site gives one lunar and two solar lines. It is important because it lies so far north at latitude 60° 42' in Unst, the most northerly of the Shetland Islands and hence the most northerly island in the British archipelago.

### 12.3. The Giants' Stones, HJ 243806

A survey of the Giants' Stones is given in Fig. 12.1. The two main stones which give the site its name are $7\frac{1}{2}$ and 5 ft high, but of the other stones the highest is $1\frac{1}{2}$ ft. We have superimposed on the survey two circular arcs, one (*ABC*) with a radius of 28 MY and one (*CDA*) with a radius of 250 MY, that is 100 MR. It will be seen that these pick up every earth-bound stone in the ring. Using the fact that the flat arc passes exactly 11 MY from the centre of the long arc we calculated carefully the lengths of the two arcs. These were 107·59 and 52·69 MY: were they intended for 107·5 and 52·5? The only other ring known to us with corners like this is Avebury, and there all arcs are

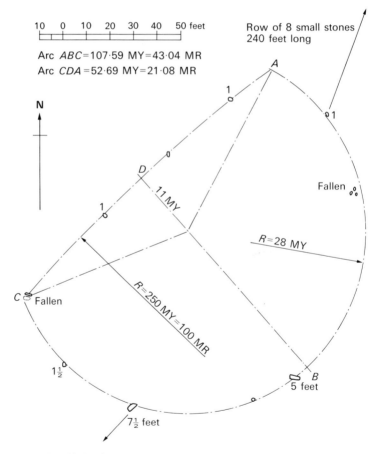

FIG. 12.1. The Giants' Stones, HU 243805 (60° 30′·6, 1° 33′).

integral in rods. The line of small stones running for 240 ft from the ring position at an azimuth of 20°·5 is perhaps a lunar line, but we did not measure the horizon altitude. A peculiarity of this site is the manner in which the large stones are placed across the arcs. Perhaps these indicated directions in their own right or perhaps re-erection has taken place.

## 12.4. The Stanydale Temple, HU 285504

C. S. T. Calder (1949) excavated this site and described it fully. He gives a good small-scale survey which naturally contains more detail than was available to us. It is obvious from the photographs he gives that much has been reconstructed but we surveyed the ring at ground level and we hope that our survey (Fig. 12.2) is representative of the original design. We have carefully superimposed two egg-shapes to which we believe the geometry of the

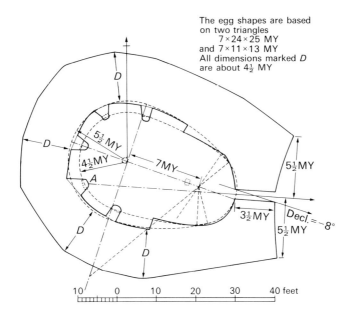

The egg shapes are based
on two triangles
7×24×25 MY
and 7×11×13 MY
All dimensions marked *D*
are about 4½ MY

FIG. 12.2. The Stanydale Temple, HU 285504 (60° 14′, 1° 29′).

site conforms. The inner egg is based on the perfect Pythagorean triangle 25, 24, 7. The outer egg may be based on a perfect triangle 13¼, 11¼, 7, but is much more likely to have been based on the triangle 13, 11, 7. The two eggs have colinear major axes and the radius of the small end of each egg is 3½ MY while the radii of the large ends are 4½ and 5½ MY. The distance between the centres is 7 MY in both cases. Particulars are given in Table 12.1.

**Table 12.1**

|          | $a$ | $b$ | $c$ | $(b^2+c^2)^{\frac{1}{2}}$ | Perimeter |
|----------|-----|-----|-----|---------------------------|-----------|
| Inner egg | 25 | 24 | 7 | 25 | 39·32 for 40 |
| Outer egg | 13¼ | 11¼ | 7 | 13¼ | 43·02 for 42½ |
| *or* | 13 | 11 | 7 | 13·04 | 43·01 for 42½ |

All dimensions in Megalithic yards.

We suggest the following explanation for the fact that the entrance passage is slewed away from the main axis. A man standing at stone $A$ would see the full orb of the sun above the horizon on the axis of the passage as it rose just before the vernal equinox. When the sunrise position lay to the right of the axis of the egg shapes the sun could not shine into the building. The first day in spring when a ray got through the passage was when the declination was $-8°·3$, and this is the declination exactly one Megalithic month before the equinox (see Thom 1967, Table 9.1 and Fig. 9.2). Similarly the last day in the autumn when the sun shone into the building was one Megalithic month after the autumnal equinox. Because of the long winter darkness the movements of the sun must always have been of the greatest importance to Shetlanders and we suggest that Stanydale was possibly a solar temple.

It is interesting to note that Calder states that the remains of the wooden posts which supported the roof were of spruce and that there had also been pine in the roof. There was no spruce in Scotland before 1548 and there has never been pine in Shetland. This seems to show that there was free communication in reasonably large vessels from Shetland to Scandinavia in Megalithic times.

### 12.5. Wormadale Hill, HU 405465

The megalith on the more or less level ground on top of Wormadale Hill is perhaps a lunar backsight. From here the top of the steep high cliff at Fitful Head nearly 20 miles distant is seen clearly but the bottom is cut off by nearer ground.

The well-defined corner so produced has an azimuth of $192°\ 01'$ and an altitude of $-21'·7$. Applying refraction $38'$ and lunar parallax $57'$ we obtain a declination of $-29°\ 08'$. Taking this to be $-(\epsilon+i+s-\Delta)$, a value of $\epsilon$ within one arc minute of the mean value found at Brogar in Orkney is yielded.

### 12.6. The Island of East Burra

Here we find a 6-ft menhir from which a 2 ft stone is visible on the horizon about ⅓ mile distant at an azimuth of $61°·5$ and altitude of $2°·9$. These figures give a declination of 16°·2 which is close to that of the May-Day/Lammas Sun.

Near the 6-ft stone there is a ring formed mainly of loose scattered stones. There are however some which are upright and earthfast. We made a survey of the earthfast stones and in the remainder of the ring we measured to points chosen as representing the curved line of the ring (Fig. 12.3). When we plotted the points we found that they lay on an egg-shaped circle based on a 5, 12, 13 triangle and having a perimeter of 74·14 MY or nearly 30 MR. Obviously the site is worthy of much greater attention than we gave it.

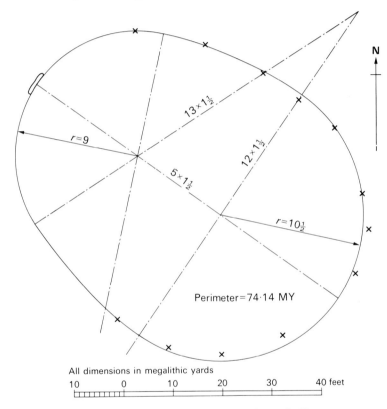

FIG. 12.3. The East Burra ring (60° 05′, 1° 19′).

## 12.7. Island of Fetlar

Shortage of time did not permit us to visit Fetlar, but two sites are reported there by James S. Laurenson, one, the Ripple Stone, the other, the Fairy Ring of Hyltadance. The Ripple Stone is 9 ft high, and the ring consists of twelve low stones spaced evenly round a circle of some 16 ft diameter.

### 12.8. Stone near Brae (near 3567)

About a mile south-west from Brae on the west side of Busla Voe there is a large, upright flat menhir. Between it and the shore of the Voe there is a small stone. This small stone seems to be in such a position that the moon at the standstill would be seen to rise at a notch. The large menhir itself is some yards too far to the west, but it is orientated correctly and the ground at the small stone is too steep to afford a foundation for a menhir of this size.

**12.9.**  We have said enough to show that Megalithic metrology, geometry, and astronomy extended to all Shetland. It is easy to see why a great interest was taken in the sun and moon. In midwinter in London at present the time between sunrise and sunset is about $7\frac{3}{4}$ hours, but in Shetland it is nearly two hours less. In Megalithic times the obliquity of the ecliptic was greater and this would have made the midwinter day still shorter.

From the north of the Island of Unst at the major standstill the moon would at that time be circumpolar for a day or two each month. This information must have been carried south and would have had an effect on the astronomical reasoning of Megalithic man. Could they have avoided the knowledge that the earth was a sphere?

# 13

## SOME OTHER SITES

### 13.1. The Temple Wood site

THE lunar observatory here has been described and discussed in Thom 1971 but some criticism has been levelled at our interpretation. Let us again point out that the position of the setting moon at the major standstill is clearly and accurately shown for both the positive and negative declinations.

It has been said that the notch in the north-west is difficult to find. It will be seen behind the circle called Temple Wood on the line through the two stones at the south end of the alignment. Even if it is not clear to the casual visitor, the original observers would not have had the slighest difficulty here as elsewhere in spotting the foresight. At each lunation as the standstill approached they would have seen the moon set further and further to the north, the monthly movement getting smaller and smaller till the most northerly position was reached at the notch. No one can mistake the south notch to the right of Bellanoch Hill.

### 13.2. Ballinaby

There are several Megalithic sites in Islay. But for our present purpose the most important is that on the west coast at Ballinaby. Here there are two menhirs, one of which is a tall slender stone perhaps 17 ft high. At the base it is roughly 3 ft by 9 inches and so the ratio of height to thickness is exceptionally high. The long sides are accurately orientated on the col at B (Fig. 13.1) $1\frac{1}{4}$ miles distant.

The col gives a declination of about $(\epsilon+i+s)$ and since there is no $\Delta$ in this the stone must show the middle position between the equinoctial and the solstitial stances. We estimate that it was used at the spring equinox about 4 a.m. and at the summer solstice about 10 p.m. when the temperatures are about 40 °F and 50 °F. Accordingly we used a refraction of 32'·4 and a parallax of 57'·2. These give, with the values of azimuth and altitude shown on the figure, a declination of 29° 17'·7. Deducting a semidiameter of 15'·5 and $i$, gives $\epsilon = 23° 53'·5$.

There is ample room for side movement when observing and altogether this must be looked on as one of the most convincing *single stone* observing sites in Britain.

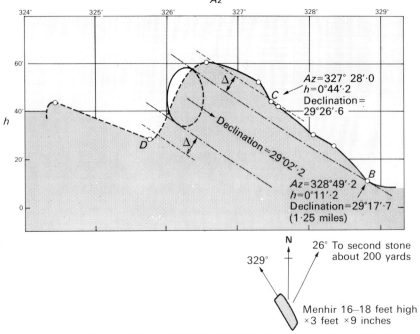

FIG. 13.1. The menhir at Ballinaby (55° 49'·0, 6° 26'·3). The moon setting with extreme
declination $(\epsilon + i) = 29° 02'·2 \pm 0'·5$.

## 13.3. Two sites near Dunbeath

At these two sites, Borgue and Cnoc Maranaith, the foresight is indicated by
the flat sides of a large slab. But in both the foresights the hills are so flat that
the path of the celestial orb is steeper than the sides of the notches. At a site
like Ballinaby the notch is unambiguous and it would not be necessary to use
memory or a handed-down description. At both of the Dunbeath sites,
however, an element of subjectivity enters into the judgement as to the exact
position of the foresight, unless an artificial marker was in fact used on the
ridge.

*Borgue—The Dogs.* The Dogs are two large boulders lying on the moor near
a large 13-ft menhir with flat sides orientated about 21°. The horizon profile
from 22° to 27° is shown in Fig. 13.2 with the moon rising at the major standstill with declination $(\epsilon + i)$. The most northerly position of the moon's
upper limb, namely $(\epsilon + i + s + \Delta)$ might be said to be shown at $A$ and of the
centre $(\epsilon + i + \Delta)$ at $B$, but as is described above the foresights seem unsatisfactory unless artificial marks were used. Nevertheless since a 13-ft stone was
used this was evidently considered to be an important site.

   With the idea that there might be an artificial foresight we made a cursory
examination of the hills, but these should be gone over in detail.

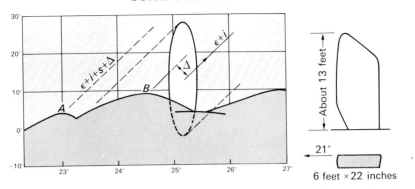

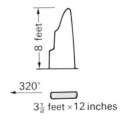

Fig. 13.2. The menhir near The Dogs, Borgue, ND 126267 (58° 13′·2, 3° 29′·4). The rising
moon at major standstill.

*Cnoc na Maranaith.* Cnoc na Maranaith is a ruinous chambered cairn on a
high ridge with extensive views all round. Near it is a slab menhir 8 ft high
orientated on the flat horizon notch shown (Fig. 13.3). It will be evident that
the observer could be certain that he was seeing the notch silhouetted on the
sun's disc only when the upper limb was a small distance above the lowest
point. Accordingly we have arbitrarily added one arc minute making the
altitude 44′·5. We took the temperature to be 50 °F and the barometric
pressure 29·4 inches. So the refraction is about 25′·8, and parallax 0′·1, and
with these and azimuth 320° 15′ the declination becomes 24° 08′·0. Deducting
a semidiameter of 15′·9 (Thom 1971, Table 4.1) the obliquity of the ecliptic
becomes 23° 53′·1 (the value in 1450 B.C.).

It is unfortunate that we cannot be certain that we have added the correct
amount to the altitude. Adding another arc minute, for example, would make
the date about 150 years earlier. We do not yet know of any reliable solstitial
site in the north of Scotland, the Orkneys, or Shetland with which this can be
compared: the lunar site at Brogar, as we have seen, yields a date of about
1600 ± 150 B.C.

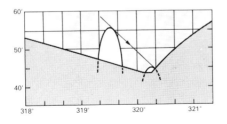

Fig. 13.3. The menhir near Cnoc na Maranaith, ND 132332 (58° 16′·8, 3° 29′·8). The
midsummer setting sun.

**Table 13.1.** *Lunar sites on west coast of Scotland*

| Site | Backsight | Foresight | Obliquity |
|------|-----------|-----------|-----------|
| Ballymeanach | 4 stones | $\begin{cases} A_1 \\ A_2 \end{cases}$ | 23° 56'·5<br>23° 56'·1 |
| Temple Wood | $\begin{cases} S_3 \\ S_1 \\ S_5 \\ Q \end{cases}$ | $A_2$<br>$A_1$<br>$A_1$<br>$A_1$ | 23° 56'·2<br>23° 55'·1<br>23° 54'·6<br>23° 53'·5 |
| Ballinaby | Menhir | | 23° 53'·5 |
| Stillaig | Stone | | 23° 52'·9 |
| Haggstone Moor | L | $A_1$ | 23° 53'·8 |

### 13.4. Lunar sites on the west coast of Scotland

In Table 13.1 will be found a selection of sites on the west coast of Scotland. With the exception of Ballinaby these are taken from Thom 1971 and were chosen because there is at each an indication of the foresight and because the profile of the horizon had been reliably determined. We have excluded Callanish I and Callanish V since the profiles there have not been measured. Also excluded are those where the intended point on the foresight is not definitely known.

The point on the profile on the appropriate figure in Thom 1971 is given in the third column. Each entry has been recalculated by the method described in §10.11 and the obliquity of the ecliptic deduced. The mean of the nine values is $\epsilon = 23° 54'·7$, but since all the lines but one are for north declinations, this should perhaps be decreased by 1 to 2 arc minutes to allow for graze. The obliquity had the value of 23° 53'·2 in 1600 B.C. so we might say that the mean date was about 1600 ± 150 years.

### 13.5. Callanish

We have not yet had an opportunity of getting from Callanish I measured profiles of Clisham or the mountains to the south from Callanish V. However we did get a theodolite profile of the hill 8·6 miles away on the north side of Loch Carloway as seen from the single stone (orientated on the hill) shown in the north-east corner of the sketch plan in Fig. 6.14 of Thom 1971. It will be seen in Fig. 13.4 that this is rather an unsatisfactory foresight as there are 2 notches.

Taking the June possibility ($i$ and $\Delta$ are of opposite sign) at 10 p.m. we find for the moon touching the bottom of the notch at $A$ a declination of 28° 38' and this with semidiameter 15'·7 and $\Delta = 9'·0$ yields a value for the obliquity of the ecliptic of $\epsilon = 23° 54'$. While this is a reasonable value, the foresight is so indeterminate as to make it useless for dating. It does, however, lend support to the idea that in cases like this it is necessary to use the notch

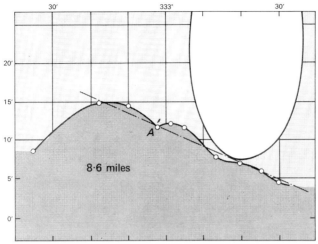

FIG. 13.4. Callanish V (58° 10′·3, 6° 42 ·3). Profile from north stone (orientated about 337°); the moon setting at major standstill.

and not the protuberances. The reason for this method of observing becomes clear when we think of the profile silhouetted on the moon's disc. It would be difficult to judge exactly when the lower limb grazed the tops, but we can see the bottom of a notch.

## 13.6. Fowlis Wester

The approximate survey in Fig. 13.5 shows what appears above the ground today, but Young (1942) and Lacailk, and Zeuner have shown that stoneholes exist below the ground and these indicate that the rings were circular and not elliptical as is assumed in Thom 1971. In 1976 we examined the horizon in detail and remeasured the fall of Creag na Criche. The point, seen by looking past the large menhir $M$, yields a declination very close to $(\epsilon + i + s)$. There is also a shallow notch in which the moon set at the minor standstill as seen from $A$, $B$ past $L$ and an additional shallow notch at 299°. The line of the two circles seems to indicate the equinox in both directions. At the equinox we expect a declination of $+0°·5$ (Thom 1967, Ch. 9).

## 13.7. The Stone at Dol

This menhir (Fig. 13.6) is one of the highest still upright in France. It is tempting to assume that it was a lunar foresight; there is an upright menhir to the west which is in the correct position for a backsight but our admittedly rough survey shows that the stones are not intervisible. Farther on in the woods there is, however, a site which seems to be, from the map, suitably placed. A difficulty here is that the stone at Dol is just outside the region covered by the large-scale maps, and surveying here is just as difficult as in Carnac.

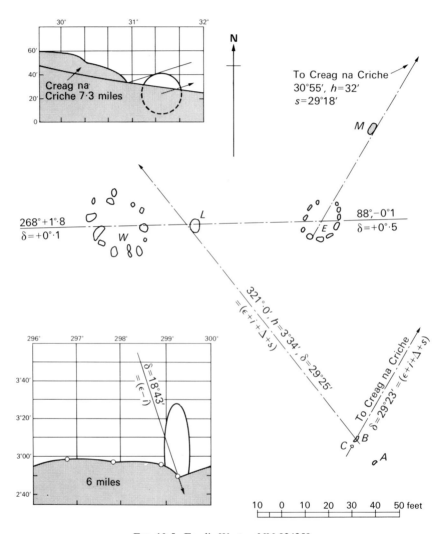

FIG. 13.5. Fowlis Wester, NN 924250.

FIG. 13.6. The menhir at Dol.

## 13.8. Crucuno

Near the hamlet of Crucuno stands a peculiar cromlech which has attracted a good deal of attention. As it is today it consists of 21 menhirs ranging from 3 to 8 ft in height, but it is known that most of these have been re-erected. The stones are built round a rectangle 30 MY by 40 MY (Fig. 3.2) so accurately placed east and west that the re-erectors, without instrumental aid, could not have been responsible for the orientation. This and the dimensions show that the site is Megalithic and dispose of the claim that the whole thing is not prehistoric.

In Thom *et al.* 1973 we show that only in the latitude of Crucuno could the diagonals of a 3, 4, 5 rectangle indicate at both solstices the azimuth of the sun rising and setting when it appears to rest on the horizon. We assumed the altitude of the horizon as $+14'$ and while we could not check this by measurement it seems from the map contours to be reasonable. The long sides of the rectangle indicate to the west the setting equinoctial sun with lower limb on the horizon.

Without distant marks, however, no accuracy would have been possible and we conclude that Crucuno was a symbolic observatory. Other astronomical possibilities are discussed in the paper mentioned above.

## 13.9. Moncrieffe House

This circle was on the side of the avenue leading to Moncrieffe House but only the higher stones showed above the grass. When the new road was proposed it was obvious that the circle was in danger and we were asked to make a survey. By this time the archaeologists had carefully excavated the site and uncovered the remains of what looked like an inner circle (Fig. 13.7). The intention was to remove this circle and re-erect it elsewhere as has been done with another circle near Inverness. To see how completely useless such a procedure really is, one has only to picture what will happen when all record of the re-erection is lost and investigators take the re-erected circle as genuine.

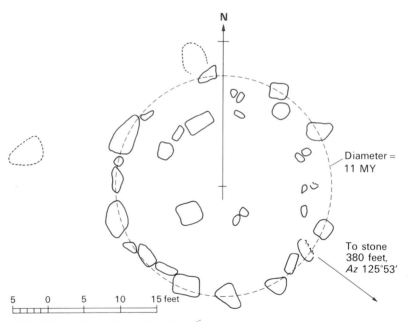

FIG. 13.7. The circle at Moncrieffe House, NO 134194 (56° 21′·5, 3° 24′·1), removed to make way for road.

# 14

## CONCLUSIONS

**14.1.** OUR method of working depends entirely on measuring lengths and angles and, while occasionally we use a rod or a bayonet to prod, we do not dig. In this we differ from archaeologists whose major weapon is the spade. We have established that a universal unit of length was in use from Shetland to Brittany and we have shown that most of Megalithic man's constructions of circles, rings, and alignments were designed to definite rules. All linear dimensions were made integral and all perimeters were nearly integral in $2\frac{1}{2}$ linear units. These rules extend from Shetland to Brittany.

A surprising fact about the unit of length is that it remained constant for such a long time. We find the same length of unit for the small circles as for the large (Thom 1967, Table 5.3) and on the assumption that small circles were built earlier than the large ones, this indicates the stability of the unit over a long period, perhaps a thousand years.

We have shown in Table 4.4 that in all of the large important sites the Megalithic yard had the same value, namely $2 \cdot 722 \pm 0 \cdot 002$ ft. It follows that measuring rods of standard length were carried throughout the whole area from Orkney to Carnac. We are not in a position to judge how much further afield the unit spread.

When we were experimenting by actually using rods under the same conditions as Megalithic man we found that perhaps the best method of comparing the length of rods was to use them to measure a long length on the ground. Since two rods are necessary for each measurement, altogether two pairs would have been necessary. The time spent in using different selections of rods would have been time well spent if it produced a set of standard rods. Whatever the method, it seems to have been possible to produce rods of standard length for century after century. They could have been made of wood. Professor J. E. Gordon has told us that the expansion of wood along the grain when soaked with water is almost negligible, being comparable with the thermal expansion.

In *Megalithic sites in Britain* (1967) and in a number of published papers we have given details of what we have found. With the idea of discovering whether Megalithic man measured to the centre of the stones or to the sides, we visited many of the smaller circles and surveyed them. These crude circles were presumably all built early in the age, but the larger, more sophisticated circles probably belong mostly to the third millenium B.C.; for example the

Ring of Stenness in Orkney is now dated at about 2700 B.C. Probably the nearby large Ring of Brogar was built a little later and the surrounding cairns forming the lunar observatory must have been later still.

## 14.2. Astronomy

The main lunar observatories from the point of view of completeness are: Brogar, Stonehenge, Callanish, and Temple Wood. But there are many other places where we find indications of accurate lunar or solar lines. In *Megalithic lunar observatories* (1971) we listed 25 under the title 'Observing sites' (Chapter 6). While some of these may be spurious, it is likely that there are many more scattered throughout the area. Why were there so many? We have seen the midsummer fires burning on the hill-tops in Austria, and in Scotland there were until recently the Beltane fires. These are all probably the remains of a method of synchronizing the calendar in different parts of the country in Megalithic times. Why then did every small community have its own observatory? We do not know the political arrangements in the area and so cannot judge to what extent each district was independent. Evidently scientific knowledge knew no political boundaries but nevertheless there may have been a desire for each district to have its own observatory. There may have been ceremonies in connection with the solstices or in connection with the lunar standstills. In addition to this there was the practical point that if weather prevented observation at one place then a chance existed that a neighbouring observatory would be more successful.

We do not know what the rings were really intended for. Most of them seem to have no astronomical significance but there are exceptions; for example, Castle Rigg shows a most interesting relation between the lines of the geometric construction and certain rising and setting points of the sun and moon on the horizon.

We might guess that all these were built early in the age, that is when an interest was first being taken in the solstice and equinox without any attempt being made to make accurate measurements. If this is correct then the accurate solstitial observatories like Ballochroy and Kintraw were constructed later.

In Thom 1971 we gave a careful analysis of the known solstitial sites in Argyllshire, namely Ballochroy, Kintraw, and Tarbert Jura. Ballochroy is for summer and winter solstice setting, Kintraw is for winter solstice setting, and Tarbert Jura is for winter solstice rising. By combining these we were able to eliminate the effect of temperature on refraction and finally obtained a value of $23° 54'\cdot2 \pm 0'\cdot7$ for the obliquity of the ecliptic; this corresponds to a date of 1750 B.C. $\pm 100$ years. Further work may change this date slightly but the indication is that these accurate solar observatories were probably built early in the second millenium B.C. It would make our study of Megalithic astronomy much easier if we knew the approximate date of the various sites.

Radio-carbon dates, incomplete though they are, show the sites to be mostly earlier than we had expected and the recalibration by the bristle cone pine method makes them earlier still. Astronomical dating by making use of the precession of the equinoxes looked promising thirty or forty years ago, but it has turned out to be disappointing. Providing that we know that an alignment was set out to show the rising point of, say, Capella, then as the declination of Capella due to precession was changing by about half a degree per century, it was thought possible to date the site. This was attempted in Thom 1967, but the large range of possible dates makes it impossible to be certain of the association of a given alignment with a definite star.

Dating by the sun or moon using the slow change in the obliquity of the ecliptic seems now to be worth while attempting, but the rate of change of obliquity was so slow (38″ per century) that we need great accuracy in the measurement of the declination lines for the sun or the moon. The difficulty of estimating the lunar parallax limits the accuracy of the method of using the moon at the standstill to about ± 100 years or even greater. Perhaps we could do better by using the sun at the solstices, but to get the best results we need a complete set of lines for sunrise and sunset at both solstices. So far we have not found a good foresight for the rising sun at the summer solstice.

It is interesting that all the estimates we have made using the obliquity of the ecliptic method at the various sites give dates early in the second millenium B.C. and yet apparently people were working at Stonehenge some 1000 years earlier. The explanation of the discrepancy is probably that the method of accurately observing the sun at the solstices or studying the lunar perturbation was not developed until late in the civilization. The habit of recording the limiting positions of the sun and the moon had, however, been developed, perhaps in the fourth millenium B.C.

There were 9·3 years between each standstill, but there would have been only some 8 years between periods of observing activity because work would have started long before the actual date of the standstill and would have continued for some time afterwards. The methods used to record the results and to pass on the information are not known. Certainly some form of writing would have been in use. It may have been pictographic and need not have had any connection with the spoken language, unless indeed the information was passed on by memorized passages. The periods, for example 173 days, had to be recorded and instructions had to be given. Presumably some of these had to be permanent, and we suggest that the cup and ring marks and some other petroglyphs contain messages. These are found on or in connection with the large standing stones, both in Britain and in France. For example the main stone in the alignments near Temple Wood carries cup marks, as does the large stone at Manemur near Quiberon. The complexity of the petroglyphs will be appreciated by an examination of the papers and books of Morris and Bailey, who have provided a mass of material which is waiting to be deciphered. If Morris is right in thinking that the petroglyphs had some connection with the astronomical use of the stones, then the code can be broken only by someone who can bring to bear a complete under-standing of the astronomical problems which faced Megalithic man and who can put himself in their position of possessing dawning knowledge. In the meantime we can only go on accumulating data by measuring and analysing every site we can find.

### 14.3. The Carnac alignments

We do not know what these were for. It is true that we have shown how the alignments at Le Ménec can be used to give a good solution for the extra-polation problem and that the curves at the beginning of the Kermario lines do give a rough solution, but neither explanation seems to be entirely satisfactory. The sector at Petit Ménec could certainly be used for extrapola-tion and could have been used with lunar observations made to the Grand Menhir, but what were all the other lines for at Petit Ménec?

It is difficult to believe that the huge alignments at Kermario were built merely to demonstrate the existence of three pairs of coupled triangles, remarkable though they may be. We have here a solution without knowing the problem. The same remark applies to Kerlescan.

The alignments at St. Pierre, Quiberon, are, we feel sure, simple sectors for extrapolating the observations made to the Grand Menhir across the bay. They are very nearly the correct length and the stones in the gardens across the road to the east do not form an extension. The rows have their own cromlech, as have Le Ménec, Kerlescan, and almost certainly Kermario. It is true that Petit Ménec apparently does not have a cromlech, unless we count the large north cromlech at Kerlescan; but was Petit Ménec not an extension of Kerlescan?

The lines at St. Barbe are almost destroyed but the remains of the great alignments of Kerzerho, through which the road to Erdeven now runs, are waiting to be surveyed. No serious study of the Finisterre alignments has yet been attempted.

**14.4.** We know but little about the people whose geometry and astronomy we have studied. We have in Orkney, at Skara Brae, almost complete examples of some of their houses. We know practically nothing of how they lived further south. They had boats of a reasonable size, certainly bigger than canoes, and they used them to cross the dangerous waters of the Pentland Firth and the much wider stretch to Shetland.

The languages that we find in Europe were in a highly developed state when written history begins. Because we have not found any of the records written by these people it would be wrong to say that they had no method of writing.

Meanwhile the knowledge of geometry and astronomy was increasing but here they have left the evidence in stone. The sites are being rapidly destroyed, but enough is still left to show how advanced they were. If we accept the findings in this book, we must accept that they could keep records of dates, numbers, etc. It is difficult to believe that all this came about without writing. Similarly it is difficult to believe that the Greek alphabet, grammar, and so on developed in a few hundred years. We must not expect that prehistoric writing followed regular lines from left to right or indeed up and down. In Chapter 5 we have studied the complicated form of some of the rings cut in the rock and we can look at Fig. 5.9 and ask ourselves what it all means. Apparently there are many places where there are cups cut in the rock; but why should a man spend hours—or rather days—cutting cups in a random fashion on a rock? It would indeed be a breakthrough if someone could crack the code of the cups.

**14.5.** All European countries have, in historic times, produced outstanding scientists. These men took knowledge as it existed in their time and advanced it—sometimes considerably. Each generation tends to underestimate the intelligence and ability of those who have gone before. Various writers have expressed the opinion that Megalithic man could not possibly have reasoned out anything about the cosmos. Our prehistoric ancestors were certainly our equals in intellectual ability. Men of great capacity would be produced in every generation. The fact that they did not have the use of pen and paper would not have prevented them from thinking, speculating, and expounding. The European languages developed before the means by which they were written down were available, and so it must have been with the beginnings of mathematics and astronomy.

### 14.6. What did Megalithic man think about the universe?
Let us see what facts Megalithic man had as a basis for his cosmology. Men of scientific bent living on the trade routes of north-western Europe were in a position to glean information from far afield. They would hear that from the northern Island of Unst the moon at the major standstill appeared to be circumpolar for a few days. Anyone can make the observation that the shadow of his own head falling on an object, no matter what its shape, appears circular and anyone who has, from the water level, watched a boat receding knows that it eventually vanishes; he knows that if he climbs a hill the boat will come again into view. He would know that eclipses of the moon occur at full moon and that the shadow as it crosses the moon is seen to be circular. This might lead to the thought 'my head is spherical and its shadow is always circular. The sun is behind me. Perhaps I am seeing a shadow of the earth on the moon.' The memory of the vanishing boat and the circumpolar moon could have suggested that the earth was a sphere.

The potential scientist would observe and think and even in the absence of any method of writing could eventually make mnemonic notes. He did not know where this was leading him any more than today's scientist really knows what the outcome of his work will be, but the earlier people were motivated by the same urge to study phenomena that drives the scientists of today.

An enormous amount of the knowledge laboriously acquired by early man has irretrievably vanished and only odd pieces come occasionally to light, often to be received with incredulity. Megalithic man has, however, left us a part of his knowledge recorded in stone. It is for us to try to read the records. We shall probably make many mistakes and occasionally have to retrace our steps. We must avoid the use of the sledgehammer and bulldozer, physically and metaphorically. It is hoped that this book makes a contribution.

# APPENDIX A

## *Calculation of azimuths from French grid coordinates*

ON the British maps, as we explained in Appendix B, Thom 1971, the grid north and geographical north are identical along the north–south line at longitude 2°W. On Breton maps the same holds along the north–south line at easting $E = 600$ km. Let $\Delta E$ be the value obtained by subtracting the easting $E_A$ of a point ($A$) in kilometres from $E = 600$. Then grid bearings from $A$ have to be decreased by

$$\frac{\Delta E \times 0\cdot00658}{\cos \phi}$$

degrees to obtain azimuths where the latitude of the point ($A$) is $\phi$.

Hence treat the coordinates of two points ($A$) and ($B$) as simple rectangular coordinates and calculate the distance and grid bearing. Then apply the above correction to obtain the azimuth of point ($B$) as seen from point ($A$).

The simple procedure given above should be sufficiently accurate for our purpose; in any case no large-scale French maps are published such as we have in Britain. Thus in general it is not possible to obtain coordinates with any great accuracy.

# APPENDIX B

## *Extrapolation to maximum declination*

**B.1.** THIS is fully described in Thom 1971 and in Thom and Thom 1972*b* so here we shall merely give an outline.

Let *g* be the declination deficiency, that is the loss in declination from the maximum in half a lunar day. Here a lunar day, the interval between two transits of the moon, is close to the interval between two rising (or setting) times. Let the corresponding distance which the observer has to move on level ground be *G*, where $G = gD \, dA/d\delta$.

Here *D* is the distance to the foresight and $dA/d\delta$ is the change in azimuth produced by unit change of declination. In Fig. B.1(a) we see the line of movement of the observer taken as being at right-angles to the line to the foresight. Suppose that on three successive nights he has established stakes at *A*, *B*, and *C*. If, for clarity, we assume that he had stepped forward towards the foresight a constant distance 2*a* each night then his positions would have been *A'*, *B'*, and *C'*. He has in fact plotted on the ground the moon's declination with 1 day represented by 2*a*.

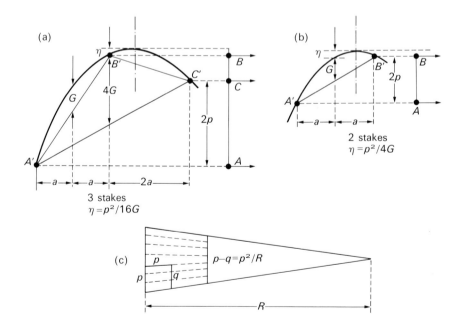

FIG. B.1. Extrapolating to the maximum from two or three observations.

Taking the curve to be parabolic the sagitta shown at $G$ is constant and shows the declination deficiency for half a day. The deficiency increases as the square of the interval and so the distance from $B'$ to the point midway between $A$ and $C$ is $4G$. The stake $B'$ had to be advanced a distance $\eta$ at right-angles to the line to the foresight to get it to the position corresponding to the maximum declination. It is not difficult to show that

$$\eta = p^2/16G$$

where $2p$ is the distance between $A$ and $C$.

If only two observations, say $A$ and $B$ (Fig. B.1(b)), were available then a stake placed midway between $A$ and $B$ had to be advanced a distance

$$G + \eta = G + p^2/4G$$

### B.2. Use of Sectors or Fans

The method of finding $p^2/4G$ or $p^2/16G$ by means of a sector is shown in Fig. B.1(c). From the geometry of the figure we find that $p - q = p^2/R$. Hence if the radius of a sector is made $4G$ the value of $\eta$ is $p - q$. There are four sectors in Caithness and two near Carnac, all with approximately the radius to suit the distance to the foresight. We do not however find any sector with a radius of $16G$, and so presumably the three-night method was not in regular use.

For a very large observatory like that centred on Le Grand Menhir Brisé the necessary side movements would have been perhaps too large. This probably worried the builders and so it is possible that the main Carnac alignments contain an attempt to develop an alternative method that could have taken account of the variation in $G$. We have suggested (Thom and Thom 1972) a method whereby Le Ménec alignments could have been used for most of the backsights but there is at present no way of showing that they were so used.

The Caithness sectors are all built of stones so small that in agricultural districts they would have been cleared away without leaving a trace. This may have happened at sites like Brogar or Temple Wood. In this connection it should perhaps be pointed out that a simpler method of making the necessary extrapolation would have been to use a triangle of base length $4G$ instead of a sector. This is described in Thom 1971.

It was essential to have some method of extrapolation, otherwise the observatory would have been useless; in fact the Brogar cairns could not have been placed as we find them.

# BIBLIOGRAPHY

ATKINSON, R. J. C., *Stonehenge*. Penguin, Harmondsworth (1960).
—— Megalithic astronomy—a prehistorian's comment. *J. Hist. Astron.*, **6**, 42 (1973).
BAITY, ELIZABETH CHESLEY, Archaeoastronomy and ethnoastronomy so far. *Curr. Anthrop.*, **14**, 389 (1973). [This article has an extensive bibliography.]
BARNATT, JOHN, *Stone circles of the Peak*. Turnstone Books, London (1978).
BROWN, P. LANCASTER, *Megaliths, myths and men*. Blandford Press, Poole (1976).
BURL, AUBREY, *The stone circles of the British Isles*. Yale University Press, New Haven, Conn. (1976).
CALDER, C. S. T., *Proceedings of the Society of Antiquaries of Scotland*, **84**, 185 (1949).
DANBY, J. M. A., *Fundamentals of celestial mechanics*. Macmillan, New York (1962).
FREER, R. and QUINIO, J.-L., The Kerlescan alignments. *J. Hist. Astron.*, **8**, 52 (1977).
HADINGHAM, EVAN, *Circles and standing stones*. Heineman, London (1975).
FREEMAN, P. R., A Bayesian analysis of the Megalithic yard. *Jl R. statist. Soc. A*, **139**, 26 (1976).
IVIMY, JOHN, *The sphinx and the megaliths*. Turnstone Press, London (1974).
KEILLER, A., *Windmill Hill and Avebury*. Oxford University Press, London (1965).
KENDALL, D. G., Hunting quanta. *Phil. Trans. R. Soc. Lond. A*, **276**, 231 (1974).
KRUPP, E. C., *The megalith builders*. Phaidon Press, Oxford (1977).
LE ROUZIC, ZACHARIE, Inventaire des monuments mégalithiques de la region de Carnac. *Bulletin de la Société Polymathique du Morbihan* (1965).
LOCKYER, SIR NORMAN, *Stonehenge and other British stone monuments*. Macmillan, London (1909).
MACKIE. EUAN W., *Sciences and society in prehistoric Britain*. Paul Elek, London (1977*a*).
—— *The search of ancient astronomies*. Doubleday, New York (1977*b*).
MICHEL, HENRI, *Scientific instruments in art and history*. (Trans. R. E. W. Maddison and F. R. Maddison.) Barrie and Rocklift, London (1967).
MICHELL, JOHN, *Astro-archaeology*. Thames and Hudson, London (1977).
MORRIS, R. W. B., *Prehistoric rock art of Argyll*. Dolphin Press, Poole (1977).
NEWHAM, C. A., *The astronomical significance of Stonehenge*. John Blackburn, Leeds (1973).
PATRICK, J. and BUTLER, C. J., On the interpretation of the Carnac menhirs and alignments by A. and A. S. Thom. *Irish Archeological Research Forum*, **1**, 29 (1974).
RENFREW, COLIN, *Before civilization*. Cape, London (1973).
RITCHIE, J. H. G., *Proceedings of the Society of Antiquaries of Scotland*, **107** (1975–6). In press.

SOMERVILLE, B., Astronomical indications in the Megalithic monument at Callanish. *J. Br. astr. Ass.*, **23**, 83 (1912).
—— Prehistoric monuments in the Outer Hebrides and their astronomical significance. *J. R. anthrop. Inst. Gt. Br. Irel.*, **42**, N.5. **15** (1912).
THOM, A., A statistical examination of the Megalithic sites in Britain. *Jl R. statist. Soc. A*, **118**, 275 (1955).
—— The megalithic unit of length. *Jl R. statist. Soc. A*, **125**, 243 (1962).
—— The larger units of length of Megalithic man. *Jl R. statist. Soc A*, **127**, 527 (1964).
—— Megalithic astronomy: indications in standing stones. *Vistas Astr.*, **7**, 1 (1965).
—— *Megalithic sites in Britain.* Clarendon Press, Oxford (1967).
—— The geometry of cup and ring marks. *Trans. ancient Monument Soc.*, **16**, 77 (1969*a*).
—— The lunar observatories of Megalithic man. *Vistas Astr.*, **11**, 1 (1969*b*).
—— *Megalithic lunar observatories.* Clarendon Press, Oxford (1971).
—— A megalithic lunar observatory in Islay. *J. Hist. Astron.*, **5**, 50 (1974).
—— and MERRITT, R. L., Some megalithic sites in Shetland. *J. Hist. Astron.*, **8** (1977).
—— and THOM, A. S., The astronomical significance of the large Carnac menhirs. *J. Hist. Astron.*, **2**, 147 (1971).
—— —— The Carnac alignments. *J. Hist. Astron.*, **3**, 11 (1972*a*).
—— —— The uses of the alignments at Le Ménec, Carnac. *J. Hist. Astron.*, **3**, 151 (1972*b*).
—— —— A Megalithic lunar observatory in Orkney: the Ring of Brogar and its cairns. *J. Hist. Astron.*, **4**, 111 (1973*a*).
—— —— The Kerlescan cromlechs. *J. Hist. Astron.*, **4**, 168 (1973*b*).
—— —— The Kermario alignments. *J. Hist. Astron.*, **5**, 30 (1974).
—— —— Further work on the Brogar lunar observatory. *J. Hist. Astron.*, **6**, 100 (1975).
—— —— A fourth lunar foresight for the Brogar Ring. *J. Hist. Astron.*, **8**, 54 (1977*a*).
—— —— The Duke of Edinburgh Lecture: Megalithic astronomy. *J. Navig.*, **30**, 1 (1977*b*).
—— —— and FOORD, T. R., Avebury: a new assessment of the geometry and metrology of the ring. *J. Hist. Astron.*, **7**, 183 (1976).
—— —— and GORRIE, J. M., The two megalithic lunar observatories at Carnac. *J. Hist. Astron.*, **7**, 11 (1976).
—— —— MERRITT, R. L., and MERRITT, A. L., The astronomical significance of the Crucuno stone rectangle. *Curr. Anthrop.*, **14**, 450 (1973).
—— —— and THOM, ALEXANDER S., Stonehenge. *J. Hist. Astron.*, **5**, 71 (1974).
—— —— —— Stonehenge as a possible lunar observatory. *J. Hist. Astron.*, **6**, 19 (1975).
—— and THOM, ALEXANDER S., Avebury: the West Kennet Avenue. *J. Hist. Astron.*, **7**, 193 (1976).
THOM, A. S. and FOORD, T. R., The Island of Eday, the Setter Stone. *J. Hist. Astron.*, **8** (1977).
WOOD, JOHN EDWIN, *Sun, moon, and standing stones.* Oxford University Press (1978).
YOUNG, A., A report on standing stones and other remains near Fowlis Wester. *Proceedings of the Society of Antiquaries of Scotland*, **77**, 174 (1942).

# AUTHOR INDEX

# SUBJECT INDEX